Thoughts
on my
Thoughts
VI

Thoughts
on my
Thoughts
VI

The <u>TALES</u> That Wagged This Veterinarian

Walter R. Hoge, DVM

Printed in the United States of America

ISBN 979-8-89114-229-9 (sc)
ISBN 979-8-89114-230-5 (hc)
ISBN 979-8-89114-231-2 (e)

Library of Congress Preassigned Control Number: 2025921315

2025.10.23

MainSpring Books
5901 W. Century Blvd
Suite 750
Los Angeles, CA, US, 90045

www.mainspringbooks.com

Thoughts on my Thoughts Book VI

250 years a nation…

That night, visions of him reaching the top first and claiming the prize sore through his mind. The glory will be his. There is nothing in the world that he can't handle when it comes to mountain terrains. He can make this final climb to the summit alone.

When his companions are asleep, he puts on his climbing gear and heads towards the summit on a clear moon lit night. His confidence soars until a cold winter storm develops, visibility drops to zero, and he can't turn back. He slips on some loose rock, slides over a cliff, finds himself dangling in midair, and can't locate a foot hold.

He is hanging from a rope in the dark, wind blowing in his ears, with little or no hope of not freezing to death. When all else has failed, he cries out "Oh dear God in Heaven, please help me!" Suddenly, from above he thinks he hears a voice say, "Cut the rope" two times. Was it from confusion caused by his body freezing? Was it God? Would he (or you) cut the rope?

Table of Contents

CHAPTER 1

MOUNTAINS TO CLIMB

A story is told about a mountain climber who liked to climb tall mountains for fun and to impress his friends. After years of preparation and training he felt he could handle any mountain terrain in the world, regardless of the degree of difficulty.

During a climbing trip, with five other men, he decided he would make the final climb to the summit, solo, so he could get there first and claim the glory, while the others slept. After the rest of the climbing party turned-in for the night, he put on his climbing gear and headed toward the summit. As he started his climb, he was very glad there was a full moon to help him see where he was going.

Although it was foolish to climb at night, alone, he did use a rope and put in good protection as he climbed. With the benefit of the full moon, he made rapid progress up the mountain, in spite of the fact he was climbing at night. His confidence soared as he neared the summit, but unfortunately, thick clouds were starting to build around the mountain, and visibility was deteriorating rapidly, as a winter storm developed. In just a few minutes visibility dropped to almost zero, as heavy clouds and fog surrounded him. It was now too late to turn back, so he continued to climb up the mountain, hoping the storm would blow by quickly.

While moving along a narrow traverse, now in total darkness, he got into some "rotten rock," and slid down the side of the ridge and over the edge of a cliff. The good news is the protection he put in held, and he was still alive after the fall; although he now found himself dangling in the air, suspended from his rope, unable to see anything around him. The bad news is, he had loosely tied his outer heavy parka across the top of his backpack while he was climbing, and he now discovered he had lost it during the fall. Slowly the cold night air from the storm began to chill him to the bone through his lightweight inner jacket. After struggling to turn himself around in a circle, and not finding anything to grab onto, in desperation he cried out, "Oh dear God in Heaven, please help me!"

Suddenly, from above he heard a strong deep voice boom out, "Cut the rope!" "What?!" As the climber listened over the wind, once again he heard a deep voice say, "Cut the rope!" Except for the cold wind, silence followed, as the climber continued to hang onto the rope, while hoping to be able to grab onto something that would enable him to climb to safety. Was the rope his only hope? What would you do? *Author unknown*

During my darkest hours I had a picture of Christ with the words, "I never said it would be easy" on His right side, and "I only said it would be worth it" on His left side – hung in clear view on my bedroom wall. It was there when:

- My wife was taken to the emergency clinic on Christmas Eve a few days after her oldest daughter's wedding.
- She underwent emergency surgery for stage 4 cancer, also known as metastatic cancer, that had spread from its original site to distant organs and other parts of her body.
- The next day, finding myself trying to give her encouragement after watching the surgeon inform her that she had terminal cancer.
- She struggled with cancer therapy and drug trials. Lost her strength, and showed premature aging.
- I was frantically googling research articles trying to find possible ways to slow down the cancer long enough until "that miracle treatment" might be found.
- She expressed that the only regret she had was that she would never be able to hold her grandchildren or watch them have children of their own.
- Her cancer treatments and drug trials caused changes that affected her appearance, physical abilities, and overall well-being.
- Loss of body weight, loss of hair and the need for a hair piece resulted in her struggling with feelings of anxiety and depression.
- She laid in a comma and then transitioned back to her Father in Heaven.
- The loss found me staying at work until late mulling over client charts, pet's lab reports, journals and delaying as long as possible going back to the dark, cold lonely environment that used to be filled with

3

an energetic and vibrant family, doing their things of life. My dog, Cinder, had even drowned in our swimming pool under the nose of this veterinarian. I was really alone and in my darkest moments of life.

During these times I would look at the picture of Christ and imagine throwing my shoe at it or crushing it into pieces on the floor. Like the mountain climber, was my only hope to hang onto the rope or was I willing to cut the rope and hope to fall into my Savior's open arms surrendering myself to His love, mercy, and protection?

Pangea (Pangaea) is the concept that all of the land masses of the earth were at one time connected as one giant super-continent. On a world map, some of the continents look like they could fit together like giant puzzle pieces (Africa and South America, for example). Does the Bible mention Pangea? Not explicitly, but possibly. Genesis 1:9 records, "And God said, 'Let the water under the sky be gathered to one place, and let dry ground appear.' And it was so." Presumably, if all the water was "gathered to one place," the dry ground would also be all "in one place." Genesis 10:25 mentions, "…one was named Peleg, because in his time the earth was divided…" Some point to Genesis 10:25 as evidence that the earth was divided after the Flood of Noah. While this view is possible, it is most definitely not universally held by Christians. Some view Genesis 10:25 as referring to the "division" that occurred at the Tower of Babel, not the division of the continents via "continental drift." Some also dispute the post-Noahic Pangea separation due to the fact that, at the current rates of drift, the continents could not possibly have drifted so far apart in the time that has transpired since the Noahic Flood. However, it cannot be proven that the continents have always drifted at the same rate. Further, God is capable of expediting the continental-drift process to accomplish His goal of separating humanity (Genesis 11:8). Again, though, the Bible does not explicitly mention Pangea, or conclusively tell us when Pangea was broken apart.

The post-Noahic Pangea concept does possibly explain how the animals and humanity were able to migrate to the different continents. How did the kangaroos get to Australia after the Flood if the continents were already separated? Young-earth creationist alternatives to the standard continental drift (plate tectonics) theory include the Catastrophist Plate Tectonics Theory, both of which place accelerated continental drift within the cataclysmic context of Noah's Flood. However, there is another explanation offered by Christian scientists that does not require a post-Noahic Pangea. According to this view, intercontinental migration most likely began while sea levels were still low during and immediately following the post-Flood Ice Age when much of the water was still trapped in ice at the poles. Lower sea levels would have left the continental shelves exposed, connecting all of the major land masses through land bridges. There are (or at least were) shallow underwater land bridges connecting all of the major continents. North America, Southeast Asia, and Australia are all attached to continental Asia. Britain is attached to continental Europe. In some places, these intercontinental bridges are only a few hundred feet below our current sea level. The theory can be summarized as follows: (1) After the Flood, an Ice Age occurred. (2) The vast amount of water that was frozen resulted in the oceans being much lower than they are today. (3) The low level of the oceans resulted in land bridges connecting the various continents. (4) Human beings and animals migrated to the different continents over these land bridges. (5) The Ice Age ended, the ice melted and the ocean levels rose, resulting in the land bridges being submerged.

So, while Pangea is not explicitly mentioned in the Bible, the Bible does present the possibility of a Pangea. Whatever the case, either view presented above presents a viable explanation for how humanity and animals were able to migrate to continents now separated by vast oceans. *Faith Blog*

There's no geological artist quite like Earth's plate tectonics. Thanks to this ongoing operation, we have mountains and oceans, terrifying earthquakes, incandescent volcanic eruptions, and new land being born every single second. Eventually, if this were to cease, the mantle will cool to such an extent that this planetwide conveyor belt will grind to a halt. At that point, you can say farewell to the carbon cycle, as well as the constant reshaping and reshuffling of landmasses that have been big drivers of evolution over eons. Currently, only Earth is known to have active plate tectonics, where the planet's crust is broken into plates that move and interact with each other. While other planets like Venus and Mars exhibit tectonic activity, they don't have the same kind of plate structure as Earth. Some moons, like Jupiter's Europa, may have a form of ice-plate tectonics. Mars, a world of failed plate tectonics, did manage to forge some impressive volcanic features, including Olympus Mons, the largest volcano in the solar system. Without moving plates, a long-lived upwelling mantle plume focused plenty of crustal melting on that one single spot.

Some experts argue that we can never accurately predict the end of plate tectonics. But scientists largely agree that such an end will arrive one day, putting Earth on a path to a geologic standstill. Earth was born 4.54 billion years ago in the pyres of the early solar system. Once entirely molten, the heat generated by its formation and radioactive materials in the rock began to escape. As the planet cooled, Earth settled into its current layered structure, with a dense inner iron core, a liquid outer core, and a brittle upper mantle and crust sandwiching the hot, plastic-like rock of the lower mantle.

Anywhere between 600 million and 3.5 billion years ago, slabs made of the crust and upper mantle—collectively known as the lithosphere—became cold and dense enough to be able to sink into the lower mantle, kicking off the era of plate tectonics. The lithosphere became divided into a jigsaw puzzle of plates that are constantly jostling across the planet's surface, driving geological action above and below the oceans. At mid-ocean ridges, mantle material rises, decompresses, and triggers profuse melting, creating oceanic lithosphere. The colder and denser edges of the slabs help pull this lithospheric plate away from these ridges and down into the depths. They usually dive beneath a less dense oceanic or continental plate in a process known as subduction. This activity generates explosive volcanoes and fresh crust at the surface.

When two continental slabs collide, they buckle, and mountain ranges like the Alps or the Himalaya form. Upwelling mantle plumes can sometimes appear beneath continental or oceanic slabs, and this ever-moving center of melting creates chains of volcanoes. At some point the mantle will cool to such an extent that the slabs can no longer sink into it, and several studies have attempted to predict when this will transpire. Mathematical models attempt to estimate how fast the mantle is cooling, based on what we know about the intensity of the planet's magmatic activity from three billion years ago to now. That, gives us a first-order estimate of when plate tectonics will end. Regardless of the precision of this figure, plate tectonics are predicted to inevitably perish. When that day arrives, it may well be the end of the world as we know it.

Earth would likely enter a single lid regime, a completed jigsaw of titanic slabs that will no longer drift or sink. Mountain building will stop, but Earth will still have an atmosphere, so erosion by wind and waves will shave down the mighty peaks to hilly plateaus. Eventually, much of the flattened continents will be underwater.

Subduction zones where two tectonic plates converge, and one plate is forced beneath the other into the Earth's mantle will no longer exist. These zones are characterized by intense geological activity, including earthquakes, volcanic eruptions, and the formation of mountain ranges and deep-sea trenches. So, while earthquakes will still happen every now and then, truly earthshattering events above magnitude 7 or so will be consigned to history. At the same time, much of the world's explosive volcanism would be extinguished—although volcanoes would not be entirely snuffed out.

Mars, a world of failed plate tectonics, did manage to forge some impressive volcanic features, including Olympus Mons, the largest volcano in the solar system. Without moving plates, a long-lived upwelling mantle plume focused plenty of crustal melting on that one single spot. While the mantle of future Earth remains warm enough to convect and partially melt, we would get similar but scattered stationary hot spots of plume-driven volcanism. We would never get anything as large as Olympus Mons on Earth, as our gravitational field is too strong, and anything that massive and tall would simply sink into the crust. Instead, our voluminous volcanoes would be flatter and far more spread out.

And as happens today, parts of the lower lithosphere would continue to peel off and fall into particularly hot parts of the mantle. This would cause mantle material to rise in its place, pushing up the crust and forming isolated mountain ranges and associated basins. This activity would cause minor earthquakes and maybe even additional pockets of volcanism. Referring to another world without fully-functional plate tectonics - These are the processes that shape Venus' surface.

Eventually, as cooling continues, those mechanisms will also cease to be, and the planet's final volcanic lights will be snuffed out. The mantle will be relatively frigid, and Earth will become a dead planet, like Mercury. Perhaps just before it does, Earth's liquid core will cool enough to end convection, causing the planet's protective magnetic field to fail. The sun's stream of energetic particles will strip away our atmosphere, and its expansion will boil away the oceans.

Predicting any future geophysical events is, even in the short term, challenging beyond current human capabilities. Despite this, it's good to think ahead. And while none of the predictive theories are perfect, they do highlight the complexity of the subject matter and where there are intriguing gaps in our knowledge of how our own home planet operates. The wildly differing models help clarify ideas about why plate tectonics happened in the first place. Things that are figured out about the future can be applied to the past. *Here's What'll Happen When Plate Tectonics Grinds to a Halt, Robin George Andrews, National Geographic, 08/29/2018.*

Consider comparing your life to taking a hike or trek and the many analogies that can be applied to our daily treks of life. As we consider this analogy, most often it comes to our minds that we want to be on the mountaintops all the time and avoid the deep valleys at all cost. What we may fail to realize is that in order to reach the summit of a mountain, we have to traverse upwards on many rough and winding trails. Once we do reach the mountain tops, if we desire to continue on with life, then we must move forward, which will require that we head back down into the valleys of life.

Climbing high mountains in life can be just as difficult and challenging as when we feel we are in the lowest of valleys. Most of us do tend to associate difficult times in our lives with the idea of being in a valley. Maybe it's a time of depression or despair. Maybe you've lost your job or are struggling financially. Maybe your job performance is just suffering. Maybe it's a relationship that is broken and appears to be shattered.

I prefer to look at life more as seasons than mountains and valleys. Each of us experiences the upward climbs and the downward slopes, sometimes multiple times each day. There are seasons of life that are hard, terribly hard. During the difficult times, it seems our world is pitch black, and we are stuck in the valley of despair. We don't know if a new day will dawn, or if the sun will ever peak above the next mountain. There are some that have been mired in the valley for years, but that is usually the exception. One personal practice that I try to remember when times are difficult is to ask myself the question, "What crisis was I having or what was I worrying about last year on this same day?" Usually, I have no clue. Then I remind myself, so shall it be next year. The momentary crisis of today will pass like the storm in the night, and soon we will see a new day dawning with all of its glorious radiance.

One truth that we tend to forget is if we want to reach the summit, climbing the mountain is also challenging. It may mean that we indeed need to make that difficult climb in order to see the sun. While the mountains in West Virginia are not nearly as tall as the Rockies, there are ravines between the mountains that are so close together they receive very little sun. So, if you live up one of those hollers, you do have to climb the mountain to see the sun. So, it is with life. If you find yourself in constant shadows, you may need to make the difficult choices and change your circumstances so that you will see and feel the warm sunlight on your face.

If you find yourself in a valley and at the base of the mountain, start climbing. But, realize that in order to reach the top, you will have to put forth more effort to climb than to remain wallowing in the mire of the valley floor. Be resolute. Be prepared. And, keep climbing. You will never see the beauty of the mountain peak unless you are willing to put in the effort of the climb.

The times of success and ease in your life, when it appears that God's blessings are being showered on you, can be just as challenging as the times in the valleys, just in a different way. The upward climb is actually much more difficult than heading back into the valley, but it is so worth the effort. If you learn and gain wisdom from each mountain top and valley experience, then each climb will take you a little higher, and each descent into a valley will not be as deep.

The truth is whether you are climbing the mountains or descending into the valleys, life may be difficult. The times when we get to rest on the mountain tops can be grand, so learn to relax, enjoy, and celebrate those times. The times when we are in the valleys are just as important, so learn to reflect, enjoy, and learn from those times.

Mountains and valleys are the realities of life. This challenges an immature line of thinking that many of us cling to – that life one day will be easy. If you learn from and apply the lessons of life, there may be seasons of rest and enjoyment, but if you are waiting to move onto easy street permanently…if it is your life's ambition to find ease and comfort, you're going to be waiting a long time. Winston Churchill put it this way, "Mountaintops inspire leaders; valleys mature them." *The Mountains and Valleys of Life, Leesha Chamberlain, 02/27/2019.*

In 2013, in his late 30's, my nephew Dustin Gardner was diagnosed with colon cancer. He had surgery in September of that same year and went through chemotherapy starting the first part of 2014. Dustin's family history shows the presence of this disease, but its presence had not been made well known. The development of colon cancer is typically a gradual process that can take several years. It usually starts as non-cancerous growths called polyps. It can take 10 to 15 years for a polyp to develop into cancer. Once cancer develops, it may progress slowly over several more years. The exact time frame depends on factors such as the type of cancer, its stage, and the patient's overall health.

All polyps will not become cancerous. However, regular colon cancer screenings can help detect and remove polyps before they turn into cancer. The recommended age for starting colon cancer screenings varies depending on individual risk factors. A family history of colorectal cancer (CRC) significantly increases an individual's risk of developing the disease. This risk is heightened, especially with a first-degree relative (parent, sibling, or child) diagnosed with CRC, potentially doubling the likelihood compared to those without a family history. The specific impact depends on factors like the number of affected relatives, their age at diagnosis, and the presence of inherited syndromes.

Colorectal cancer rates are rising in younger adults. While it's still less common than in older adults, the increase is significant enough to warrant attention and changes in screening recommendations. The US Preventive Services Task Force, for example, lowered the recommended age for colon cancer screening from 50 to 45 for average-risk individuals.

During the weekend of Memorial Day in 2014, I invited Dustin's family to what I called a "Survivors Dinner" at the Sand Piper restaurant, in Idaho Falls, Idaho, to celebrate his conquering colon cancer and my miracle cure of prostate cancer that was diagnosed in 2013, initiated by a chance find of a doctor's letter to my father about his prostate cancer written 18 years previously. The letter encouraged me to see a urologist that led to the discovery of cancer cells that were at a stage where they often escape the gland and metastasize to other parts of the body - a death sentence.

Other than missing one year because of a stroke, we have had this "Survivors Dinner" yearly through and including the writing of this article, 2025, with 15 in attendance. During these years, we discussed how fortunate our families are that we have survived life threatening events that would have changed our lives dramatically if there weren't some special experiences, miracles, that had helped us through the dark moments. We also discussed how the brain's natural process of forgetting results in a decrease in the accessibility to these memories over time. While it's natural for memories, even of incredible events, to fade with time, active efforts to remember and reflect on them can help preserve their power and meaning in our lives.

New experiences and information can overwrite or interfere with the retrieval of older memories, including those of miracles. If these memories are not regularly revisited or retold, they are more prone to fading. Without conscious effort to recall and reflect on the miracle, the details can become less accessible. It's human nature to forget, even when it comes from God's interventions in our lives.

Actively remembering and reflecting on miraculous events can help keep them fresh in our minds. Writing down the details or sharing them with others can be helpful in this regard. For those who see miracles through a faith lens, engaging in spiritual practices like prayer, scripture study, and attending religious services can reinforce the memory of past miracles and their significance.

Since our last "Survivors Dinner", I've thought a lot about the miracles that have occurred in the lives of those who were in attendance and how I would like to write down at least what I recall and those events mentioned by the survivor's families that classified why they were candidates for my wife and I to host a yearly "Survivors Dinner."

- Over forty years ago, my sister, Bobbie, was struck on the head by a horse and found wondering in a field near her home. As she later laid in a comma, the attending physician diagnosed a severe concussion and advised her husband, Melvin, that he should prepare his family for a possible funeral.

A concussion is usually temporary and has symptoms like loss of consciousness, severe headache, vomiting, and seizures. However, worsening neurological symptoms can indicate a life-threatening situation. In severe cases, even a single concussion can cause significant brain swelling (cerebral edema). If the swelling is severe enough, it can compress the brainstem, which controls vital functions like breathing and heart rate, leading to death. Bobbie currently enjoys visits from her great and great, great grandchildren.

- My sister, Pat, sheepishly traveled to her home in Blackfoot to inform her father that she was planning to have another baby (I believe #7) and would like a physical exam before making that decision. Dad gave her an exam and also collected a Pap Smear. This procedure involves using a small brush or spatula to collect cells from the cervix and the transformation zone (the area where cervical cancer typically develops). The smear found cervical cancer in an area that the Pap Smear procedure, during that time, usually didn't reach deep enough to diagnose the cancer. Pat did not want to have radiation therapy because of the effects expected while trying to care for her 6 children. The surgeon removed the cancerous area and any lymph tissue he could find around the area. Pat is now in her 70's and a great-grand-mother of many children.

- My nephew, Andrew Gardner, had a near drowning experience when trapped under a raft during an inflatable raft experience. My wife and I visited him at a hospital in Boise, Idaho during his recovery. His lungs would become permanently damaged – a condition he will live with for the rest of his life.

When someone near-drowns, they inhale water, which can irritate the lungs and disrupt the normal functioning of the air sacs (alveoli). Water, whether fresh or salt, can wash away or destroy surfactant, a substance that helps keep the air sacs open. This can result in damaging of the thin membrane separating the air sacs from the blood vessels, leading to fluid leakage into the lungs (pulmonary edema). The fluid buildup in the lungs is often noncardiogenic, meaning it's not caused by heart problems, but rather by the lung injury itself.

Severe cases of near-drowning can lead to ARDS (acute respiratory distress syndrome) that is a life-threatening condition where the lungs become severely inflamed and filled with fluid, making it difficult to breathe. The damage to the lungs can impair the transfer of oxygen into the blood, leading to low blood oxygen levels (hypoxemia). This can result in various lung injuries or systemic inflammation including severe pneumonia (caused by microorganisms in aspirated water). Pneumonia is an infection of the lungs that can lead to sepsis - a life-threatening condition that occurs when the body's immune system overreacts to an infection. This overreaction can lead to widespread inflammation of the air sacs (alveoli) and organ damage. The inflammation can lead to the accumulation of fluid or pus in the lungs, which can interfere with breathing.

Even if someone seems fine after a near-drowning incident, delayed complications like pneumonia or further lung injury can develop due to the initial aspiration. In some cases, near-drowning can lead to long-term lung problems or even brain damage due to oxygen deprivation.

- My brother-in-law, Lance, was presented with a newborn that was diagnosed as having encephalitis. Neonatal (first 28 days of a newborn) encephalitis is a serious condition where the brain becomes inflamed, most often due to viral or bacterial infections in newborns. It can lead to seizures, brain damage, and long-term developmental issues like cerebral palsy. Cerebral palsy is a group of disorders that affect movement, balance, and posture due to damage to the developing brain before or during birth. This damage occurs in the areas of the brain that control motor function, leading to a range of symptoms and disabilities.

Infections can be acquired during pregnancy, birth, or shortly after. In newborns, encephalitis prognosis varies significantly between viral and bacterial infections. Bacterial encephalitis, though less common, carries a higher risk of severe neurological damage or death, while viral encephalitis can also have serious long-term consequences, but outcomes can vary widely depending on the specific virus and individual factors.

Fortunately for the family, the pediatrician had recently treated his first case of encephalitis and could tell the young parents that there were two different causes of this disease and develop the best plan for treatment. If the baby had one form, bacterial, the prognosis was poor (bacteria – only some antibiotics can cross the blood-brain barrier (BBB) into the brain and even those that can may not reach therapeutic levels in the cerebrospinal fluid. The BBB, along with the blood-cerebrospinal fluid barrier, protects the brain from harmful substances but also makes treating brain infections challenging.

If encephalitis was occurring from a viral infection, the prognosis was much better – however, long-term consequences were still possible. Today, that child is an adult with children of her own, she has no symptoms of every having encephalitis.

- I have a niece that was living in a family with substance abuse. There was restitution to be paid, the traumatic loss of a spouse occurred, and there were difficult times raising her children as a single parent. She now works long hours as a licensed nurse and oversees her elderly parent's needs – making it possible for them to continue living in their home.

We all have mountains to face during our lives. Some are small and take little effort to overcome, but then life throws us those mountains that we cannot even see the top of them let alone conquer them. Turning back to the mountain climber who found himself dangling in the air, suspended from his rope, unable to see anything around him, his outer parka lost, not finding anything to grab onto, and contemplating the reality of freezing to death. He cries out, "Oh dear God in Heaven, please help me!"

Suddenly, from above he hears a strong deep voice boom out two times, "Cut the rope!" We leave him hanging there clinging onto the rope, while hoping to be able to grab onto something that would enable him to climb to safety.

Many Christians believe the Bible is God's primary way of communicating with humanity, revealing His character, will, and plan for salvation; the Holy Spirit can speak to individuals through a "still, small voice," prompting them towards good or warning them against evil; and, some believe God's creation reveals His power, wisdom, and glory.

God can use events, both positive and negative, to guide or teach us. He may speak through the words or actions of friends, family, pastors, or even strangers; some believe God uses dreams and visions to reveal His plans or messages; a sense of conviction, peace, or guidance can be attributed to God's voice within.

Many Christians believe that God's ultimate revelation of Himself is through Jesus Christ, who is referred to as the "Word of God". Ultimately, how God speaks to individuals can be a personal and subjective experience. Some may experience God's presence through powerful, dramatic events, while others may find Him in the quiet moments of everyday life.

God spoke to Moses primarily through a burning bush and also "face to face" like a friend, though he did not see God's actual face. The burning bush experience, where God called out to Moses and identified himself, marked the beginning of God's direct communication with Moses. *AI*

But, would the mountain climber (or you) have faith enough to trust Him and "cut the rope" that you perceive as your only anchor of hope? The story of the mountain climb ends: Except for the wind, silence followed, as the climber continued to hang onto the rope, while hoping to be able to grab onto something that would enable him to climb to safety. Unable to see his true situation, the climber concluded, as most people would, that hanging onto the rope was his only hope.

The following day, the rest of his climbing party discovered him frozen to death, still dangling from his rope - only eight feet above a large out-cropping of rock. Had the climber cut the rope, he would have dropped down to a relatively safe area, near his backpack, where he could have built a fire, using some of the surrounding scrub brush, and probably survived the night. *Author unknown*

I thought about this scenario and what I would probably have done. I have faith in there being a God the Eternal Father, that His son, Jesus Christ, has been resurrected and atoned for all our sins, in Gethsemane and on the cross, and that His Gospel has been given for the joy and benefit of man both on this earth and in the hereafter. Still when push turned to shove – would I have the guts to cut that rope? Probably not unless I looked at my situation from a practical point of view. "Here I am hanging from a rope with little to no hope of not freezing to death. Have I heard voices from the Holy Spirt, my delirium from weakness and loss of body temperature or something "blowing in the wind" that is unsettled, elusive, or not easily grasped – like the wind itself.

Thinking about what I would go through during the process of my tissue freezing during hypothermia, I have been led to believe it is generally considered a bad way to die. While some individuals experiencing hypothermia report a sense of peacefulness or euphoria as they lose consciousness, the process involves a significant amount of suffering leading up to that point. The body's physiological response to cold temperatures, including shivering, confusion, and loss of coordination, can be distressing. Additionally, the eventual shutdown of vital organs and the brain's ability to function properly can be a painful process. So, voices or not, I would probably cut the rope to get it over with. And, if I landed safely near my backpack and survived the ordeal, I would praise my Heavenly Father for the miracle of saving my life.

As time went on, my personal miracle would probably fade as is the tendency that even in the face of compelling evidence, it is a recurring theme throughout history and across cultures. One would probably find a beautiful painting of a four-leaf clover or a horse shoe over my mantle with writing underneath showing a date and inscription: "Walter's stroke of luck and may God bless us all."

CHAPTER 2

EXTRACTING FROM MOTHER EARTH

Extraction is a vital step in obtaining pure bioactive natural compounds for medical, scientific and commercial use. Interest in extracting natural products for applications across the food, pharmaceutical, and cosmetic industries has grown rapidly, driving demand for newer, more efficient extraction methods. Natural products have been used by humans for millennia for their therapeutic, cosmetic, and nutritional benefits. Today, these compounds continue to play a critical role in drug discovery and other industries. Extraction is the process of separating out the desired component(s) from a chemical mixture. It is a key step in using any bioactive natural compound. Advances in technology and research have led to the development of innovative approaches for extracting and isolating natural products. These methods have the potential to expand the understanding of natural product chemistry and unlocking new sources of valuable compounds.

The first efforts by humans to make extractions from natural products probably coincided with the discovery of fire. Ancient cultures worldwide used extraction processes, primarily utilizing water as an extraction medium. Later on, distillation and alcohol extraction (preparation of tinctures) methods were adopted and refined. The choice of solvent is the first important decision to be taken when designing an extraction procedure, as extraction solvents play a key role in determining the extracted compounds' quality, quantity, and selectivity. The choice of extraction solvent depends on the chemical properties of the natural products being extracted and the desired end product. Solvents commonly used for natural product extraction include polar solvents such as water, methanol, ethanol, and acetone and non-polar solvents such as hexane, chloroform, and ethyl acetate. Each solvent has specific properties that make it suitable for extracting compounds of specific polarity. For example, ethanol–water mixtures are recommended for the extraction of phenolics. However, acetone has been proven efficient in the extraction of polyphenols from lychee flowers compared to methanol, water and ethanol. Solvents also play a role in the safety and potential environmental impact of the extraction process. It is important to consider the toxicity and flammability of solvents, as well as their potential effect on the environment. In this respect, organic solvents have a number of disadvantages: most of them are volatile and toxic and contribute significantly to environmental pollution. With the development of green chemistry, the design of green and sustainable extraction methods of natural products has become a hot research topic. Among proposed green solvents, ionic liquids, natural deep eutectic solvents, supercritical and subcritical fluids and solvents from natural and renewable sources stand out as the most promising approaches for current solvent innovation.

The most common extraction method for natural products is typically solid-liquid extraction (the process of removing a solute component from the solid using a liquid solvent). Several solid-liquid extraction techniques have been applied to purify bioactive constituents from plants and microorganisms. Traditional methods include maceration, percolation, and Soxhlet extraction. Soxhlet extraction is a laboratory technique that uses a solvent to extract compounds from a solid material. It's a continuous extraction process that's often used to analyze environmental samples, food, and beverages. A solvent is heated to its boiling point, the solvent vapor rises and condenses in a condenser, the condensed solvent drips down onto the solid material, the solvent dissolves the desired compounds from the solid material, and the solvent is siphoned back into the flask for reuse. Alcohol extraction produced from the distillation process of yeast fermentation of organic material can be used as a type Soxhlet extraction. However, in this case the fermented liquid, such as wine or mash, is heated in a still, the alcohol evaporates and rises to the top of the still where it is collected and condensed into a concentrated (high-proof) solution.

Recently developed extraction techniques for natural products are more energy efficient and result in shorter extraction times compared to earlier methods. Such techniques include ultrasound-assisted extraction, microwave-assisted extraction and pressurized solvent extraction. The choice of extraction solvent and method depends on the type of natural raw material being extracted, the target compounds, and the desired end product. Based on the law of similarity and intermiscibility (like dissolves like), solvents with a polarity value near the solute's polarity are likely to perform better and vice versa. When selecting the extraction method, it is necessary to take into consideration the stability of the desired product: temperature must be chosen carefully in order to avoid degradation. Current methods for natural product extraction offer several benefits, including improved efficiency, reduced extraction time, and reduced solvent usage. However, there are also some challenges: Some methods, such as supercritical fluid extraction and microwave-assisted extraction, can be expensive due to the specialized equipment required to perform them. Given the costs involved, these same methods may also be challenging to scale up for commercial production. However, they also offer opportunities for increased productivity, potential selectivity, and sustainability. Therefore, researchers must carefully evaluate these methods to determine their suitability for specific applications and weigh the benefits against the costs and limitations. *BMC Chem, ...extraction & isolation of natural products, 06/30/2023*

The extraction of natural dyes leading to the current textile industry started from humble beginnings. Historically, dyes came from nature, with primary sources consisting of animals or plants. The majority of these came from roots, berries, bark, leaves, wood, and other organic, naturally occurring substances such as fungi. Archaeologists have even found evidence of textile dyeing going back to the Neolithic period, otherwise known as the New Stone Age, which began around 10,200 BC. In China, there is evidence that dyes were created from insects, barks, and plants, beginning about 5,000 years ago.

These dyes, while effective, were rudimentary and simplistic, often depicting ruddy colors (e.g., reds, browns, and oranges) that faded with use. The more luxurious dyestuffs (substances that produce a dye) which produced brilliant and permanent colors, such as the natural invertebrate dyes, didn't gain major popularity until the medieval era. Around that same period, plant-based dyes such as woad, indigo, saffron, and madder root became important trade goods throughout Asia and Europe. Spanish treasure fleets then introduced cochineal beetle (see Natural Dyes chapter) and the heartwood of logwood to Europe, thus expanding the amount of available dye colors.

When Europe carried colonists to America, the dyes came with them. These natural dyes continued to dominate the global textile market, until in 1856 William Perkin created mauveine (a rich synthetic purple) from aniline which comes from the indigo-yielding plant, Indigofera anil. He was in his apartment boiling nitric acid and benzene in smuggled Institute of Learning class glass flasks, and precipitated an unexpected reaction. A chemical had formed inside the tubes with the color of pale, crushed violets. In an era obsessed with dye-making any colored chemical was considered a potential dye – and a quick dip of a piece of cotton into the flask revealed the new chemical could color cotton. Moreover, this new chemical did not bleach or bleed. Perkin called it aniline mauve. By the mid-1860s, a glut of new synthetic dyes, in shades of lilac, blue, magenta, aquamarine, red, and blue flooded the cloth factories of Europe. In 1857, Perkin, barely nineteen years old, was inducted into the Chemical Society of London as a full fellow, one of the youngest in its history to be thus honored. Then, in 1869, the red dye found in madder root was the first natural pigment to be synthetically duplicated, which began the steady decline of dyes produced from natural sources. By the late 1870s, synthetic chemists in Germany had created more molecules than they knew what to do with. "Practical chemistry" had become almost a caricature of itself: an industry seeking a practical purpose for the products that it had so frantically raced to invent. *The History of Textile Dyes, Brahms Mount, 09/09/2022*

In 1878, a twenty-four-year-old medical student, Paul Ehrlich, hunting for a thesis project, proposed using cloth dyes – aniline and its colored derivatives – to stain animal tissues. At best, Ehrlich hoped that his dyes might stain the tissues and make microscopy easier. But to his astonishment, the dyes were far from indiscriminate darkening agents. Aniline derivatives stained only parts of the cell, silhouetting certain structures and leaving others untouched. The dyes seemed able to discriminate among chemicals hidden inside cells – binding some and sparing others. In 1882, working with Robert Koch, he discovered yet another novel chemical stain, this time for mycobacteria, the organisms Koch had discovered as the cause of tuberculosis. He began to hunt for antimicrobial chemicals, in part because he already knew that chemical dyes could specifically bind microbial cells. He infected mice and rabbits with the parasite responsible for the dreaded sleeping sickness, *Trypanosoma brucei*, then injected the animals with chemical derivatives to determine if any of them could halt the infection. After several hundred chemicals, Ehrlich and his collaborators had their first antibiotic hit: a brilliant ruby-colored dye derivative that Ehrlich called Trypan Red. In 1910, Ehrlich announced that he had discovered yet another molecule with "specific affinity" – this one a blockbuster. The new drug cryptically called compound 606, was active against a notorious microbe, *Treponema pallidum*, which caused syphilis. At this time, syphilis was endemic and compound 606, containing arsenic and Trypan Red dye, not only was a bullet to cure active syphilis but neurosyphilis as well. He named the drug Salvarsan, from the word salvation.

Ehrlich's "magic bullets" had one last target to fell: cancer. He was slowly inching towards his ultimate goals: the malignant human cell. Between 1904 and 1908, he rigged several elaborate schemes to find an anticancer drug using his vast arsenal of chemicals: He tried amides (used as local anesthetics including lidocaine, bupivacaine and ropivacaine commonly used for pain control during minor surgery or invasive procedures such as biopsies, small excisions or dental work); anilines (come from the burning of plastics and tobacco, or from the breakdown of pollutants in outdoor air - small amounts can be found in corn, grains, rhubarb, apples, beans, and rapeseeds, coal etc. Used to make many products, including dyes, herbicides, and rubber accelerators); sulfa derivatives (also known as sulfonamide, are a group of drugs that have antibacterial, antiviral, and other properties); arsenics (toxic naturally occurring element that can be found in soil, water, air, plants, and animals. It can also be introduced into the environment by human activities like mining, fracking, and burning coal); bromides (can come from many sources, including the environment, agriculture, and human activities. Some leafy vegetables and herbs can contain high levels of bromide, bromide is found in coal-fired power plants, oil and gas brine, and shale formations, in some pharmaceuticals, personal care products, and in some fabric dyes. They are more carcinogenic than chlorinated products. Bromides, were historically used as sedatives and anticonvulsants in medicine and were discontinued due to concerns of toxicity; and alcohols (they are hydrocarbons that can be found in beverages, household products, and medicines. Some alcohols are toxic and can cause serious health problems – inflammation of the optic nerves, kidney failure, cancer, high blood pressure, liver disease stroke, GI problems and weakened immune system. Ethanol is found in alcoholic beverages, mouthwash, cooking extracts, and some medicines. It is the only product made for human consumption. Isopropyl alcohol is used for rubbing alcohol, lotions, and some cleaning products. Methanol is used in windshield-wiper fluid, de-icing products, paint removers, and some Windex products. Ethylene glycol is used in radiator antifreeze, degreasing agents, foam stabilizers, and metal cleaners).

None of them worked to kill cancer cells. What was poison to cancer cells, he found, was inevitably poison to normal cells as well. But the search for the ultimate, discrimination anticancer drug proved fruitless. His pharmacological bullets, far from marginal, were either too indiscriminate or too weak. He surmised that, with cancer, it was the similarity of the cancer cell to the normal human cell that made it nearly impossible to target. To target the abnormal cell, one would need to decipher the biology of the normal cell.

In 1928 a young English physician named Lucy Wills, freshly out of the London School of Medicine for Women, traveled on a grant to Bombay to study anemia. Wills was an exotic among hematologists, an adventurous woman driven by a powerful curiosity about blood and willing to travel to a faraway country to solve a mysterious anemia on a whim. She found that anemia in Bombay could not be cured from tested yeasty concoctions or by vitamin B12. It was soon discovered that the "magic bullet" missing turned out to be an orange-yellow material called folic acid, vitamin B9, substance found in fruits, vegetables and brewer's yeast. Folic acid is a crucial building block for DNA and thus vital for cell division. In the human body, there are more than 300 billion cells produced daily and if folic acid is absent (as in the men and women starved of vegetables, as in Bombay) the production of new blood cells in the bone marrow halts. Millions of half-matured cells spew out, piling up like half-finished goods bottlenecked in an assembly line.

In 1946, Dr. Sidney Farber while working on the links with vitamins, bone marrow and normal blood, began to wonder if folic acid might help restore normal blood counts in children with leukemia. Childhood leukemia is a type of cancer that affects the white blood cells. It is the most common cancer in children, accounting for about 30% of all childhood cancers. Symptoms can vary depending on the type and severity of the disease. Common symptoms may include: Fatigue, fever, bruising easily, bleeding gums or nosebleeds, bone pain, swollen lymph nodes, enlarged liver or spleen, loss of appetite, and weight loss.

Farber wondered whether administering folic acid given to children with leukemia might restore normalcy to their blood. Following a tenuous trail, he obtained some synthetic folic acid, recruited a cohort of leukemic children, and started injecting folic acid into them. in the months that passed, Farber found that folic acid, far from stopping the progression of leukemia, actually accelerated it. In one patient, the already high white cell blood count nearly doubled. In another, the exploding malignant cells infiltrated the skin. Farber stopped the experiment in a hurry. Pediatricians at the Children's Hospital were furious about Farber's trial. The folic acid analogues had not just accelerated the leukemia; they had likely hastened the death of the children. But Farber was intrigued. If folic acid accelerated the leukemia cells in children, what if he could cut off its supply with other drugs – an antifolate? Could a chemical that blocked the growth of white blood cells stop leukemia? Could the anemia of the mill workers in Bombay be re-created therapeutically in the medical units of Boston?

It turned out that the chemical reactions to make folic acid brought a serendipitous bonus. Since the reactions had several intermediate steps, researchers could create variants of folic acid through slight alterations in the recipe. These variants of folic acid – closely related molecular mimics – possessed counterintuitive properties. One that nearly mimics the natural molecule can bind to the receptor or enzyme and block its action, like a false key jamming a lock. These were precisely what Farber had been fantasizing about. In 1947, the first package of antifolate arrived at Farber's laboratory. Farber snatched the drug as soon as it arrived: Hoping at best for a minor reprieve from advanced leukemia in a young boy, began to inject the antifolate. The marked increases in white blood cells suddenly stopped rising and hovered at a plateau. Then the count began to drop, the leukemia blasts gradually flickering out in the blood and then all but disappearing. The cancer hadn't vanished – under the microscope, there still were malignant cells. In early 1948, the boy's alertness, nutrition and activity were equal to his twin's.

For Dr. Sidney Farber's groundbreaking work in cancer treatment, particularly in leukemia, where he discovered that by blocking the action of folic acid with a drug called aminopterin, he could achieve temporary remissions in children with acute leukemia, essentially laying the foundation for modern chemotherapy; this finding was significant because it showed that targeting a specific vitamin pathway could inhibit cancer cells.

But treating cancer with antifolate there was always the same catch. After a few months of remission, the cancer would inevitably relapse, ultimately flinging aside even the most potent drugs. The cells would return in the bone marrow, then burst out into the blood. Yet the remissions, even if temporary, were still genuine remissions and historic. About 1/3rd of the initial treatment group remained alive for four to even six months after diagnosis. In leukemia, six months of survival was an eternity. *From: The Emperor of all Maladies, Siddharth A. Mukherjee, 2010 & several other references*

From a brilliant ruby-colored dye, a derivative that Ehrlich called Trypan Red, and arsenic he announced in 1910 and that he had discovered yet another "magic bullet" molecule with "specific affinity" – this one turned out to be a blockbuster. The new drug cryptically called compound 606, was active against a notorious microbe, *Treponema pallidum*, which causes syphilis. At this time, syphilis was endemic and compound 606 not only was a "magic bullet" to cure active syphilis but neurosyphilis as well.

To an orange-yellow colored B9 vitamin (known as folate) found in fruits, vegetables and brewer's yeast - the lacking of which was found in the 1920s to cause folate-deficiency anemia in Bombay. Farber found another "magic bullet" (known as antifolate) that could suppress acute leukemia at least for a short period of time in young children? It killed cancer cells but could not cure cancer.

Antifolates, particularly methotrexate (MTX), are still widely used in the treatment of childhood leukemia, as they are considered a key component of chemotherapy regimens for pediatric acute lymphoblastic leukemia (ALL) due to their effectiveness in targeting rapidly dividing cancer cells: making them a significant part of current treatment protocols for child leukemia patients.

CHAPTER 3

WONDERS OF THE POMEGRANATE

The actual dyeing process is not described in the Bible. Dyed materials are mentioned as early as the time of the Exodus. Material for the Tabernacle is described as "blue and purple and scarlet stuff" (Exodus 26:1,31). Josephus described the Temple materials as "woven of four stuffs, byssus as a symbol of the earth, whence the flax grows; purple, the sea which was dyed with the blood of fishes; hyacinth, the air; and scarlet, the fire" (Antiq. III. vii). Dyeing with its infinite possibility in color variations had its secret formula. All ancient crafts were family affairs and the best techniques and materials were trade secrets. With the rise of the new science of chemistry the secret formulas were made known. The dye used must have a natural affinity for the cloth used, or a mordant (inorganic oxide that combines with the stain or dye and there by fixes it to the material) must be added to make the color fast. Wool, the most common cloth in Biblical times, was easy to dye. Natural wool came in a variety of colors running from white and yellow through tans and browns.

By the use of different dyes on these various wools it was possible to make the "many-colored robes" (Ps 45:14). Linen was more difficult to dye, but linen was used in the Tabernacle (Exod 35:6) and the Temple (2 Chron 2:7). Cotton was easy to dye. Its home was India and by the time of Esther it was used in Persia (Esth 1:6). Some silk was dyed before it left the Far East for Antioch, while some was dyed in Mediterranean cities. Fine leather also was dyed.

The most important red used in dyeing ran from a brilliant hue to a scarlet (Isa 1:18). It was produced from cochineal insects (see Natural Dyes chapter). A cheaper commonly used dye was secured from the root of the madder plant. The best blue dye was that extracted from the Mollusca Purpura and Murex which flourished on the Phoenician coast. The expensive garments which symbolized rank and nobility were dyed purple from the secretion of the Mollusca. During intertestamental times indigo came into Palestine from India. Yellows were made from safflower, turmeric and pomegranate. The dominant color of cloth described in the NT is purple (Mark 15:17; Luke 16:19; John 19:2,5; Acts 16:14). When the Apostle Paul went to Philippi, Lydia from Thyatira, "a seller of purple goods" (Acts 16:14) was one of the first to respond to the Gospel. *Encyclopedia of the Bible – Dye, Dyeing*

Pomegranates have a long history of use in natural dyeing, dating back thousands of years. The rinds of the fruit, particularly, are rich in tannins, which allow them to produce a range of colors, from soft yellows to deep browns, and even greens, greys, and blacks. The fruit's symbolic significance also led to its use in textiles, adding to its cultural importance. Pomegranates were used for dyeing in ancient Mesopotamia, and in Mughal India, they were used to create ceremonial and celebratory fabrics. In Mexico, pomegranate rinds have been used for centuries to dye wool, producing rich, earthy tones. Pomegranate dye was a popular choice for dyeing Oriental carpets due to its ability to create yellows that are lightfast with other natural dyes. A lightfast dye is a dye that resists fading or discoloration when exposed to light, particularly sunlight or artificial light sources. This property is crucial for ensuring the longevity and vibrancy of colored materials, especially in artwork, textiles, and other applications where color permanence is desired.

Pomegranate is a fruit used in traditional and modern medicine for a variety of ailments due to its rich antioxidant and anti-inflammatory properties. It has a long history of use in treating intestinal parasites, diarrhea, and other gastrointestinal problems; extracts and juices have been used to address gum bleeding, mouth ulcers, and other oral health concerns; traditional medicine utilizes pomegranate for sore throat, skin conditions, and even as a general tonic; its juice, may help lower blood pressure, reduce LDL cholesterol, and improve overall cardiovascular health; pomegranate extracts have shown potential in alleviating symptoms and preventing complications of both rheumatoid and osteoarthritis; they can help with wound healing and may offer protection against skin diseases; research suggests pomegranate's antioxidant and anti-inflammatory properties may play a role in preventing certain cancers, including prostate and breast cancer; and, studies are exploring pomegranate's effects on diabetes, athletic performance, and even Alzheimer's disease. *AI*

The pomegranate has three symbolic values: (1) The pomegranate's calyx (sepals) has the appearance of a crown, which is suggestive of kings, queens, and royalty (queenship/kingship is also associated with the temple.). (2) During the spring season, the pomegranate tree is covered with lovely scarlet flowers; scarlet serves as a reminder of the blood of Christ. Similarly, the pomegranate juice is blood red, also an image of Jesus's blood. (3) The pomegranate's numerous seeds suggest fertility and eternal increase (granate, from pomegranate, originates from Latin, meaning "having seeds". *175 Temple Symbols and Their Meanings, Donald W. Parry, 2020.*

Although the pomegranate is an ancient symbol steeped in tradition, it has re-emerged in contemporary culture, not only because of its beauty and rich history, but because the pomegranate is quite desirable for its healthy, antioxidant qualities. The word pomegranate, "rimon" in Hebrew, is derived from the Latin words "pomum" (apple) and "granatus" (seeded). Grown in the Mediterranean region for several thousand years, this remarkable fruit is rich in symbolism and there are specific references to the pomegranate in the Bible.

In the Old Testament skillful workers embroidered representations of the pomegranates into the hem of the high priest's robe; the pomegranates were alternated with bells of gold (see Ex. 28:33-34). Additionally, hundreds of images of pomegranates existed on the columns of Solomon's temple (see 1 Kgs. 7:20; see also 7:18, 42; Chr. 3:16; Jer. 52:22-23). King Solomon is said to have designed his crown based on the "crown" of the pomegranate. The significance of the Jewish pomegranate is further exemplified by its appearance on ancient coins of Judea, one of only a few images that appear as a holy symbol.

Jewish tradition teaches that the pomegranate is a symbol of righteousness because it is said to have 613 seeds, which corresponds with the 613 mitzvot, or commandments, of the Torah. For this reason and others, it is customary to eat pomegranates on Rosh Hashanah. Moreover, the pomegranate represents fruitfulness, knowledge, learning, and wisdom. Many Jewish scholars believe that the pomegranate was the "forbidden fruit" of the Garden of Eden. Furthermore, the pomegranate is listed in the Bible as one of the seven species (shivat haminim) of fruits and grains that are special products of the Land of Israel. *Wikipedia.*

It is written that the story of the "forbidden fruit" growing on the tree of Knowledge and Evil in the Garden of Eden begins with the creation of the world... Following the creation periods... "And on the seventh day God ended his work, and all things which He had made; and He rested. And God blessed the seventh day, and sanctified it. And these are the generations of the heaven and of the earth, when they were created, in the day that the Lord God, made the heaven and the earth. And every plant of the field before it was in the earth, and every herb of the field before it grew. God, created all things, of which He had spoken, spiritually, before they were naturally upon the face of the earth. For God had not caused it to rain upon the face of the earth. And He had created all the children of men; and not yet a man to till the ground; for in Heaven, He created them; and there was not yet flesh upon the earth, neither in the water, neither in the air;

Lord God spoke and there went up a mist from the earth, and watered the whole face of the ground. And He, formed man from the dust of the ground, and breathed into his nostrils the breath of life; and man became a living soul, the first flesh upon the earth, the first man also; nevertheless, all things were before created; but spiritually were they created and made according to His word. And the Lord God planted a garden eastward in Eden, and there He put the man whom He had formed. And out of the ground made the Lord God caused to grow every tree, naturally, that is pleasant to the sight of man; and man could behold it. And it became also a living soul. For it was spiritual in the day that He created it; for it remaineth in the sphere in which God created it, yea, even all things which He prepared for the use of man; and man saw that it was good for food. And the Lord God planted the tree of life also in the midst of the garden, and also the tree of knowledge of good and evil. And the Lord God commanded the man, saying: Of every tree of the garden thou mayest freely eat, but of the tree of the knowledge of good and evil, thou shalt not eat of it, nevertheless, thou mayest choose for thyself, for it is given unto thee; but, remember that I forbid it, for in the day thou eatest thereof thou shalt surely die.

And the Lord God said unto His Only Begotten, that it was not good that the man should be alone; wherefore, l will make a help meet for him. And the Lord God, caused a deep sleep to fall upon Adam; and he slept, and God took one of his ribs and closed up the flesh in the stead thereof; and the rib, which God had taken from man, He made a woman and brought her unto the man. And Adam said: This I know

now is bone of my bones, and flesh of my flesh; she shall be called Woman, because she was taken out of man.

And I, the Lord God, spake unto Moses saying: Satan, who confronted you, is the same which was from the beginning and he came before me, saying—Behold, here am I, send me, I will be thy son, and I will redeem all mankind, that one soul shall not be lost, and surely I will do it; wherefore give me thine honor. But, behold, my Beloved Son, which was my Beloved and Chosen from the beginning, said unto me—Father, thy will be done, and the glory be thine forever.

Wherefore, because that Satan rebelled against me and sought to destroy the agency of man, which I the Lord God had given him, and also, that I should give unto him mine own power; by the power of mine Only Begotten, I caused that he should be cast down; he became Satan, yea, even the devil, the father of all lies, to deceive and to blind men, and to lead them captive at his will, even as many as would not hearken unto my voice. In the pre-existence Satan had drawn away many (1/3 of the hosts of Heaven) after him and he sought also to beguile Eve, for he knew not the mind of God, wherefore he sought to destroy the world.

Satan spoke to Eve by the mouth of a serpent and said: Ye shall not eat of every tree of the garden? Eve said unto the serpent: We may eat of the fruit (pomegranate?) of the trees of the garden; but of the fruit of the tree which thou beholdest in the midst of the garden, God hath said—Ye shall not eat of it, neither shall ye touch it, lest ye die. The serpent said unto the woman: Ye shall not surely die; God doth know that in the day ye eat thereof, then your eyes shall be opened, and ye shall be as gods, knowing good and evil.

And when the woman saw that the tree was good for food, and that it became pleasant to the eyes, and a tree to be desired to make her wise, she took of the fruit thereof, and did eat, and also gave unto her husband with her, and he did eat. The eyes of them both were opened, and they knew that they had been naked. And they sewed fig leaves together and made themselves aprons. The Lord God, called unto Adam, and said unto him: Where goest thou? Adam replied that he heard His voice in the garden, and was afraid, because he beheld that he was naked, and hid himself. The Lord God, said unto Adam: Who told thee thou wast naked? Hast thou eaten of the tree whereof I commanded thee that thou shouldst not eat, if so thou shouldst surely die? And God, said unto the serpent: Because thou hast done this thou shalt be cursed above all cattle, and above every beast of the field; upon thy belly shalt thou go, and dust shalt thou eat all the days of thy life; Adam cursed shall be the ground for thy sake; in sorrow shalt thou eat of it all the days of thy life. Thorns also, and thistles shall it bring forth to thee, and thou shalt eat the herb of the field. By the sweat of thy face shalt thou eat bread, until thou shalt return unto the ground—for thou shalt surely die—for out of it wast thou taken: for dust thou wast, and unto dust shalt thou return.

And the Lord God said unto His Only Begotten: Behold, the man has become as one of us to know good and evil; and now lest he put forth his hand and partake also of the tree of life, and eat and live forever, I will send him forth from the Garden of Eden, to till the ground from whence he was taken." *See Pearl of Great Price, Moses Chapters 2-4, 1880.*

Pomegranates continue to be a motif often found in Christian religious decoration. They are often woven into the fabric of vestments and liturgical hangings or wrought in metalwork. Pomegranates figure in many religious paintings by the likes of Sandro Botticelli and Leonardo da Vinci, often in the hands of the Virgin Mary or the infant Jesus. The fruit, broken or bursting open, is a symbol of the fullness of Jesus' suffering and resurrection. In the Eastern Orthodox Church, pomegranate seeds may be used in kolyva, a dish prepared for memorial services, as a symbol of the sweetness of the heavenly kingdom.

Because the pomegranate is so rich in history and symbolism, it is represented in modern culture in everything from pomegranate jewelry to all kinds of pomegranate gifts, which are appropriate for many occasions. Pomegranate Judaica is quite popular today due to the continued interest in this ancient, healthy, and mysterious fruit. In fact, the beauty of this historical fruit translates so well into modern jewelry and art, it can be seen on everything from pomegranate necklaces, bracelets and earrings, to the pomegranate mezuzah. The rich red color and symbolism of the pomegranate makes it the perfect subject for jewelry makers and artists alike. *Wikipedia*

The myth of Persephone, the goddess of the underworld, prominently features her consumption of pomegranate seeds, requiring her to spend a certain number of months in the underworld every year. The number of seeds and therefore months vary. During the months that Persephone sits on the throne of the underworld beside her husband Hades, her mother Demeter mourned and no longer gave fertility to the earth. This was an ancient Greek explanation for the seasons of the year.

My pomegranate tree reminds me of the approaching fall by the splitting open of its fruit and the birds pecking away at the seeds. If I don't harvest the crop soon the fruit will be gone. Knowing this, I still find myself procrastinating the harvest: The stems connected to the fruit take more than sharp scissors to cut, the limbs are spiny and gloves are advised, the seeds take effort to separate from the husk and the pigmentation of the fruit can cause indelible stains on fabrics.

In modern times, the pomegranate still holds strong symbolic meanings for the Greeks. When one buys a new home, it is conventional for a house guest to bring as a first gift a pomegranate, which is placed under/near the home altar of the house, as a symbol of abundance, fertility, and good luck. I like to think that having a living productive pomegranate tree in my back yard is symbolic, like the Greeks, of love and peace in our home. *Wikipedia*

CHAPTER 4

NATURAL DYES

Scale insects are small insects, of dramatically variable appearance and extreme sexual dimorphism. Adult females typically have soft bodies and no limbs, and are concealed underneath domed scales, extruding quantities of wax for protection. Some species are hermaphroditic, with a combined ovotestis instead of separate ovaries and testes. Males, in the species where they occur, have legs and sometimes wings, and resemble small flies. Scale insects are herbivores, piercing plant tissues with their mouthparts and remaining in one place, feeding on sap. The excess fluid they imbibe is secreted as honeydew on which sooty mold tends to grow. The insects often have a mutualistic relationship with ants, which feed on the honeydew and protect them from predators. There are about 8,000 described species. The oldest fossils of the group date to the Late Jurassic, preserved in fossilized tree resin called amber. Some scale insects are serious commercial pests, they are difficult to control as the scale and waxy covering protect them effectively from contact insecticides. Some species are used for biological control of pest plants such as the prickly pear, Opuntia.

Others produce commercially valuable substances including carmine and kermes dyes, and shellac lacquer.

The cochineal insect, Dactylopius coccus, is a scale insect from which the natural dye carmine is derived. A primarily sessile (meaning the parasite has an inability to move actively or spontaneously and is permanently attached to the substrate or to the base, hence, not freely moving) is native to tropical and subtropical South America through North America (Mexico and the Southwest United States), this insect lives on cacti in the genus Opuntia, feeding on plant moisture and nutrients. The insects are found on the pads of prickly pear cacti, collected by brushing them off the plants, and dried.

The insect produces carminic acid that deters predation by other insects. Carminic acid, typically 17–24% of dried insects' weight, can be extracted from the body and eggs, then mixed with aluminum or calcium salts to make red and purple dyes called carmine dye, also known as cochineal. Today, carmine is primarily used as a colorant in food and in lipstick (E120 or Natural Red 4). Other species in the genus Dactylopius can be used to produce "cochineal extract", and are extremely difficult to distinguish from D. coccus, even for expert taxonomists; the scientific term D. coccus and the vernacular "cochineal insect" are sometimes used, intentionally or casually, and possibly with misleading effect, to refer to other species.

Carmine dye was used in the Americas for coloring fabrics and became an important export good in the 16th century during the colonial period. Production of cochineal is depicted in the Codex Osuna (1565). After synthetic pigments and dyes such as alizarin were invented in the late 19th century, use of natural-dye products gradually diminished. Fears over the safety of artificial food additives renewed the popularity of cochineal dyes, and the increased demand has made cultivation of the insect profitable again, with Peru being the largest producer, followed by Mexico, Chile, Argentina and the Canary Islands.

Cochineal insects are soft-bodied, flat, oval-shaped scale insects. The females, wingless and about 5 mm (0.20 in) long, cluster on cactus pads. They penetrate the cactus with their beak-like mouthparts and feed on its juices, remaining immobile unless alarmed. After mating, the fertilized female increases in size and gives birth to tiny nymphs. The nymphs secrete a waxy white substance over their bodies for protection from water loss and excessive sun. This substance makes the cochineal insect appear white or grey from the outside, though the body of the insect and its nymphs produces the red pigment, which makes the insides of the insect look dark purple. Adult males can be distinguished from females in that males have wings, and are much smaller.

The cochineal disperses in the first nymph stage, called the "crawler" stage. The juveniles move to a feeding spot and produce long wax filaments. Later, they move to the edge of the cactus pad, where the wind catches the wax filaments and carries the insects to a new host. These individuals establish feeding sites on the new host and produce a new generation of cochineals. Male nymphs feed on the cactus until they reach sexual maturity. At this time, they can no longer feed and live only long enough to fertilize the eggs. They are, therefore, seldom observed. In addition, females typically outnumber males due to environmental factors.

Feeding cochineals can damage and kill the plant. Other cochineal species feed on many of the same Opuntia, and the wide range of hosts reported for D. coccus likely is because of the difficulty in distinguishing it from other Dactylopius species.

Scale insects are herbivores, piercing plant tissues with their mouthparts and remaining in one place, feeding on sap. The excess fluid they imbibe is secreted as honeydew on which sooty mold tends to grow. The insects often have a mutualistic relationship with ants, which feed on the honeydew and protect them from predators. There are about 8,000 described species.

Several natural enemies can reduce the population of the scale insects on hosts. Of all the predators, insects seem to be the most important group. Insects and their larvae such as pyralid moths, which destroy the cactus, and predators such as lady bugs, various flies, and ants have been identified, as well as numerous parasitic wasps. Many birds, rodents (especially rats), and reptiles, also prey on cochineal insects.

Cochineals are farmed in the traditional method by planting infected cactus pads or infesting existing cacti with cochineals and harvesting the insects by hand. The controlled method uses small baskets called Zapotec nests placed on host cacti. The baskets contain clean, fertile females that leave the nests and settle on the cactus to await fertilization by the males. In both cases, the cochineals must be protected from predation, cold, and rain. The complete cycle lasts three months, during which time the cacti are kept at a constant temperature of 27 °C (81 °F). At the end of the cycle, the new cochineals are left to reproduce or are collected and dried for dye production.

Workers collect the female cochineal insects from their host plants. The insects are killed by immersion in hot water or by exposure to sunlight, steam, or the heat of an oven. Each method produces a different color that results in the varied appearance of commercial cochineal. The insects must be dried to about 30% of their original body weight before they can be stored without decaying. It takes about 70,000 insects to make 1 pound (0.45 kilograms) of cochineal dye. The two principal forms of cochineal dye are cochineal extract, a coloring made from the raw dried and pulverized bodies of insects, and carmine, a more purified coloring made from the cochineal. To prepare carmine, the powdered insect bodies are boiled in ammonia or a sodium carbonate solution, the insoluble matter is removed by filtering, and alum is added to the clear salt solution of carminic acid to precipitate the red aluminum salt. Purity of color is ensured by the absence of iron. Stannous chloride, citric acid, borax, or gelatin may be added to regulate the formation of the precipitate. For shades of purple, lime is added to the alum.

Traditionally, cochineal was used for coloring fabrics. Cochineal dye was used by the Aztec and Maya peoples of North and Central America as early as the second century BC. Inhabitants of Peru have been producing cochineal dyes for textiles since early in the Middle Horizon period (600–1000 CE). Cochineal dye was extensively used in the Pre-Columbian era, often for ceremonial textiles and those worn by rulers. The dye bonds best with animal fibers rather than plant fibers and was most effective for dying wool from alpacas and other Camelidae, rabbit fur, and feathers. It was also used on cottons and plant-based fabrics, to less effect.

During the colonial period, with the introduction of sheep to Latin America, the use of cochineal increased. It provided the most intense color and it set more firmly on woolen garments compared to clothes made of materials of pre-Hispanic origin such as cotton or agave and yucca fibers. In general, cochineal is more successful on protein-based animal fibers (including silk) than plant-based material.

Once the European market discovered the qualities of this product, the demand for it increased dramatically. Carmine became the region's second-most-valuable export next to silver. The dyestuff was used throughout Europe and was so highly prized, its price was regularly quoted on the London and Amsterdam Commodity Exchanges (with the latter one beginning to record it in 1589). By the 17th century cochineal was a commodity traded as far away as India.

The production and the use of luxury colors and textiles were regulated in countries such as Spain and Italy. Dyestuffs produced from the cochineal insect were used for dyeing the clothes of kings, nobles, and the clergy. In 1454, Pope Paul II officially changed the color of the robes worn by Catholic cardinals from "Cardinal's purple" to vibrant red. By 1558, their red robes would have been created with American cochineal. By the 1600s, cochineal also gave the English "Redcoats" their distinctive officers' uniforms. Carmine became strong competition for other colorants such as madder root, kermes, Armenian cochineal, brazilwood, and Tyrian purple. It became the most important insect dye used in the production of hand-woven oriental rugs, almost completely displacing *lac insect* dye (a natural red pigment derived from the lac insect, has been used as a food coloring agent for centuries). It was also used for handicrafts, and tapestries. Spanish influence also changed the way in which Aztecs used pigments, particularly in their manuscripts. The use of cochineal in manuscripts was replaced by Spanish dyes like minium and alizarin crimson.

During the colonial period in Latin America, many indigenous communities produced cochineal under a type of contract known as Repartimiento de Mercancías. This was a type of "contract forwarding" agreement, in which a trader lent money to producers in advance, with a "call option" to buy the product once it was harvested. Communities with a history of cochineal production and export have been found to have lower poverty rates and higher female literacy, but also smaller indigenous populations.

In 1777, French botanist Nicolas-Joseph Thiéry de Menonville, presenting himself as a botanizing physician, smuggled the insects and pads of the Opuntia cactus to Saint Domingue. This particular collection failed to thrive and ultimately died out, leaving the Mexican monopoly intact. After the Mexican War of Independence in 1810–1821, the Mexican monopoly on cochineal came to an end. Large-scale production of cochineal emerged, especially in Guatemala and the Canary Islands; it was also cultivated in Spain and North Africa. The demand for cochineal fell sharply in the middle of the 19th century, with the appearance of artificial dyes such as alizarin crimson. This caused a significant financial shock in Spain as a major industry almost ceased to exist. The delicate manual labor required for the breeding of the insect could not compete with the modern methods of the new industry, and even less so with the lowering of production costs. The "tuna blood" dye (from the Mexican name for the Opuntia fruit) stopped being used and trade in cochineal almost totally disappeared in the course of the 20th century. For a time, the breeding of cochineal was done mainly for the purposes of maintaining the tradition rather than to satisfy any sort of demand. However, the product has become commercially valuable again. One reason for the increasing interest in natural dyes is consumer concern over the possibility that some commercial synthetic red dyes and food colorings may be carcinogenic. Being natural is not a guarantee of safety, but studies show that cochineal is neither carcinogenic nor toxic. Cochineal does, however, have a slight potential to trigger an allergic reaction. *Wikipedia*

Uses of cochineal: Approved by FDA as a natural red food coloring for use in various products like yogurt, candy, ice creams, drinks, food, meat and cosmetics; used to create vibrant reds, purples, and pinks; pigments for paints; has been used in traditional medicine, and some extracts are used in pharmaceutical products; the stain carmine, used in microbiology, is often made from cochineal extract; and colored wool and cotton are important materials for Mexican folk art and crafts.

Today, cochineals are harvested mainly in Peru and the Canary Islands on plantations of prickly pear cacti, the bugs' preferred host. There, the insects are sun-dried, crushed, and dunked in an acidic alcohol solution to produce carminic acid, the pigment that eventually becomes carmine or cochineal extract, depending on processing. About 70,000 insects are needed to produce a pound of dye. Cochineal is often labeled as carmine, E120, or Natural Red 4 on ingredient lists, depending on the region.

Until 2009, cochineal was one of many dyes that fell under the umbrella term "natural color" on ingredients lists. But because cochineal provokes severe allergic reactions in some people, the Food and Drug Administration requires carmine and cochineal extract to be explicitly identified in ingredients lists.

Aside from its role as an allergen, cochineal has no known health risks, although those who keep kosher or choose not to eat animal products will want to keep their distance. In addition to food, cochineal is used as a dye in cosmetics products, including lipstick, and at least one person has reported a severe allergic reaction to a cochineal dye used in a pill coating.

Cochineal may be made from bugs, but other synthetic red dyes such as Red No. 2 and Red No. 40, which carry far greater health risks, are derived from either coal or petroleum byproducts. Compared with these sources, bugs might sound positively appetizing. Unless you're allergic to it, cochineal extract probably isn't a health concern. *AI*

CHAPTER 5

COLOR ADDITIVES

Across the U.S., a longtime push to ban synthetic dyes in food is gaining renewed momentum, with critics of the dyes insisting it's not a matter of if, but when. States have cited the Make America Healthy Again (MAHA) movement, led by Health and Human Services Secretary Robert F. Kennedy Jr., as a driving force, along with concerns among parents and some scientists that dyes might contribute to behavioral problems in kids - a link the Food and Drug Administration says it is monitoring but hasn't established. In the first three months of the 2025, 20 states introduced nearly 40 bills aimed at cracking down on artificial dyes and other food additives, the most in any year, according to the Food Safety Environmental Working Group.

The FDA has approved 36 color additives, including nine synthetic dyes used in foods and beverages. Among them was Red No. 3, approved for use in foods in 1907, though the agency banned it in January over concerns about possible cancer risks. They're commonly used in products marketed to kids, including candy, breakfast cereals and soda, because their bright, vibrant hues are particularly eye-catching, experts say. *NBC News, Berkeley Lovelace Jr., -3/23/2025.*

A color additive, as defined by regulation, is any dye, pigment, or other substance that can impart color to a food, drug, or cosmetic or to the human body. Color additives are important components of many products, making them attractive, appealing, appetizing, and informative. Added color serves as a kind of code that allows us to identify products on sight, like candy flavors, medicine dosages, and left or right contact lenses. One of the U.S. Food and Drug Administration's (FDA) roles is to assure that color additives are safely and appropriately used.

Color additives are classified as straight colors, lakes, and mixtures. Straight colors are color additives that have not been mixed or chemically reacted with any other substance (for example, FD&C Blue No. 1 or Blue 1). Lakes are formed by chemically reacting straight colors with precipitants and substrata (for example, Blue 1 Lake). Lakes for food use must be made from certified batches of straight colors. (One exception is carmine, which is a lake made from cochineal extract (see Natural Dyes chapter). Lakes for food use are made with aluminum cation as the precipitant and aluminum hydroxide as the substratum. Mixtures are color additives formed by mixing one color additive with one or more other color additives or non-colored diluents, without a chemical reaction (for example, food inks used to mark confectionery).

"Color" includes white, black, and gray. In addition, any chemical that reacts with another substance and causes formation of a color may be a color additive. For example, dihydroxyacetone (DHA), when applied to the skin, reacts with the protein of the skin to impart color. Even though DHA is colorless, it acts as a color additive when used for this purpose and is regulated as a color additive. There is no "generally recognized as safe" (GRAS) exemption to the definition of a color additive. The Federal Food, Drug, and Cosmetic Act (FD&C Act) provides that a substance that imparts color is a color additive and is subject to premarket approval requirements unless the substance is used solely for a purpose other than coloring.

Naturally occurring color additives from vegetable and mineral sources were used to color foods, drugs, and cosmetics in ancient times. Paprika, turmeric, saffron, iron and lead oxides, and copper sulfate are some examples. The early Egyptians used artificial colors in cosmetics and hair dyes. Wine was artificially colored beginning in at least 300 BC. In 1856, William Henry Perkin discovered the first synthetic organic dye, called mauve. Discoveries of similar dyes soon followed and they quickly became used to color foods, drugs, and cosmetics. Because these dyes were first produced from by-products of coal processing, they were known as "coal-tar colors."

Federal oversight of color additives began in the1880s. The assessment of color-imparting ingredients in foods was among the first public initiatives undertaken by the U.S. when, in 1881, the U.S. Department of Agriculture's (USDA) Bureau of Chemistry began research on the use of colors in food. Butter and cheese were the first foods for which the federal government authorized the use of artificial coloring. By 1900, many foods, drugs, and cosmetics available in the U.S. were artificially colored. However, not all of the coloring agents were harmless and some were being used to hide inferior or defective foods. A careful assessment of the chemicals used for coloring foods at the time found many blatantly poisonous materials such as lead, arsenic, and mercury being added. In many cases, the toxicities of the starting materials for synthesizing coloring agents were well known and could be toxins, irritants, sensitizers, or carcinogens.

In 1906, Congress passed the Food and Drugs Act, which prohibited the use of poisonous or deleterious colors in confectionery and the coloring or staining of food to conceal damage or inferiority. The USDA had initial enforcement authority for this act. In 1907, the USDA issued Food Inspection Decision (F.I.D.) 76, which contained a list of seven straight colors approved for use in food. Subsequent F.I.D.'s in the early part of the century established a voluntary certification program and listed new colors. In 1927, responsibility for enforcing the Food and Drugs Act of 1906 was given to the newly established FDA. (The agency was first called the Food, Drug, and Insecticide Administration and was given its current name in 1930.) By 1931, there were 15 straight colors approved for use in food, including six of the seven in use today: FD&C Blue No. 1 (Brilliant Blue FCF), FD&C Blue No. 2 (Indigotine), FD&C Green No. 3 (Fast Green FCF), FD&C Red No. 3 (Erythrosine), FD&C Yellow No. 5 (Tartrazine), and FD&C Yellow No. 6 (Sunset Yellow).

In the 1920s and 1930s, it became clear that the Food and Drugs Act of 1906 did not go far enough to protect the public health from misbranded, adulterated, and even toxic products, including an eyelash dye that blinded some women. The Federal Food, Drug, and Cosmetic Act of 1938 further increased government oversight of food and drugs and, for the first time, passed legislation for the regulation of cosmetics and medical devices. For color additives, the 1938 FD&C Act mandated the listing of those coal-tar colors (other than coal-tar hair dyes) that were "harmless and suitable" for use in foods, drugs, and cosmetics. In addition, the act: contained adulteration and misbranding provisions for the use of coal-tar colors in foods, drugs, and cosmetics; required the listing of new colors; and made mandatory the previously voluntary certification program for batches of listed colors, with associated fees. Color additive lakes were in use by this time and were included in the provisions of the 1938 FD&C Act. The initial listing of lakes for food use under the act restricted their use to coloring shell eggs (egg dyeing).

In response to the 1938 Act, through public hearings FDA created the FD&C, D&C, and Ext. D&C nomenclature for certifiable color additives. FDA also established labeling and recordkeeping provisions, identified diluents that could be added to color additives, and established procedures for requesting certification of color additives and adding new color additives to the permitted list.

In the fall of 1950, many children became ill from eating an orange Halloween candy containing 1-2% FD&C Orange No. 1, a color additive approved for use in food. That same year, U.S. House Representative James Delaney began holding hearings on the possible carcinogenicity of pesticide residues and food additives. These events prompted FDA to reevaluate all of the listed color additives. In the next few years, FDA found that several caused serious adverse effects and proceeded to terminate their listings. During that time, it also became clear that coal was no longer the primary raw material source for the manufacture of color additives.

The Color Additive Amendments of 1960 defined "color additive" and required that only color additives (except coal-tar hair dyes) listed as "suitable and safe" for a given use could be used in foods, drugs, cosmetics, and medical devices. The 1960 Amendments prescribed the factors that FDA must consider in determining whether a proposed use of a color additive is safe, as well as the specific conditions for safe use that must be included in the listing regulation. FDA updated the procedural regulations for the petition process in response to these amendments. Under these amendments, the approximately 200 color additives that were in commercial use at the time were provisionally listed and could be used on an interim basis until they were either permanently listed or terminated due to safety concerns or lack of commercial interest. Permanently listing a color additive for a proposed use was prohibited unless scientific data established its safety. The 1960 Amendments also contained a "Delaney Clause" that prohibited the listing of a color additive shown to be a carcinogen. The clause states that "A color additive shall be deemed unsafe. . . if the additive is found. . . to induce cancer when ingested by man or animal, or . . . after other relevant exposure of man or animal to such additive."

After 1960, FDA gradually removed color additives from the provisional list either by permanent listing or by termination of listing. Today about half of the "1960" color additives remain listed; only color additive lakes remain provisionally listed and initiatives are underway to permanently list them. FDA has regulatory oversight for color additives used in foods, drugs, cosmetics, and medical devices. FDA lists new color additives or new uses for listed color additives that have been shown to be safe for their intended uses in the Code of Federal Regulations (CFR), conducts a certification program for batches of color additives that are required to be certified before sale, and monitors the use of color additives in products in the U.S., including product labeling. These activities stem from FDA's role in enforcing the color additive provisions of the FD&C Act, the Fair Packaging and Labeling Act, and other applicable laws, including the recently enacted Public Health Security and Bioterrorism Preparedness and Response Act of 2002 that requires domestic and foreign manufacturers of color additives used as ingredients in foods to register with FDA by December 12, 2003.

Color additives used in foods, drugs, cosmetics, and medical devices must comply with individual listing regulations issued by FDA. The use of an unlisted color additive, the improper use of a listed color additive, or the use of a color additive that does not conform to the purity and identity specifications of the listing regulation may cause a product to be adulterated according to the provisions of the FD&C Act. FDA may take enforcement action against such products. Most products contain only a small amount of color additive, so it takes only a small quantity to potentially adulterate a large amount of product.

All color additives required to be listed by FDA fall into two categories: those that are subject to FDA's certification process and those that are exempt from the certification process. Color additives subject to batch certification are synthetic organic dyes, lakes, or pigments. Those for food use are chemically classified as azo, xanthene, triphenylmethane, and indigoid dyes. Although certifiable color additives have been called coal-tar colors because of their traditional origins, today they are synthesized mainly from raw materials obtained from petroleum.

Color additives exempt from certification generally include those derived from plant or mineral sources. Most are straight colors; with one exception, cochineal extract (and its lake, carmine) that is derived from an insect (see Natural Dyes chapter). Certification of exempt color additives must comply with the identity and purity specifications and use limitations described in their listing regulations. Users of these color additives are responsible for ensuring that the color additives comply with the listing regulations. The decision about the need for batch certification is made during the agency's review of a petition requesting a listing for the color additive. Batch certification is required when the composition needs to be controlled to protect the public health. Some color additives may contain impurities of toxicological concern, such as carcinogenic constituents.

Prior to certification, the batch cannot be used in food, drug, cosmetic, or medical device products and must be stored separately from batches already certified. Upon receipt of the sample, FDA personnel evaluate its physical appearance and chemically analyze it. At least 10 analyses are performed, for purity (total color content), moisture, residual salts, unreacted intermediates, colored impurities other than the main color (called subsidiary colors), any other specified impurities, and the heavy metals lead, arsenic, and mercury. The results are reviewed for compliance with the identity and specifications described in the listing regulation for the color additive. If the sample is found to meet these requirements, FDA issues a certificate for the batch that identifies the color additive, the batch weight, the uses for which the color additive is certified, the name and address of the owner, and other information as required. FDA also assigns a unique lot number for the batch and the name of the batch changes. *Food Safety Magazine, October/November Issue, 2003.*

Many of the most commonly used food colors are synthetic petroleum-derived chemicals that do not occur in nature. These synthetic dyes often substitute for real, nutritious ingredients, such as fruits and vegetables, and are often used to make foods more attractive, especially those manufactured for and marketed to children. And, unlike some additives, dyes don't keep food from spoiling or fend off bacteria that cause food poisoning. They simply exist to help food companies make brightly colored foods look more appealing to eat. Research shows that the many synthetic dyes used in food may cause harmful health effects, particularly in children. Many advocacy groups insist it is time for the FDA to reevaluate the use of these unnecessary color additives. In general, the term "synthetic dyes" includes the following dyes and any approved lakes produced there from: Blue 1, Blue 2, Green 3, Red 3, Red 40, Yellow 5, and Yellow 6. There are two other synthetic dyes approved for very limited uses in the U.S. that you are unlikely to encounter: Citrus Red and Orange B. According to the USDA Branded Foods Database, more than 36,000 American food products contain Red 40, and more than 8,000 foods sold in the US contain carcinogenic Red 3.

Since synthetic food dyes are commonplace on supermarket shelves and in school foods, they're likely in the foods eaten on a regular basis. One can't identify foods that contain dyes simply by looking at colors alone. The only way to reliably identify—and fully avoid—dyed foods is by reading the ingredient lists on package labels. Synthetic dyes, if present, must be listed by name on ingredient lists in almost all foods, although there is some slight flexibility in how they are listed. Blue 1, for example, may appear as FD&C Blue 1, Blue #1, or Blue No. 1. But other color additives like titanium dioxide, which potentially damages DNA when eaten, can just be listed as "artificial color" or "color added."

The FDA initially approved synthetic food dyes between 1969 and 1987, when few studies were available. Since then, there have been clinical trials (including randomized, double-blind trials) investigating whether synthetic dyes can impact neurobehavioral outcomes in children, and new laboratory studies of neurotoxic effects in animals have become available. In 2021, California's Office of Environmental Health Hazard Assessment (OEHHA) completed a comprehensive evaluation of all available studies and concluded that synthetic food dyes could "cause or exacerbate neurobehavioral problems in some children. OEHHA's peer-reviewed assessment used a state-of-the-art approach combining systematic reviews and evidence integration. To reach its conclusions, it integrated evidence from 27 clinical trials in humans, as well as studies of laboratory animals that shed light on how food dyes might impact the body (including studies on cells and neurotransmitters). These types of clinical trials in humans provide vital scientific evidence, directly showing these dyes may have effects on children.

Notably, OEHHA also concluded that the FDA's "safe levels," or Acceptable Daily Intakes (ADIs), are inadequate to protect children from these harmful effects. Since 2010, the European Union has required a warning label on foods that contain certain synthetic food dyes to alert consumers to the potential impacts on kids' neurobehavior.

Potential health concerns: Some studies suggest that synthetic food dyes may exacerbate hyperactivity, inattention, and other behavioral issues in children, especially those with conditions like attention-deficit/hyperactivity disorder (ADHD); certain dyes, like Red 40, Yellow 5, and Yellow 6, have been associated with allergic reactions and hypersensitivity in some individuals; some studies have raised concerns about the potential carcinogenicity of certain dyes, with some dyes found to be contaminated with carcinogens; some dyes, like Yellow 5, have been shown to be genotoxic in some studies, meaning they can potentially damage genetic material; Red 3 has been linked to cancer in animal studies and has been banned from cosmetics, but is still used in some foods; Red 40 dye is one of the most commonly used synthetic food dyes and has been linked to hyperactivity and other behavioral problems in some children; and Yellow 5 and Yellow 6 have also been associated with hyperactivity and other behavioral problems in some children.

The FDA has concluded that the dyes it approves do not pose significant health risks, but some studies suggest that certain children may be sensitive to them and that most of the studies evaluating the safety of food dyes were performed decades ago. *Synthetic food dyes: A rainbow of risks, M.M. Bailey, 04/15/2024.*

"There really hadn't been much of a grassroots movement attempting to ban synthetic dyes until that shifted this 2024 election cycle," said Jerold Mande, an adjunct professor of nutrition at the Harvard T.H. Chan School of Public Health, who is also a former FDA senior adviser and former deputy undersecretary for food safety at the Agriculture Department. "I really think Make America Healthy Again (MAHA) is playing a big role in this." It's by no means a new movement: The FDA began taking steps to look into a possible link between dyes and behavioral problems in kids in the 1970s, when a California allergist and pediatrician proposed a possible connection. The agency investigated it even further following a 2007 study published in the Lancet, which said artificial dyes resulted in increased hyperactivity in kids. In 2011 and 2019, the FDA also reviewed data but determined no causal relationship could be established for children who haven't already been diagnosed with behavioral disorders. Scientists and physicians have called for more research on the topic. The FDA did not respond to a request for comment. The FDA has said that it "has reviewed and will continue to examine the effects of color additives on children's behavior."

While the FDA hasn't made a connection, that hasn't stopped government officials and outside groups from insisting there is one — or alleviated concerns from parents. Studies have shown that there are some behavioral problems in schools that many feel are contributed by the dyes in food children are given during school hours.

Kennedy, who oversees the FDA, has also previously claimed dyes are linked to hyperactivity and learning disorders. He cited a 2021 report from the California Office of Environmental Health Hazard Assessment that reviewed 27 trials in children and concluded food dyes can interfere with normal behavior in some kids. He is vowing to eliminate artificial dyes from the nation's food supply, telling executives from major food companies in a closed-door meeting this month that he wants them all gone by the end of his term, according to an HHS official.

While some research has suggested a link between certain dyes and an increase in hyperactivity and moodiness or irritability in children, the evidence still isn't conclusive, which may explain why the FDA is taking so long. Questioning how Kennedy would go about banning the chemicals: "The research is really, really hard to do. To see if there's evidence some kids respond badly to color dyes, you can't do it in people. You can't take a bunch of kids and give some of them food dyes and another bunch of kids not and see what happens. Even so, it may become harder for food companies to defend the use of the chemicals — especially because they don't preserve food or provide a nutritional benefit." *NBC News, Berkeley Lovelace Jr., 03/23/2025.*

Who knows the future how artificial dyes will be used in US's food items. On Oct. 1, 2024, the FDA began implementing a reorganization impacting many parts of their agency. They are also in the process of updating FDA.gov content to reflect these changes.

In the EU, artificial food dyes are permitted but must be listed with their specific E number and may require a warning label, especially regarding potential effects on children's activity and attention. While not banned outright, some dyes like the "Southampton Six" (including Red 40, Yellow 5, and Yellow 6) require a warning label stating they "may have an adverse effect on activity and attention in children." This approach reflects a more precautionary stance compared to the US, where such warnings are not mandated. Maybe using the EU approach is a good start in the US while the FDA is reorganizing many parts of their agency.

CHAPTER 6

POND SCUM OR WHAT

Nominative determinism is the theory that people are drawn to careers or interests that resonate with their names, suggesting a psychological link between name and profession. Last names that directly or indirectly reflect a person's profession are called aptonyms or aptoronyms, and some examples include: Smith (metalworker), Baker (baker), Carpenter (wood), Cook (food), Miller (grinds grain into flour), Taylor (tailor), Fisher (catcher of fish), Arzt (German for physician), Hogg/Hoge (keeper of swine – during my youth I raised pigs. My favorite one had the registered name of Miss Royal Charm IV) and Doktor (Doctor). Dr Dick Chopp, the Texan urologist is known for performing vasectomies. When my wife had a portion of her large and small intestine repaired, it was done by Dr. Gutman. During my presurgical exam for back surgery several months following a stroke, Dr. Yeh told me that I was going to have such pain that I would hate him. I told him that I would not hate him if I had a lot of pain and I couldn't imagine hurting any more than I was from the arthritis in my lower disks I had ruptured 35 years previously. Other than a spinal leak that gave me a head ache and kept me lying flat on my back for several days, from day one I had less pain than before surgery. On my first post op visit Dr Yeh asked me how I was feeling. I asked him how he pronounced his name? He had a questioning look on his face (probably thought I was having another stroke) and replied that his name was pronounced Yeah. I told him, "I feel Yeah!" as I lifted my hands in the air with gratitude. Whenever I hear or see the word yeah, I have a psychological link with the name Yeh - a casual form of yes. When you're hanging out with someone you really look up to and they ask you if you want to go to a party, play it cool by saying "Yeah, sure," instead of "Yes!" After that visit we had a relaxed wonderful relationship. Especially when he later performed surgery on my son involving the same vertebral disks. We asked him why the both of us? His casual cool response was, "You have both been blessed with the same genetic defect."

Spiritually, the name Paisley, of Scottish origin, is often associated with "church" or "place of worship" and can also evoke a sense of tradition, faith, and a connection to Scottish heritage, as well as positive qualities like creativity and imagination. The name Paisley comes from the Scottish town of the same name, which itself is derived from the Scottish Gaelic word "pislig," meaning "church". While not explicitly spiritual, the name is often associated with positive qualities like creativity, imagination, and a connection to spirituality. Some sources also suggest alternate meanings for Paisley such as "wanderer" or "pilgrim". While originally a surname, Paisley has become a popular first name, especially for girls, and is known for its feminine, bohemian flair. The name is also known for its association with the distinctive Paisley fabric pattern, which originated in India and was popularized in the town of Paisley, Scotland. Whilst there's no concrete evidence, it's believed that the paisley pattern was derived from the Zoroastrian symbol of a cypress tree combined with a floral spray, to represent life and fertility. The most recognized symbol of Zoroastrianism is the Faravahar, a winged figure representing the human soul and its journey, with elements symbolizing good thoughts, words, and deeds, and the struggle between good and evil. The popularity of the paisley print became prevalent in the 16th century, famously associated with luxurious Kashmir shawls.

According to Roman historian Pliny, glass-making was discovered accidentally by the Phoenicians around 5000 BC, while cooking on the desert sand. However, the earliest man-made glass objects were found later around 3500 BC in Egypt and Mesopotamia, with magnifying lenses no doubt being made soon after the discovery. The earliest known lens currently unearthed is the Nimrud lens (750 BC) found at the Assyrian palace of Nimrud in modern-day northern Iraq. It is believed to have been used as a magnifying glass, or as a burning-glass to start fires. Lenses were certainly well known by the time of the Greeks, with even the dramatist, Aristophanes, referring to them in his Comedy of the Clouds in 424 BC, a reference found stating, "Have you ever seen a beautiful, transparent stone at the druggists', with which you may kindle fire?", and Socrates referring them as a crystal lens. Uses of these early lenses included starting fires, cauterizing wounds, and for their magnifying properties. In the 1st century AD we find the first written record of magnification with the Roman Seneca the Younger explaining: "Letters, however small and indistinct, are seen enlarged and more clearly through a globe or glass filled with water." And Emperor Nero reportedly using an emerald as a visual aid to see gladiatorial games. The most powerful ancient lens yet discovered was found in Crete dating back to the 5th century BC and had the ability to magnify clearly up to seven times and even as much as twenty times, albeit with considerable distortion. 20x magnification is useful for observing small objects like insects, bacteria, and other microscopic details. A 20x microscope lens with a 0.28 μm resolution per sensor pixel, for example, can resolve objects down to 0.28 μm. Paramecium, a unicellular ciliate protozoan, typically ranges in size from 50 to 300 micrometers (μm) in length, depending on the species.

The tear drop looking Paramecia lives in a symbiotic relationship with green algae, living inside of them, and is a genus of eukaryotic, unicellular, ciliates. They are widespread in freshwater, brackish, marine environments, and are often abundant in stagnant basins and ponds. Some species are readily cultivated and they have been widely used in classrooms and laboratories to study biological processes. Paramecium species are commonly used as model organisms of the ciliate group and have been characterized as the "white rats" off the phylum Ciliophera. Paramecia reproduce both asexually through binary fission (divides into two identical sisters) and sexually through conjugation, a process involving genetic exchange between two individuals. After conjugation, the paramecium divides, and each new cell inherits a copy of the macronucleus and micronucleus. In 1718, the French mathematics teacher and microscopist Louis Joblot published a description and illustration of a microscopic poisson (fish), which he discovered in an infusion of oak bark in water and named this creature "slipper", and the phrase "slipper animalcule" remained in use as a colloquial epithet for Paramecium, throughout the 18th and 19th centuries. The name "Paramecium" – was coined in 1752 when the name generally became "Animalcules which have no visible limbs or tails, and are of an irregularly oblong figure."

A Paramecium propels itself by whip-like movements of the cilia (hair lick structures), which are arranged in tightly spaced rows around the outside of the body. The beat of each cilium has two phases: a fast "effective stroke," during which the cilium is relatively stiff, followed by a slow "recovery stroke," during which the cilium curls loosely to one side and sweeps forward in a counter-clockwise fashion. The densely arrayed cilia move in a coordinated fashion, with waves of activity moving across the "ciliary carpet," creating an effect sometimes likened to that of the wind blowing across a field of grain. The Paramecium spirals through the water as it progresses. When it happens to encounter an obstacle, the "effective stroke" of its cilia is reversed and the organism swims backward for a brief time, before resuming its forward progress. This is called the avoidance reaction. If it runs into the solid object again, it repeats this process, until it can get past the object.

Paramecium feed on microorganisms such as bacteria, algae, and yeasts. To gather food, the Paramecium makes movements with cilia to sweep prey organisms, along with some water, through the oral groove (vestibulum, or vestibule), and into the cell. The food passes from the cilia-lined oral groove into a narrower structure known as the buccal cavity (gullet). From there, food particles pass through a small opening called the cytostome, or cell mouth, and move into the interior of the cell. As food enters the cell, it is gathered into food vacuoles, which are periodically closed off and released into the cytoplasm, where they begin circulating through the cell body by the streaming movement of the cell contents, a process called cyclosis or cytoplasmic streaming. As a food vacuole moves along enzymes from the cytoplasm enter it, to digest the contents. As enzymatic digestion proceeds, the vacuole contents become more acidic. Within five minutes of a vacuole's formation, the pH of its contents drops from 7 to 3. As digested nutrients pass into the cytoplasm, the vacuole shrinks. When the fully digested vacuole reaches the anal pore, it ruptures, expelling its waste contents outside the cell.

There are also green algae living inside the paramecium's cytoplasm. It forms a mutualistic relationship where they both benefit. The algae provide the paramecium with sugars and oxygen through photosynthesis. In return, the paramecium provides protection and resources like nitrogen and carbon dioxide to the algae. The algae gain protection from the environment and access to essential nutrients from the paramecium. The paramecium benefits from the sugars and oxygen produced by the algae.

The question of whether Paramecium exhibit learning has been the object of a great deal of experimentation, yielding equivocal results. However, a study published in 2006 seems to show that Paramecium caudatum may be trained, through the application of a 6.5-volt electric current, to discriminate between brightness levels. This experiment has been cited as a possible instance of cell memory, or epigenetic learning in organisms with no nervous system.

In an article "Introducing Paisley Paramecium" 05/14/2019, Newton Paisley wrote: "My last name is Paisley. I know - kind of hilarious for a textile designer. I've always felt quite connected to the swirly world of the paisley pattern, from psychedelic Pucci of the 1970s to its ancient structured Persian ancestors and everything in between. Anyway, five years ago when I was making my first foray into the design world, I met someone who learned I was a textile-mad biologist and said I should "be called Susy Paramecium not Susy Paisley" (a paramecium, is a tear-drop shaped microorganism). The idea for a paisley design based on real microorganisms popped into my head and I have been gently thinking about it ever since. It has been a surprise to find myself falling in love with the tiniest creatures in Earth, having always studied big beasties like bears. I've been learning about organisms so small that millions can fit in a drop of water, and billions in a gram of soil. Microbes inhabit the widest range of habitats from sub-freezing temperatures, to water hotter than boiling, from lava, to the atmosphere miles above Earth, to glaciated mountain peaks and to the deepest ocean trenches. They include the strongest animals on Earth, the biggest producers of oxygen and greatest storers of carbon.

I wanted the design to evoke droplets of water as well as using the conventions of the paisley design. I also intended it to be reminiscent of stitching and lace, as the fabric of nature is fragile and intricately interwoven and embellished. I could exercise a bit of freedom in the coloration, and can further expand on this in the future, as many of these species are really quite transparent. The species in my design are all aquatic - living in both fresh and sea water. They include many species of free-floating plankton, both zooplankton (more like animals) and phytoplankton (which are more like plants). Phytoplankton form the base of the marine food web. The health of all marine creatures, from fish fry to whales, is dependent the health of phytoplankton. They are also of serious conservation concern: warming oceans have caused levels of phytoplankton to decline 40% since 1950.

The largest organisms in my design, yet still only a couple of centimeters in length, are aeolid nudibranchs. Facelina auriculata, was discovered by Müller in 1776, the year of American independence. These little beauties are very variable in color with poetic common names like 'clown', 'splendid', 'dancer', and 'dragon'. Because their coloring is so variable, and in honor of 1776 and the American Independence, I whipped out my artistic license, and made my nudibranchs largely Red, White and Blue. Around the centrals circles are unicellular paramecia (the tear dropped paisley-shaped creatures), and amoebas (single cell that moves in a blob like manner). Also, a water bear - a tardigrade. The rest of the creatures around that central circle are copepods - a group which, combined, forms the largest biomass on the Earth. And they are freakishly strong. Relative to their size, typically about 1mm long, copepods are also the world's fastest animal, being able to jump at a rate of about a half a meter per second. Their incredible strength, relative to their size, makes them more than ten times stronger than any other known species on the planet and even stronger than any human-made motor produced to date. They don't only qualify as superheroes for their strength and speed. It is estimated that copepods absorb 1-2 billion tons of carbon per year. This makes them the largest carbon sink in the world, handily transporting massive amounts of carbon to the deep sea.

The whole living world relies on these beings, only 1% of which have been identified never mind appreciated. So, this is my paisley tribute to these intriguing mini-miracles - so symmetrical and precise in form and yet totally bizarre - that are literally everywhere and yet invisible to the naked eye."

Why these thoughts? Recently I was attending church and mentioned to my friend that he was wearing a beautiful Paramecium tie. Correcting me, he informed me that it was a beautiful Paisley tie. Who was correct?

1– The Paisley pattern, a distinctive teardrop or leaf-shaped motif, has a rich history rooted in Persia and India, evolving into a global textile design. Its origins are often traced back to the Zoroastrian symbol of a cypress tree combined with a floral spray, representing life and fertility. The pattern gained prominence with the luxurious Kashmir shawls, which became coveted items of fashion in the 16th century, particularly among Persian royalty. British colonialists introduced the design to Europe in the 17th century, and the town of Paisley, Scotland, became a center for replicating and mass-producing the pattern on various textiles.

2– The most powerful ancient magnifying lens yet discovered was found in Crete dating back to the 5th century BC and had the ability to magnify clearly up to seven times and even as much as twenty times, albeit with considerable distortion. 20x magnification is useful for observing small objects like insects, bacteria, and other microscopic details. A 20x microscope lens with a 0.28 µm resolution per sensor pixel, for example, can resolve objects down to 0.28 µm. Paramecium typically ranges in size from 50 to 300 micrometers (µm) in length, depending on the species. This leads me to suspect the development of the Paisley pattern was influenced from observing paramecium found in high numbers in stagnant ponds.

3– In Newton Paisley's article, "Introducing Paisley Paramecium", appears to describe the best way to name the tie. The beautiful Paisley/Paramecium tie pattern probably was first discovered looking through a magnification lens amongst pond scum sometime after the 5th century BC. Looks like my friend and I were half right. I should have told him: "What a beautiful Paisley/Paramecium tie!"

CHAPTER 7

MICROBES WILL WIN SOONER OR LATER

After Pearl Harbor and the entry of the United States into the war, the rapid mobilization and training of men for the US Navy led to the "sudden formation of 'military cities' composed mostly of transients" of up to 100,000 recruits at a time, a disruption in the movement and crowding of people that was followed by a striking rise in the incidence of streptococcal group A infections which often resulted in strep throat or scarlet fever. This disease may develop into rheumatic fever which is an inflammatory disease that can develop after the bacterial infection. The body's immune system overreacts to the infection, leading to inflammation in various parts of the body resulting in: Joint pain and swelling, fever, skin rash, heart inflammation (carditis), and neurological problems (such as involuntary movements or seizures).

Long-term damage to the heart valves can lead to heart failure and surgery to repair the damaged heart valves. This can be avoided by early diagnosis and treatment of strep throat or scarlet fever with antibiotics, anti-inflammatory medications (such as aspirin or corticosteroids), good hygiene practices - such as hand washing, and avoiding contact with sick people. Rheumatic fever is rare in developed countries due to widespread antibiotic use. It is more common in children and young adults. The risk of developing rheumatic fever is higher after a second or subsequent strep throat infection.

Today we think of "strep throat" as a mostly harmless and readily treatable infection, but during World II streptococcal infections were a burden not just because of the days lost to men feeling unwell, but the very serious arthritic conditions, heart valve complications, pneumonia, kidney infections, and meningitis that often followed such infections. The complications of rheumatic fever could be fatal or lifelong; a good indication of the severity of this outbreak is that the Navy built two large convalescent hospitals just to care for rheumatic fever patients struck down by this epidemic. A comprehensive epidemiological study of hemolytic streptococcus in the US Navy published in 1949 estimated that at least one million personnel contracted a streptococcal infection in the U.S. Navy between 1941 and 1945. These figures are only for the US Navy and there are no comparable studies for the army.

The conditions of the training camps and radio schools were a study in the fostering of conditions favorable to the spread of infectious disease: The recruit usually arrived at a Naval Training Center after a long trip in an overheated troop train. He was first given a physical examination and housed in a Receiving Barrack which was commonly overcrowded and probably seeded with epidemic strains of hemolytic streptococcus. When his company was formed, he was assigned to a barrack in a recruit camp. This barrack had been vacated for only a few hours prior to his entrance. The former occupants of the barrack had probably experienced a high incidence of streptococcal infections and had had a high carrier rate on departure. Crowding of the barrack to 50% above the planned capacity was common…the recruit had to learn to swim in an indoor pool of warm chlorinated water and then stand "outdoor watches" in fog, rain, snow, or freezing temperatures. Moreover, training with gas masks was done without any cleaning of the masks in between trainees. The Naval technique for polishing the floors was rubbing with steel wool followed by dry sweeping, a process often done just before bed with the windows closed. Conditions were stressful and sleep was limited. Everyone who was sick was treated in the medical quarters, and these were one-story steam-heated buildings with double-decked bunks and little means of isolation. That the conditions themselves were fostering disease rates was in little doubt, as similar patterns were not seen in the civilian population.

In response to the outbreak, the Navy shifted from treating infected patients to mass prophylaxis with sulphadiazine, a sulfonamide derivative introduced to the American market in 1940. They began prophylactic treatment with 10,000 recruits at the Farragut Naval Training Center camps in Idaho (now a state park and public recreation located in northern Idaho at the southern tip of Lake Pend Oreille in the Coeur d'Alene Mountains) during December 1943, and extended it to all enlisted personnel at that location during March of 1944. After an initial indication that this would help with the problem, by June of 1944 prophylactic application of sulphadiazine had ceased to make a difference to infection and morbidity rates. In September 1944 extensive testing of the various strains of streptococcal bacteria cultured from patients revealed that the majority of them were sulphadiazine resistant. Testing of cultures collected in the pre-sulfonamide era showed that previously sulfonamide-sensitive strains had acquired resistance. Although it was difficult for the researchers to tell whether prophylaxis or treatment or both had caused the emergence of resistance, or whether a resistant strain had been carried into the camp from civilian life and then expanded in the milieu of the camp, it was clear that Farragut – the place where prophylaxis had been piloted - subsequently became the first focal point from which sulfonamide resistant strains of hemolytic streptococcus were disseminated to the rest of the Navy training camps.

A similar program of prophylaxis was initiated by the US Army in 1943, and although the ostensible target was meningitis and not hemolytic streptococcus, the drug and the outcome were the same. An epidemic of meningococcal meningitis was felling new recruits, who were more susceptible to the infection than troops with more than a year's experience of service; one post in 1943 reported an infection rate of 42.2 per 1000 per annum at the epidemic's peak, and deaths from meningitis were second only to tuberculosis (caused by the bacterium Mycobacterium tuberculosis), over the course of the war. Leaning on the successful use of sulphadiazine as therapy for those infected, the decision was taken to try and rid Army training camps of carriers who harbored the bacillus (bacteria that can cause a variety of diseases, including anthrax, food poisoning, and other infections) in the nose without falling ill.

In the autumn of 1943, The Office of the Surgeon General established as Army policy the administration of sulphadiazine to all new recruits. A one-time dose of 2 grams of sulphadiazine as prophylactic measure was judged sufficient for ridding carriers of meningococci, but already by the following year the incidence of sulphadiazine-resistant strains had become clear. A hastily organized study of the phenomenon showed an apparent shift toward a more drug resistant distribution among meningococci, and four of five strains of gonococcus (apparently tested by accident) were also sulphadiazine-resistant.

The solution at the time seemed to be more chemoprophylaxis, on more fronts, not less. Dust and bedding as potential reservoirs of infectious bacteria became a major focus of military efforts to curb transmission of streptococcus and meningococcus in their training centers. Oiling of the floors with an emulsion of oil and Roccal, (a quaternary ammonium compound - QAC disinfectant), was complemented by infusing blankets with the mixture. The oil was intended to weigh down the dust and keep it out of the air while the Roccal was meant to kill the bacteria. While the results were encouraging in tests of bacterial load, these interventions did not have much of an impact on the actual rates of transmission.

QACs were also increasingly used to disinfect mess utensils during this period. Research showing poorly washed utensils to be a vector of transmission of tuberculosis and influenza after World War I led to scalding water washing as the recommended preventative measure; the advent of quaternary ammonium compounds provided an alternative mode of disinfection where access to hot enough water was limited. They also had the apparently attractive feature of remaining on the surface of the utensils because of their wetting properties, in contrast to soaps and chlorine that had to be washed off to avoid bad tastes and smells.

It is difficult to assess the exact volume and range of QACs that were brought to bear on these settings aside from those used as test sites for the new protocols, as other substances such as chlorine bleach and phenols (cresol solutions and Lysol, they are effective against a wide range of microorganisms and are commonly now used in household cleaners and healthcare settings) were also used for disinfection.

Concern about venereal disease was another major driver of the use of disinfectants. Canadian soldiers were given "packets" containing permanganate solution and calomel lotion, which was a 30% mercury-based disinfectant. American soldiers either treated themselves or visited medical orderlies for application of what were thought to be preventative disinfectants after sex in an effort to curb the transmission of syphilis and gonorrhea; the recommended course of action was washing the genitals with permanganate (potassium permanganate, appears as a dark purple or bronze-like crystal. It's used in water treatment, soil remediation, and as a topical antiseptic) followed by 5 min of rigorous application of calomel (mercury compound at one time used to treat syphilis). These same soldiers, having reached the field of battle, were given packets of sulfonamide powder intended for sprinkling into wounds while waiting for evacuation or treatment.

The mix of old and new chemotherapeutic disinfectants is therefore likely to have been extensive and to have varied from location to location and person to person. Nonetheless, it is clear that the antibacterial action of QACs was an explicit focus of Navy medical research, and concerted efforts to curb infections through disinfectants, as well as sulfonamide prophylaxis and therapy were occurring simultaneously in military settings throughout World War II. Ironically, the expanded use of QACs was often undertaken explicitly because of the appearance of drug-resistant strains of bacteria in hospital and military settings. As with sulfonamides, production numbers for QACs in the 1940s also give us insight into the increasing scale of their application.

At the same time that the lives and bodies of people, particularly troops, were uprooted and thrown into disarray by the turbulence of war, changes in animal husbandry were simultaneously generating novel conditions for disease, prophylaxis and treatment in animals in the United States. The two were of course interlinked, as global trade networks were disrupted and the importance of domestic food production increased. Leading up to World War II, the intensification of agriculture enabled by developments in nutrition, housing, transport, and breeding meant an enormous growth in the size of flocks, cow and pig herds, and milking operations. For poultry, the introduction of vitamin D meant a transition from flocks of tens or hundreds living outdoor to flocks of thousands raised on indoor growing floors, conditions that fostered large scale outbreaks of pullorum, a bacterial disease of chicks, and coccidiosis, an intestinal affliction caused by protozoa. The same companies developing sulfonamides and new disinfectants for use in human medicine were also aiming for the agricultural market. Many of these companies were already engaged in the animal nutrition market through the synthesis or fermentation of vitamin concentrates, as well as various mineral or amino acid supplements.

Sulfonamides for the treatment of pullorum and intestinal diseases in chickens were used beginning in 1939, and were increasingly an industrial research focus throughout the 1940s. Arsenical medications, in declining use in human medicine, were at the same time finding a renewed career in treating intestinal parasites and growth promotion.

The excitement in veterinary laboratories following the demonstration that protozoan diseases might be prevented or cured by chemotherapy was similar to that exhibited earlier in medical fields after the discovery that bacterial diseases could be arrested using sulfonamides…the pharmaceutical industry employed chemists, parasitologists, veterinarians, nutritionists, advanced poultry producers, statisticians, and marketing specialists to discover and develop new anticoccidial drugs. Many of the best scientists from university staffs were employed or became consultants in this expanding industry. *Mechanisms of emerging resistance associated with non-antibiotic antimicrobial agents: a state-of-the-art review,08/21/2023.*

Antimicrobials and resistance suggest that not all interactions of bacteria with antibiotics can be explained within the frames of the classical bullet-target concept. For example, recent work on antibiotic resistance mechanisms used the "kin selection" concept, since this resistance mechanism operates at the population/system level. This well-established theory for the macro-organismal world seems also applicable to the microbial world, where a small number of antibiotic-resistant bacteria provide protection for the antibiotic sensitive cells, thus ensuring the survival of the whole population under the antibiotic assault. Moreover, in complex biofilm consortia, the protection against antibiotics is offered to all community members, irrespectively of the kinship, which requires a conceptual framework operating at the system level. Thus, the conceptual base of microbe–antibiotic interaction has been broadening beyond the bullet-target model to reflect the complexity of these interactions.

The current state in the field of antimicrobials, resistance, and chemotherapy is certainly not limited to clinical microbiology as it was in the early years of the antibiotic era. It is not a single grand challenge; it is rather a complex problem requiring concerted efforts of microbiologists, ecologists, health care specialists, educationalists, policy makers, legislative bodies, agricultural and pharmaceutical industry workers, and the public to deal with. In fact, this should be of everyone's concern, because, in the end, there is always a probability for any of us at some stage to get infected with a pathogen that is resistant to antibiotic treatment. Moreover, even the behavioral patterns, such as hygienic habits or compliance with antibiotic treatment regimens, may have consequences that are not limited only to individual health issues but, on a larger scale, contribute to the interaction with the resistomes around us. The resistome is the total collection of genes or genetic material that confers antimicrobial resistance within a microbial community. It encompasses all antibiotic resistance genes, including those found in both pathogenic and non-pathogenic bacteria, as well as their precursors. The resistome also includes genes that contribute to resistance against other antimicrobial agents like biocides and heavy metals.

Modification of the existing antimicrobials was initiated (and successfully implemented) during the period, when the rate of discovery of novel drug classes suddenly dropped in the 1970s, and the growing resistance problem forced researchers to look into the possible modification of the existing arsenal that could confer improved activity, less sensitivity toward resistance mechanisms, and less toxicity. Although this approach still successfully provides effective antimicrobials for the market, one of the lessons learned is that sooner or later bacteria will acquire resistance.

The antibiotic treatment choices for already existing or emerging hard-to-treat multidrug-resistant bacterial infections are limited, resulting in higher morbidity and mortality rates. There are potential alternatives to antibiotic treatment: 1-passive immunization such as antibodies received from a mother to her in utero child or immune globulin injections to prevent a disease such as a rabid animal bite, infection or toxin; 2-monoclonal antibodies for cancer therapy; or 3-using viruses as bacteriophages (phages) to target and kill bacteria.

However, the mainstream approach relies on the discovery and development of newer, more efficient antibiotics. The vast majority of antimicrobial classes in use today have been isolated in the golden era of antibiotic discovery from a limited number of ecological niches and taxonomic groups, mainly from soil Actinomyces. Actinomycetes are a group of bacteria that produce many antibiotics, including β-lactams, tetracyclines, macrolides, aminoglycosides, and glycopeptides. These antibiotics are used in clinics to treat a variety of conditions. Examples of natural antibiotics produced by actinomycetes: Streptomycin, Vancomycin, lipopeptide Daptomycin and others. Actinomycetes also produce anticancer agents, such as doxorubicin, bleomycin, and calicheamicins. These bacteria are also used in biotechnology and agriculture. Further exploration of this ecological niche, coupled with newer technologies such as cell-free assays and high-throughput screening, however, did not produce any novel drug classes in the past 20+ years.

Some possible approaches to tap the novel antimicrobial diversity is the exploration of ecological niches other than soil, such as the marine environment, borrowing antimicrobial peptides and compounds from animals and plants, mimicking the natural lipopeptides of bacteria and fungi, accessing the uncultivated portion of microbiota through exploring their microbial diversities, and the use of the synthetic routes pioneered during the early years of the antibiotic era. The latter approach becomes dominant in the search for drugs aimed at newly identified targets in a bacterial cell. Other strategies may include drugs engineered to possess dual target activities.

The vast majority of current antibiotics, even heavily modified, target the same cellular processes as their natural or synthetic predecessors. The range of these targets is limited to the components of translational machinery (refers to the cellular components and processes involved in protein synthesis, specifically the translation of mRNA into proteins), cell wall biosynthesis, DNA/RNA metabolism and some other cellular processes. With the extensive range of genomes sequenced, it becomes possible to implement the idea of a "magic bullet" in a more elaborate way, with essential targets defined much more precisely at the molecular level. This needs to be complemented by the availability of chemically diverse compound collections to screen for the target/drug combinations. The comparison of metabolic pathways in commensal and pathogenic bacteria and drugs targeting their pathogenic traits have been used to help identify drug/target combinations that can be used in treating virulent pathogens.

The main problem being faced with antibiotic therapy is that after a new antibiotic is introduced, resistance to it will, sooner or later, arise. This scenario has been seen on multiple occasions, and thus there is a continuing race between the discovery and development of new antibiotics and the bacteria that will respond to this selective pressure by the emergence of resistance mechanisms.

So how to protect the power of antibiotics and extend their lifespan? There are many factors contributing to the emergence and dissemination of antibiotic resistance and the problems require a complex approach. A significant factor to consider apparently is the use of antibiotics by humans. Not surprisingly, the level of antibiotic-resistant infections strongly correlates with the level of antibiotic consumption. There may be requests from patients to prescribe antibiotics when there is no need for them, as in the case of viral infections, and which should be explained to them. Indeed, the lack of knowledge about antibiotic resistance positively correlates with the higher prevalence of resistance. The important part is also to comply with the drug use regimen, which may be difficult in the case of infections requiring long-term therapy with multiple antibiotics as in the case of TB. The contributing factor to the dissemination of antibiotic resistance, even in the case of absolute compliance, may be the practice of empirical prescription of antibiotics (which accounts for the vast majority of prescriptions). An empirical prescription of antibiotics is when antibiotics are given before the results of a blood culture and antibiotic susceptibility test are known. This is done based on a clinical presentation and the most likely pathogens. The situation is different in countries where the sales of antibiotics are inadequately regulated, and antibiotics are available without prescription. In the absence of regulation, the personal decisions on antibiotic purchase and use are governed by cultural and economic reasons. Self-medication lacks the attributes of a successful therapy, such as proper diagnosis, suitable antibiotic choice, correct usage, compliance, and treatment efficiency monitoring, thus contributing to the mounting resistance problem.

Domesticated animals also get infected and require antibiotic therapy. The agricultural use of antibiotics, however, is not limited exclusively to this use. Antibiotics are also used for the growth promotional and prophylactic purposes in food animals, as well as for a broader and less-targeted treatment in aquaculture and horticulture. The experience of the Scandinavian countries, where the programs of optimal disease preventive management routines and proper use of antimicrobials, combined with the withdrawal of antibiotic growth promoters, were implemented in food animal production. These measures resulted in reduction in the use of antimicrobials and helped prevent the creation of a relatively favorable situation for antimicrobial resistance. With the ban of growth promoting antibiotics in 2006, other EU countries have been implementing similar measures to limit the occurrence and dissemination of antibiotic resistance from agricultural sources.

The history of massive production and use of antibiotics by humans is very short on the evolutionary scale, but even this short-term (albeit large-scale) practice has produced very interesting results demonstrating the interminable adaptive capabilities of bacteria, which allow them to withstand massive antibiotic insults and generate some formidable examples of hard-to-treat infections that we call "superbugs." Although no broad baseline data collection on antibiotic resistance genes has been performed at the onset of antibiotic use, recent studies suggest that the most likely source of these genes is the environmental antibiotic resistome. The functional role of antimicrobials and the corresponding resistance genes in natural ecosystems is hypothesized as a signaling/regulatory rather than a bullet/target relationship. Confirmatory to this suggestion are also the other therapeutic properties of antimicrobials, well beyond the initial range of use as anti-infective agents. Bacteria do not respect the boundaries of ecological compartments, and there is always a continuous flow by genetic information between different ecological compartments. Once the potential antibiotic resistance genes enter, even in small numbers or low frequencies, into the commensal/pathogenic human/ animal microbiota, the antibiotic selection immediately leads to the amplification and dissemination of these genes. There is some evidence on the environmental origin of some clinically relevant resistance genes. The predecessor/ ancestral genes for antibiotic resistance are not necessarily the genes conferring resistance per se in natural ecosystems. In this scenario a quinolone resistance emerged, the enzyme involved in DNA metabolism in environmental bacteria also happens to be protecting against this synthetic antibiotic, and, once the encoding gene entered into the human/ animal microbiota on a mobile element, a strong selective pressure leads to its amplification and dissemination into the commensal and pathogenic microbiota.

Another important aspect is the release of antibiotics and the corresponding pre-selected and amplified antibiotic resistance gene pool from the human and animal ecological compartments back into the environment. What are the consequences of this? Does the resulting multidrug combination in the environment accelerate the evolution toward antimicrobial resistance? What are the consequences of the presence of sublethal concentration antibiotics in the environment? What is the impact of the environmental stresses, such as, for example, the SOS (Save Our Souls) response-inducing UV radiation, on the horizontal dissemination of antibiotic resistance genes? An SOS response to UV light refers to a cellular mechanism in bacteria, primarily E. coli, where exposure to ultraviolet radiation triggers a coordinated response to repair DNA damage by activating a set of genes that produce proteins necessary for detecting and fixing the lesions, essentially acting as a distress signal to repair damaged DNA; this process is often associated with increased mutation rates due to the involvement of error-prone DNA polymerases. Essentially, when bacteria experience DNA damage from UV radiation, their SOS response activates pathways that facilitate the transfer of mobile genetic elements carrying antibiotic resistance genes to neighboring bacteria, contributing to the spread of resistance within a population. What is the rate of decay of the released antibiotic resistance genes in the environment, given the improved survival strategies of mobile genetic elements? Could the environment provide a broader playground for the mobile antibiotic resistance encoding elements to promote their own diversity? And what are the chances for antibiotic resistance genes to re-enter the human and animal food chain? There are pressing needs to answer these questions to build the broader strategies that would help to preserve the power of antibiotics. *A Brief History of the Antibiotic Era: Lessons Learned and Challenges for the Future, Front Microbiology, Rustam I Aminov, 12/08/2010*

One of the reasons behind the sudden concern over antibiotic use can be attributed to the discovery void that we are currently experiencing. This void is defined by the lack of new antibiotics being discovered. As bacteria are evolving and mutating, we are equipped with fewer new antibiotics to stop their spread. One of the key reasons behind this void boils down to a simple reason. The creation of new antibiotics became not profitable enough for Big Pharma, especially compared to other medications that a person takes for an entire lifespan. The economic incentive is driving lifestyle drugs rather than antibiotics, which are only taken for a few days to a couple weeks. But the blame does not solely rest in the hands of Big Pharma.

There are various other social factors influencing antibiotic resistance. Within the general public, concerns surround the tendency to self-medicate, low adherence to full antibiotic treatment, and easy accessibility to antibiotics. Within the private sector, medical professionals are faced with patient demands and expectations, economic incentives, high costs of diagnostic testing, high patient load, and a lack of continuing medical education. Professionals in the public sector, often face similar issues surrounding a lack of education and diagnostic facilities.

The awareness of antibiotic resistance has led to the development of guidelines to improve public health. Improving access to clean water, sanitation, and vaccines reduces the need for antibiotics. Antibiotic stewardship to improve hospital infection control, changing political and economic incentives encourages antibiotic development, reducing the use of antibiotics in the agricultural industry, limiting the antibiotics consume through our diet and education and accountability will hopefully keep us informed and responsible enough to ensure the safety of our future health. *Antibiotics: The good, the bad and the ugly, Institute for Public Health, 07/23/2020*

Microorganisms use the very same (and probably some additional but still unidentified) natural mechanisms to protect themselves against the massive antibiotic assaults continuously launched by the humankind since the time of discovering antibiotics. Although the majority of infections were overcome by the developing living organisms during the almost four billion years of evolution, during this time the microbial world has accumulated an enormous diversity of metabolic and protective mechanisms that can be mobilized in response to man's attempted destruction. Microorganism's SOS (save our souls) abilities to adapt to any life-threatening event, tells us one and all that sooner or later they will acquire resistance and win.

CHAPTER 8

TETRACYCLINES

Contrary to the common belief that the exposure to antibiotics is confined to the modern "antibiotic era," research has revealed that this is not the case. The traces of tetracycline, for example, have been found in human skeletal remains from ancient Sudanese Nubia dating back to 350–550 CE. The distribution of tetracycline in bones is only explicable after exposure to tetracycline-containing materials in the diet of these ancient people. Another example of ancient antibiotic exposure is from a histological study of samples taken from the femoral midshafts of the late Roman period skeletons from the Dakhleh Oasis, Egypt. These samples showed discrete fluorochrome labeling consistent with the presence of tetracycline in the diet at that time. The postulated intake of tetracycline in these populations possibly had a protective effect because the rate of infectious diseases documented in the Sudanese Nubian population was low, and no traces of bone infection were detected in the samples from the Dakhleh Oasis.

Tetracyclines are unique among antibiotics in that they are strong chelators (a molecule that binds to metal ions, forming a stable ring-like structure called a chelate) and are incorporated into the hydroxyapatite mineral (HA) portion of bones as well as teeth enamel. HA is a naturally occurring mineral form of calcium apatite, primarily found in bones and teeth. It's the main component of tooth enamel and bone mineral, contributing to their hardness and strength. In bone, HA crystals are typically plate or needle-shaped and play a crucial role in bone regeneration and structural stability. Tetracycline incorporation in developing bones and teeth is associated with permanent staining and provides markers of metabolically active areas during tetracycline exposure. Traces of exposure to other antibiotics in ancient populations are much more difficult to detect, and only surviving customs and anecdotal evidence may point to these occurrences. For example, anecdotes about the antibiotic-like properties of red soils in Jordan that were used historically (and are still being used as an inexpensive alternative to pharmaceutical products today) for treating skin infections have led to the discovery of a number of antibiotic-producing bacteria and concomitant antibiotic production in these soils. The actinomycete bacteria isolated from these soils produced actinomycin, which are polypeptide antibiotics that bind to a pre-denatured DNA conformation and have very little chance to be preserved in ancient samples.

Another possibility of exposure to antimicrobials in the pre-antibiotic era could be through the remedies used for millennia in traditional/alternative medicine, in particular in traditional Chinese medicine (TCM). The best-known example is the discovery of a potent anti-malarial drug, qinghaosu (artemisinin), which was extracted in the 1970s from Artemisia plants, used by

Chinese herbalists for thousands of years as a remedy for many illnesses. Antimicrobial activity seems present in a number of other herbs used in TCM and the discovery of active components in these ancient remedies may enrich the arsenal of antimicrobials used by the mainstream medicine. At the same time, selective pressures imposed by these antimicrobial activities during the long-term history of TCM may have been one of the factors contributing to the accumulation of antibiotic resistance genes in human populations. *A Brief History of the Antibiotic Era: Lessons Learned and Challenges for the Future, Front Microbiology, Rustam I Aminov, 12/08/2010 + AI.*

Discovered as natural products from actinomycetes soil bacteria, the tetracyclines were first reported in the scientific literature in 1948. They were noted for their broad spectrum antibacterial activity and were commercialized with clinical success beginning in the late 1940s to the early 1950s. The second-generation semisynthetic analogs and more recent third-generation compounds show the continued evolution of the tetracycline scaffold toward derivatives with increased potency as well as efficacy against tetracycline-resistant bacteria, with improved pharmacokinetic and chemical properties. Their biologic activity against a wide spectrum of microbial pathogens and their uses in mammalian models of inflammation, neurodegeneration, and other biological systems indicate that the tetracyclines will continue to be successful therapeutics in infectious diseases and as potential therapeutics against inflammation-based mammalian cell diseases.

In early 1948, five-year-old Toby Hockett was rushed by his parents to Johns Hopkins Children's Hospital in

Washington, DC, with severe abdominal pain, and diagnosed with a ruptured appendix. Although emergency surgery was successful, a serious infection and complications set in, and the few antibiotics clinically useful at the time proved ineffective, leaving him facing imminent death. However, a new experimental antibiotic had recently arrived on campus for clinical use, a compound that had hardly been used in humans and was still being evaluated as a new chemotherapeutic agent. In this post–WWII era, antibiotics were considered novel therapeutics, with penicillin being heralded as a "wonder drug" having saved countless lives on the battlefields. It was also a period of chemical discovery, where the scientific methods of microbiology and organic chemistry were merging, and the promises of infectious disease chemotherapy became a major drive of medical research in academia and the chemical industry. Since the antibiotics of the day failed Toby Hockett, his parents in desperation consented for him to be treated with the yellow-colored compound recently sent by the Lederle Laboratories Division of American Cyanamid, under the name AureomycinTM. It was a risk without choice; "I remember being put on the operating table, screaming and crying, and seeing the gas mask coming down on my face and being in that hospital for a very long time after that," he recalled. Within months he fully recovered and was one of the first of many people whose lives were saved by Aureomycin.

Aureomycin had been discovered almost five years earlier in the early 1940s by Lederle, whose mission to generate new compounds and drugs, particularly antibiotics, had begun even earlier in the late 1930s. Industrial chemical producers in this era were aware of the discovery and commercial value of penicillin, and it changed the course of their business. Normally they were resigned to producing consumer products, but now they began hiring scientists from many medical disciplines and started screening chemicals, biologics, immune-sera, and other promising and potential molecules against a host of diseases in a spirit of optimism, growth, and medical discovery that was unprecedented in the history of the emerging pharmaceutical industry. In 1938, Cyanamid president William B. Bell unveiled to his executives a new mission statement, "You may come up with nothing, but you may discover a single drug that may conquer even one major disease, then the public will be well served and our company will prosper," thus formalizing the company's entry into the area of antibiotic discovery. The discovery of the tetracyclines in the early 1940s antibiotic discovery was progressing rapidly from the chemical diversity derived from the soil fungi actinomycetes. It was evident that the microbial world produced a wealth of natural products and antibiotic compounds capable of fighting microbial diseases. But it was their medical and financial potential that drove the expansion of many pharmaceutical companies within the United States.

They then began a search for an antibiotic they felt should rival streptomycin, enlisting as consultant 71-year-old Benjamin Minge Duggar, a retired professor of plant physiology and economic botany from the University of Wisconsin, to head their soil screening department. Duggar was world renowned for his extensive knowledge and study of soil fungi; he collected soil samples from all over the world sent to him by friends from sites he instructed would yield actinomycetes soil bacteria, or "ultra-molds" as he called them, those with ground coverings left undisturbed and natural. The samples were subjected to culture and broth dilution assays performed by his technicians, in which the microorganisms were plated, and the colonies assayed for antibiotic activity against a panel of Gram-positive and Gram-negative bacteria. Although many soil organisms were known to produce antibiotics, most were toxic or had undesirable properties, and the team encountered many false leads. One sample, however, drew their attention early on. It was dug from a dormant timothy hayfield on the University of Missouri campus, outside Columbia, Missouri. It yielded an unusual yellow-colored colony that inhibited the growth of all their strains in an initial panel of bacteria, and produced remarkably large zones of growth inhibition in agar. This was an unheard-of property at this point, as compared to the few antibiotics available for comparison. They further found that even crude extracts of the colony retained remarkable antibacterial activity against lethal scrub typhus and the rickettsia, such as Rocky Mountain spotted fever, an infection for which there was no cure. Soon enthusiasm about its broad range of activity and potency against lethal pathogens led to the labeling of the unknown substance as a "broad spectrum" antibiotic, becoming one of the first in medical history to attain this title. Duggar named the compound aureomycin in reference to its yellow color and the gold-colored Streptomyces strain from which it was extracted. He continued the study of the ultra-mold and its medical microbiology, taxonomy, and physiology, naming it Streptomyces aureofaciens and first publishing his results in 1948. This established Aureomycin as a new and potent broad spectrum antibacterial agent that was safe and effective, although its exact chemical structure had yet to be determined. Soon Aureomycin was produced in commercial quantities. By December 1, 1948, the drug was approved by the FDA for clinical use and was an immediate success in the clinic, saving countless lives against a broad spectrum of infectious diseases, and generating notoriety and profits for the company. By 1950, there had been gathered thousands of soil samples from around the world and the soil bacterium Streptomyces rimosus was found. This organism produced a compound with similarity in color to Aureomycin, but it was slightly more water soluble and had better bioactivity, giving it a medical and competitive edge over Aureomycin in the treatment of infectious diseases. The compound was named Terramycin in reference to terra, Latin for earth, and perhaps its origin, Terre Haute, Indiana. It was approved by the FDA in 1950, competing directly with Aureomycin while gaining success in the treatment of a broad spectrum of infectious diseases. The chemical structures of both Aureomycin and Terramycin, however, were difficult to solve and remained elusive for both companies, although they shared their respective compounds with each other in order to determine their common structural features and substructures and settle their disparate molecular identities. By 1952, The core scaffold for this new family of antibiotics became descriptively known as the tetracyclines. The naphthacene ring system and its structural locants of the first-generation antibiotics: chlortetracycline, oxytetracycline, and tetracycline, approved by the FDA. Second-generation tetracyclines are a group of antibiotics that includes doxycycline, minocycline, and lymecycline.

They are used to treat acne, bacterial infections, Lyme disease, and other conditions.

In the late 1980s antibiotic resistance was becoming more prevalent in the clinic, prompting pharmaceutical companies to expand their antibiotic discovery programs. Soon their lead compound tigecycline entered clinical studies and was approved by the FDA for hospital use in 2006. This was the first new third-generation tetracycline to enter the market in over 35 years and one specifically designed to confront tetracycline-resistant mechanisms. As of 2006, tigecycline was found to be clinically active within acceptable MIC ranges against Gram positive isolates obtained globally, including resistant organisms, such as MRSA (methicillin-resistant S. aureus), vancomycin-resistant enterococci, and penicillin-resistant S. pneumoniae. Against Gram negative pathogens, particularly Enterobacteriaceae and Acinetobacter, tigecycline also shows clinical antibacterial response.

While the fields of antibiotic and tetracycline resistance expanded rapidly during the 1980s, this time period also brought another surprising finding concerning the tetracyclines when bioarcheologists found, tetracycline like fluorescent bands in the bone of skeletal remains of a tribe from ancient Sudan dated from the Late Antiquity period, 350 A.D., from an area that was once known as Nubia. Over 70 individuals from all age groups were studied, and they showed consistent and significant osteon bone labeling by tetracycline that only occurs with chronic and repeated tetracycline exposure. These findings were derided by their peers, attributing the bone labeling to surface contamination by tetracycline produced by mold like bacteria, but the team hypothesized that the Nubians routinely fermented grains as part of their diet-producing beer gruels, and that Actinomycetes could have accidentally contaminated their vats, and once discovered by the Nubians, could have been purposefully propagated for their use.

More recently, the chemical identity of the bone fluorescent bands where the bone fluorophore was extracted and characterized by HPLC-mass spectrometry, was found to contain significant amounts of the antibiotic tetracycline. These findings show that tetracyclines were produced by the ancient Nubians and could have been one of the first antibiotics produced via fermentation, predating penicillin by almost 2000 years. It was also evident that the fermentation of tetracyclines was not an isolated event, inasmuch as fluorophore-labeled ancient bone has been found in other local geographical areas and in other distant regions.

Individuals from all age groups were studied and showed consistent and significant osteon bone labeling by tetracycline that only occurs with chronic and repeated tetracycline exposure. Tetracyclines have a high affinity for calcium, which allows them to bind readily to the mineral matrix of bones and teeth, leading to their incorporation into these structures during active mineralization, causing a noticeable discoloration when administered during tooth development, particularly in children (or young animals); this is why tetracycline use is often discouraged during pregnancy ad early childhood. *Antimicrobial Therapeutics Reviews, The history of the tetracyclines Mark L. Nelson1 and Stuart B. Levy, 12/2011 – plus additional AI findings*

The Hymn to Ninkasi is a song of praise to Ninkasi, the Sumerian goddess of beer, and contains an ancient recipe for brewing. Written down around 1800 BCE, the hymn is no doubt much older. Evidence for brewing beer in the Mesopotamian region dates back to 3500-3100 BCE at the Sumerian settlement of Godin Tepe in modern-day Iran where, in 1992 CE, archaeologists discovered chemical traces of beer in a fragmented jar dating to the mid-fourth century BCE. The same site also yielded evidence for early wine-making and it is thought that the idea of brewing beer arose from baking. The fermentation process evident in grains may have been left out inspired the creation of both wine and beer.

Godin Tepe was a Sumerian outpost, first inhabited in 5000 BCE, which became a significant town and fortress along the famous Silk Road trade route. That evidence for the brewing of beer should be discovered there is not surprising as beer was the drink of choice among the ancient Sumerians; one of the most common pictographs found in Sumerian cuneiform is the one for beer. The Ebla Tablets (discovered in Syria in 1974 CE) dating from 2500 BCE, provide evidence that Ebla, another Sumerian outpost, was brewing significant quantities of beer at that time using many different recipes. As only fresh water was used in beer, and had to be boiled, it was healthier to drink than water from the canals which could be polluted by animal waste. Scholar Jeremy Black writes: Beer was a staple in Mesopotamia and its surroundings from prehistoric times, as the fermentation process was an effective method of killing bacteria and waterborne disease. Its manufacture was recorded and controlled by scribes even in the earliest written records, from the late fourth millennium BCE. Beer was consumed by people at all levels of society and offered to gods and to the dead in libation rituals.

Beer also contained nutrients other beverages did not and, as Black notes, was a staple in the daily diet of the people throughout Mesopotamia. Laborers were provided with beer as part of their daily rations (a practice also observed in Egypt) and, based on art works as well as writings, it was a drink enjoyed by the lowest laborer to the highest noble and was consumed through a straw. The straw, developed by the Babylonians, was first invented by the Sumerians specifically for the purpose of drinking beer. From the evidence of art works found throughout Mesopotamia, it is clear that beer was consumed daily in great quantities by the people. The commercialization of beer is evidenced by The Alulu Tablet from the city of Ur, an ancient receipt for the delivery of beer by the brewer Alulu, dated to 2050 BCE.

Beer was also the drink of the gods. This is evident from a number of myths such as the poem Inanna and the God of Wisdom where the goddess Inanna and the god of wisdom Enki get drunk together and in the poem Enki and Ninmah, the goddess Ninhursag loses prestige when she is beaten in a drinking game by Enki. As in the case of goddesses like Nisaba (patroness of grains, accounts, writing, and scholarship), Ninkasi was both the brewer of beer and the beer itself. Nisaba was not just the goddess of grain but the actual grain and, once she became goddess of writing, she was not just an impartial overseer of the craft but the craft itself; the same is true of Ninkasi. Her spirit and essence infused the beer produced under her guidance.

The priestesses of Ninkasi were the first brewers and women, generally, brewed beer in the home until commercial production of the beverage began and men started taking over. Even so, most ancient depictions of brewers show them as women in both Mesopotamia and Egypt. Ninkasi was said to make the beer fresh every day from the best ingredients and her priestesses would have followed suit as the hymn is, again, not only a praise song but also instructions on how to brew beer.

In an age where few people were literate, the Hymn to Ninkasi, with its steady cadence, provided an easy way to remember the recipe for brewing beer. One began with flowing water, then made Bappir (twice-baked barley bread) and mixed it with honey and dates. Once the bread had cooled on reed mats it was mixed with water and wine before being put into the fermenter. After the brew had finished the fermentation process it was placed in the filtering vat "which makes a pleasant sound" and then placed "appropriately on a collector vat" from which the filtered beer was then poured into jars. According to the hymn, the pouring of the beer was "like the onrush of the Tigris and Euphrates" which is taken to mean that, like those two rivers, beer brought life to those who drank it.

The hymn was most likely sung while the ancient Sumerians brewed their beer and was passed down by master brewers to their apprentices. Beer was valued highly in ancient Mesopotamia and an expert brewer would have lived quite comfortably once the brew was manufactured commercially. Sumerologist (scholar who specializes in the study of Sumerian culture, language, and history), Samuel

Noah Kramer notes how "beer had its divine and sublime qualities for the Sumerian poets and sages, but it was, as noted, also the drink of the gods. Ninkasi's name literally translates as 'the lady who fills the mouth' and beer was thought to have healing and elevating qualities which could only improve one's life. Although she was the goddess 'born in sparkling-fresh water', it was beer that was her first love. Ninkasi's love of beer, and attention to her craft, provided the drink of the gods to mortals." *Hymn to Ninkasi, Goddess of Beer, Ryan Moorhen, 01/18/2018*

Tetracyclines are believed to be one of the first antibiotics produced by fermentation. Fermentation is a metabolic process where microorganisms break down carbohydrates in the absence of oxygen, producing various by products like acids, alcohol, and gases. Nubians routinely fermented grains as part of their diet-producing beer gruel and one of the contaminated biproducts from the organism Actinomycetes, yellow colored tetracyclines, when eaten was laid down in their bones and teeth. This was especially found in children that were in rapid growth stages of their bones and teeth. It appears that the constant presence of tetracyclines in the diet was the reason that the rate of infectious diseases documented in the Sudanese Nubian population was low, and no traces of bone infection were detected in the samples from the Dakhleh Oasis.

However, tetracycline is not associated with less tooth decay. In fact, it's known to have adverse effects on teeth when ingested during tooth development, primarily causing discoloration and potentially weakening tooth enamel, which can increase the risk of decay.

To make beer, the water had to be boiled, making it safer to drink beer than water from the canals which could be polluted by animal waste. The fermentation process was also an effective method of killing bacteria and waterborne disease. Also, beer contains nutrients not found in potable water. It was a staple diet as early as 3500-3100 BCE. It appears that children's diets during this era included a fair amount of alcohol from beer and its gruels.

According to an AI search: The type of illnesses you can develop after 10 to 20 years of regularly drinking more than 14 units (one unit is defined as 10 milliliters (ml) or 8 grams (g) of pure alcohol) a week include: mouth cancer, throat cancer and breast cancer; stroke; heart disease; liver disease; and brain and other damage to the nervous system.

In 3100 BC, the average life expectancy was generally between 28 and 33 years. This low number is due to high infant and childhood mortality rates. If someone survived past these early years, their chances were of living into their 40s. I wonder how many of the Nubians over 10 to 20 years of age suffered from signs of chronic alcohol ingestion? I wonder if family members of alcoholics experienced the anxiety, depression and shame modern families have that are related to their loved one's addiction? Also, were their family members often the victims of emotional or physical outbursts and did they have family members, addicted to alcohol, that tried to shield their family from the impact of alcohol abuse by distancing themselves?

I suspect the Old Testament advice, "Do not get drunk on wine, which leads to debauchery" (a broad term that includes drunkenness that often leads to sexual immorality, and other forms of unrestrained living) was good advice as much in the BCE era as it is today, *Ephesians 5:18*. Also, according to Buddha: The "six holes" which cause the loss of wealth (and health) are desire for intoxicating drinks and behaving foolishly, staying up late at night and losing the mind in frivolity, indulging in musical and theater entertainments, gambling, associating with evil companions, and neglecting one's duties.

CHAPTER 9

PENICILLIN MAY HAVE SAVED AND THREATENED MY LIFE

We usually associate the beginning of the modern "antibiotic era" with the names of Paul Ehrlich and Alexander Fleming. Ehrlich's idea of a "magic bullet" that selectively targets only disease-causing microbes and not the host was based on an observation that aniline and other synthetic dyes, which first became available at that time, could stain specific microbes but not others. Ehrlich argued that chemical compounds could be synthesized that would "be able to exert their full action exclusively on the parasite harbored within the organism." This idea led him to begin a large-scale and systematic screening program (as we would call it today) in 1904 to find a drug against syphilis, a disease that was endemic and almost incurable at that time. This sexually transmitted disease, caused by the spirochete Treponema pallidum, was usually treated with inorganic mercury salts but the treatment had severe side effects and poor efficacy. In his laboratory, together with chemist Alfred Bertheim and bacteriologist Sahachiro Hata, they synthesized hundreds of organoarsenic derivatives of a highly toxic drug Atoxyl and tested them in syphilis-infected rabbits. In 1909 they came across the sixth compound in the 600th series tested, thus numbered 606, which cured syphilis-infected rabbits and showed significant promise for the treatment of patients with this venereal disease in limited trials on humans. It was a derivative of a brilliant ruby-colored dye that Ehrlich called Trypan Red. Despite the tedious injection procedure and side effects, the drug, marketed by Hoechst under the name Salvarsan, was a great success and, together with a more soluble and less toxic Neosalvarsan, enjoyed the status of the most frequently prescribed drug until its replacement by penicillin in the 1940s. Amazingly, the mode of action of this 100-year-old drug is still unknown, and the controversy about its chemical structure has been solved only recently.

The systematic screening approach introduced by Paul Ehrlich became the cornerstone of drug search strategies in the pharmaceutical industry and resulted in thousands of drugs identified and translated into clinical practice, including, of course, a variety of antimicrobial drugs.

During the earlier days of antibiotics research, this approach led to the discovery of sulfa drugs, namely sulfonamidochrysoidine (Prontosil), which was synthesized by Bayer chemists Josef Klarer and Fritz Mietzsch and tested by Gerhard Domagk for antibacterial activity in a number of diseases. Prontosil, however, appeared to be a precursor to the active drug, and the active part of it, sulfanilamide, was thus not patentable as it had already been in use in the dye industry for some years. As sulfanilamide was cheap to produce and off-patent, and the sulfanilamide moiety was easy to modify, many companies subsequently started mass production of sulfonamide derivatives. The legacy of this oldest antibiotic on the market is possibly reflected in one of the most broadly disseminated cases of drug resistance: sulfa drug resistance, which is almost universally linked with class 1 integrons. (Integrons are genetic elements in bacteria that capture and reassemble genes from other mobile elements. They are common in bacteria and play a major role in the spread of antibiotic resistance.) Moreover, once the sulfa drug resistance is established on a mobile genetic element, it may be difficult to eliminate because the resulting construct confers a fitness advantage to the host even in the absence of antibiotic selection. Despite this, many continuously modified derivatives of this oldest class of synthetic antibiotics are still a viable option for therapy, and the action of and resistance to sulfanilamide is one of the best examples for the arms race between man and microbes.

The discovery of these first three antimicrobials, Salvarsan, Prontosil, and penicillin, was exemplary, as those studies set up the paradigms for future drug discovery research. The paths, followed by other researchers, resulted in a number of new antibiotics, some of which made their way up to the patient's bedside. The period between the 1950s and 1970s was indeed the golden era of discovery of novel antibiotic classes, with no new classes discovered since then. Therefore, with the decline of the discovery rate, the mainstream approach for the development of new drugs to combat emerging and re-emerging resistance of pathogens to antibiotics has been the modification of existing antibiotics.

Probably many of us are familiar with the somewhat serendipitous event on the September 3, 1928 that led to the penicillin discovery by Fleming (1929). Although the antibacterial properties of mold had been known from ancient times, and researchers before him had come upon the similar observations regarding the antimicrobial activity of Penicillium from time to time, it was his formidable persistency and his belief in the idea that made the difference. For 12 years after his initial observation, A. Fleming was trying to get chemists interested in resolving persisting problems with purification and stability of the active substance and supplied the Penicillium strain to anyone requesting it. He finally abandoned the idea in 1940, but, fortunately, in the same year an Oxford team led by Howard Florey and Ernest Chain published a paper describing the purification of penicillin quantities sufficient for clinical testing. Their protocol eventually led to penicillin mass production and distribution in 1945. Fleming's screening method using inhibition zones in lawns of pathogenic bacteria on the surface of agar-medium plates required much less resources than any testing in animal disease models and thus became widely used in mass screenings for antibiotic-producing microorganisms by many researchers in academia and industry. Fleming was also among the first who cautioned about the potential resistance to penicillin if used too little or for a too short period during treatment.

Unknown to many, however, is the fact that the first hospital use of a drug that we would name an antibiotic today was the so-called Pyocyanase prepared in1899 from Pseudomonas aeruginosa. It was noticed that the bacterium as well as the prepared extracts were active against a number of pathogenic bacteria and thus they tried to use the extract for treatment of various diseases. As the results of these treatments were not consistent and the preparation itself was quite toxic for humans, the treatment was eventually abandoned. Further investigations confirmed the production of antibiotic substances by Pseudomonas aeruginosa, also display potent antibacterial activities.

The discovery of these first three antimicrobials, Salvarsan, Prontosil, and penicillin, was exemplary, as those studies set up the paradigms for future drug discovery research. The paths, followed by other researchers, resulted in a number of new antibiotics, some of which made their way up to the patient's bedside. The period between the 1950s and 1970s was indeed the golden era of discovery of novel antibiotics classes, with no new classes discovered since then. Therefore, with the decline of the discovery rate, the mainstream approach for the development of new drugs to combat emerging and re-emerging resistance of pathogens to antibiotics has been the modification of existing antibiotics. *A Brief History of the Antibiotic Era: Lessons Learned and Challenges for the Future, Front Microbiology, Rustam I Aminov, 12/08/2010*

The discovery of penicillin, one of the world's first antibiotics, marks a true turning point in human history — when doctors finally had a tool that could completely cure their patients of deadly infectious diseases. Many school children are taught to recite the basics. Penicillin was discovered in London in September of 1928. As the story goes, Dr. Alexander Fleming, the bacteriologist on duty at St. Mary's Hospital, returned from a summer vacation in Scotland to find a messy lab bench and a good deal more.

Upon examining some colonies of Staphylococcus aureus, Dr. Fleming noted that a mold called Penicillium notatum had contaminated his Petri dishes. After carefully placing the dishes under his microscope, he was amazed to find that the mold prevented the normal growth of the staphylococci.

It took Fleming a few more weeks to grow enough of the persnickety mold so that he was able to confirm his findings. His conclusions turned out to be phenomenal: there was some factor in the Penicillium mold that not only inhibited the growth of the bacteria but, more important, might be harnessed to combat infectious diseases. As Dr. Fleming famously wrote about that red-letter date: "When I woke up just after dawn on September 28, 1928, I certainly didn't plan to revolutionize all medicine by discovering the world's first antibiotic, or bacteria killer. But I guess that was exactly what I did." Fourteen years later, in March 1942, Anne Miller became the first civilian patient to be successfully treated with penicillin, lying near death at New Haven Hospital in Connecticut, after miscarrying and developing an infection that led to blood poisoning. But there is much more to this historic sequence of events.

Actually, Fleming had neither the laboratory resources at St. Mary's nor the chemistry background to take the next giant steps of isolating the active ingredient of the penicillium mold juice, purifying it, figuring out which germs it was effective against, and how to use it. That task fell to Dr. Howard Florey, a professor of pathology who was director of the Sir William Dunn School of Pathology at Oxford University. He was a master at extracting research grants from tight-fisted bureaucrats and an absolute wizard at administering a large laboratory filled with talented but quirky scientists. This landmark work began in 1938 when Florey, who had long been interested in the ways that bacteria and mold naturally kill each other, came across Fleming's paper on the penicillium mold while leafing through some back issues of The British Journal of Experimental Pathology. Soon after, Florey and his colleagues assembled in his well-stocked laboratory. They decided to unravel the science beneath what Fleming called penicillium's "antibacterial action."

One of Florey's brightest employees was a biochemist, Dr. Ernst Chain, a Jewish German émigré. Chain was an abrupt, abrasive and acutely sensitive man who fought constantly with Florey over who deserved credit for developing penicillin. Despite their battles, they produced a series of crude penicillium-mold culture fluid extracts. During the summer of 1940, their experiments centered on a group of 50 mice that they had infected with deadly streptococcus. Half the mice died miserable deaths from overwhelming sepsis. The others, which received penicillin injections, survived.

It was at that point that Florey realized that he had enough promising information to test the drug on people. But the problem remained: how to produce enough pure penicillin to treat people. In spite of efforts to increase the yield from the mold cultures, it took 2,000 liters of mold culture fluid to obtain enough pure penicillin to treat a single case of sepsis in a person. In September 1940, an Oxford police constable, Albert Alexander, 48, provided the first test case. Alexander nicked his face working in his rose garden. The scratch, infected with streptococci and staphylococci, spread to his eyes and scalp. Although Alexander was admitted to the Radcliffe Infirmary and treated with doses of sulfa drugs, the infection worsened and resulted in smoldering abscesses in the eye, lungs and shoulder. Florey and Chain heard about the horrible case during dinner one evening and, immediately, asked the Radcliffe physicians if they could try their "purified" penicillin. After five days of injections, Alexander began to recover. But Chain and Florey did not have enough pure penicillin to eradicate the infection, and Alexander ultimately died.

In the summer of 1941, shortly before the United States entered World War II, Florey and Heatley flew to the United States, where they worked with American scientists in Peoria, Ill., to develop a means of mass producing what became known as the wonder drug. Aware that the fungus Penicillium notatum would never yield enough penicillin to treat people reliably, Florey and Heatley searched for a more productive species. One hot summer day, a laboratory assistant, Mary Hunt, arrived with a cantaloupe that she had picked up at the market and that was covered with a "pretty, golden mold." Serendipitously, the mold turned out to be the fungus Penicillium chrysogeum, and it yielded 200 times the amount of penicillin as the species that Fleming had described. Yet even that species required enhancing with mutation-causing X-rays and filtration, ultimately producing 1,000 times as much penicillin as the first batches from Penicillium notatum.

During the war, penicillin proved its mettle. Throughout history, the major killer in wars had been infection rather than battle injuries. In World War I, the death rate from bacterial pneumonia was 18 percent; in World War II, it fell, to less than 1 percent. From January to May in 1942, 400 million units of pure penicillin were manufactured. By the end of the war, American pharmaceutical companies were producing 650 billion units a month. Ironically, Fleming did little work on penicillin after his initial observations in 1928. Beginning in 1941, after news reporters began to cover the early trials of the antibiotic on people, the unprepossessing and gentle Fleming was lionized as the discoverer of penicillin. And much to the quiet consternation of Florey, the Oxford group's contributions were virtually ignored.

That problem was partially corrected in 1945, when Fleming, Florey, and Chain — but not Heatley — were awarded the Nobel Prize in Physiology or Medicine. In his acceptance speech, Fleming presciently warned that the overuse of penicillin might lead to bacterial resistance. In 1990, Oxford made up for the Nobel committee's oversight by awarding Heatley the first honorary doctorate of medicine in its 800-year history. *The real story behind penicillin, PBS, Dr. Howard Markel, 09/27/2013*

Before my teens, my father, his pharmacist friend (Wally Schumacker) and Wally's older than me son (name I can't remember), stayed in a cabin on the Middle Fork of the Salmon River in central Idaho. It is part of the larger "River of No Return" wilderness area and due to its remote location is a popular destination for challenging whitewater rafting, fly fishing and stunning scenery. The nickname "River of No Return" historically refers to the Main Salmon River, but it is also fitting for the Middle Fork due to the difficulty of navigating upstream against its powerful currents and rapids.

I have a vivid memory of this trip because of two events that occurred while we were there. One was while Wally was collecting fire wood a fairly large section of a branch became lodged under the skin of the pharmacist's arm. My dad got his doctor's bag out of the car, placed an instrument deep into the open wound and pulled out the foreign body. Luckily the pharmacist had alcohol flowing through his veins to deaden his senses and pain and the doctor had some left in the bottle of probably 80 proof (40% ethanol alcohol) or higher to flush the debris and microorganisms from the area.

In a medical setting, usually poisonous if taken eternally, rubbing alcohol (70% isopropyl alcohol -140 proof) is used. It acts as a disinfectant and cleaner for: surfaces, equipment, and objects in hospitals, laboratories, and households; for first aid, to treat minor scrapes, cuts, burns, and insect bites; to clean electronics, smartphones, keyboards, and other office equipment; to make soaps, perfumes, and skin and hair solutions; and many other applications. 70% isopropyl alcohol is the preferred concentration for standard disinfection because it's 30% water dilution helps it stay on surfaces longer, allowing more contact time to kill microbes. I don't know if the 40% drinking ethanol stayed on the surfaces of Wally's arm long enough to kill the microbes. I do know that the smell permeated the area well into the evening.

During the night we the two sons slept in sleeping bags in the station wagon. We were convinced by our parents that sleeping in the car would be a great outdoor experience. However, we knew the real reason was that the two of them alone inside the cabin would allow them to do some things their wives were best not to hear about.

Sleeping in the station wagon on the second night, I had a splitting headache, felt hot and needed a cool drink of water. Quietly I got out of the vehicle and walked to a running stream near the cabin. I knelt down, splashed water on my face and while attempting to drink from the creek I fell face first into the cold mountain stream. The next day I didn't feel good and my friend mentioned that I was holding my neck as if it were stiff. I tried to look and act ok, but it didn't work. My father pulled out his medical bag for the second time and took my temperature. It was very high, my neck was stiff and sore, and I wasn't answering questions to his liking. He told me that I appeared to have a severe infection that was affecting my brain. He filled two glass syringes, each bearing a long needle, near to the top with a white fluid, and told me to drop my pants and shorts, and bend over the cabin table. He then emptied one syringe of white liquid deep into the muscles of my right buttocks and one deep into my left buttocks. He mentioned that he was giving me a high dose of penicillin in hopes it would quickly kill the organism he suspected was invading my body.

I later learned, a stiff neck can be caused by a number of infections, including meningitis, vertebral osteomyelitis, and deep neck infections. These infections can spread to the brain and spine if not treated promptly. Meningitis is a bacterial, viral, or fungal infection that inflames the membranes that protect the brain and spinal cord. Symptoms include fever, stiff neck, headache, nausea, vomiting, light sensitivity, and changes in mental state. According to a 02/06/2025 Google search: The drug of choice for treating meningitis is cephalosporin antibiotic derivatives. The alternative therapy is penicillin G, Doxycycline or chloramphenicol. I was born in 1946 and penicillin was mass marked beginning in 1945 which was about 8-10 years before I received those injections. The other antibiotics were not available at that time.

Several years later, I had an anaphylactic reaction, requiring an epinephrine injection, after receiving another dose of penicillin. Dad told me that I may have developed an allergy to mold from the high dose of penicillin he previously gave me during our trip to the Middle Fork of the Salmon River. Also, he told me that I probably should not take penicillin again.

While attending veterinary school in my twenties, my overall allergies worsened when I was exposed to the large animal bedding and food barns, guinea pigs and rabbits. I had skin tests for allergies and the tests showed a highly positive reaction to mold as well as other plant and animal material. I was advised by an allergist that I should go into research and teaching if I really wanted to be a veterinarian.

Desensitization injections were a complete failure. However, for several years in the future, whenever I had an allergy attack the area of the desensitization injection site on my left arm swelled and displayed an itchy red bump. From that time on I reported that I was allergic to penicillin when asked by a doctor.

However, at the age of 79, researching this subject I found that: Having a mold allergy doesn't necessarily mean you're allergic to penicillin. Penicillin is made from the same mold, but modern penicillin is separated from the mold and purified. Many early allergies were due to impurities.

Synthetic penicillin is not produced naturally, but are instead created from a chemical precursor and are called semi-synthetic penicillin. The Penicillium mold is fermented to create a brew that is chemically or enzymatically broken down to form 6-aminopenicillanic acid (6-APA) and the 6-APA is used to make different types of penicillin.

People with a mold allergy aren't at a higher risk of developing a penicillin allergy. Symptoms of a penicillin allergy are: Skin rash, hives, itching, fever, swelling, shortness of breath, wheezing, runny nose, itchy, watery eyes, and anaphylaxis. Inhaled mold spores and fragments can be caused by mold in damp basements, closets, bathrooms etc. and symptoms tend to worsen during the summer.

Anaphylaxis is a severe, life-threatening allergic reaction that can occur rapidly after exposure to an allergen. Epinephrine is the first-line and only recommended medication for treating anaphylaxis. It counteracts the life-threatening symptoms of difficulty breathing, throat swelling, and a sudden drop in blood pressure. The fast, pounding heart, nervousness and anxiety caused by epinephrine - made this a terrifying experience for me.

Knowing this and having had two of these terrifying experiences, no matter what current research has found about the new synthetic penicillin, I always report my allergies to molds and the anaphylactic epinephrine reactions I have experienced.

The plot thickens. Since my late 50's my allergies have all but disappeared. Not pressing my luck, I do still take an antihistamine once daily. AI research commented: "Yes, allergies can change with age, and some people may find their allergies subside or even disappear over time. Possible reasons for allergies improving with age may be from the body's immune system naturally changing and becoming less reactive to allergens as people get older. This phenomenon is sometimes attributed to a quieting of the immune response in midlife; some individuals may gradually develop a tolerance to their triggers after repeated exposure over the years, though this is observed more often with pet allergies; and, changes like spending more time indoors, moving to a new region with different environmental allergens, or other shifts in lifestyle can reduce exposure to triggers and lead to allergy improvement."

I personally believe that the primary factor reducing the intensity of my allergies is gradually developing a tolerance to their triggers after repeated exposure over the years (like dog and cat allergies can) working as a veterinarian. Allergists told me that I would probably develop asthma if I didn't get away from constant exposure to the allergens. Asthma has an allergic and genetic factor – maybe "good anti-asthma genes" and tolerance to allergen triggers, like dogs and cats, helped keep me in practice for over 50 years.

CHAPTER 10

WAXES

Waxes are a diverse group of organic compounds that play essential roles in both biological and industrial contexts. Chemically, they are characterized by their hydrophobic nature, meaning they repel water, and their solid state at room temperature. However, waxes become malleable when heated slightly above room temperature, allowing them to be shaped and molded into various forms. The molecular structure of waxes typically includes long-chain hydrocarbons, fatty acids, esters, and alcohols. This composition gives waxes their unique properties, such as water resistance, low solubility in water, and high melting points. These properties make waxes indispensable in a wide range of applications, from providing a protective barrier in plants and animals to serving as ingredients in cosmetics, pharmaceuticals, and industrial products.

In nature, waxes form a vital part of the cuticle on the surfaces of leaves, fruits, and stems, helping to prevent water loss and protect against pests and pathogens. They also play crucial roles in the insulation and waterproofing of feathers, fur, and skin in animals, aiding in their survival and adaptation to diverse environments.

In the industrial sector, waxes are used in a variety of applications, including candle making, coatings for paper and textiles, and as ingredients in cosmetics, polishes, and pharmaceuticals. Their versatility and biocompatibility make them highly desirable materials for a wide range of products.

Waxes are commonly used in the food industry to improve the appearance, retain moisture, prevent spoilage and increase the shelf life of various food products. They are typically applied as thin coatings on the surface of fruits, vegetables, and certain confectionery items. Some common foods that may contain waxes include: Fruits, such as apples, citrus fruits (e.g., oranges, lemons), cucumbers, tomatoes, and avocados, are often coated with waxes to enhance their appearance and prolong their shelf life. These waxes help reduce moisture loss and prevent mold growth during storage and transportation. Certain vegetables, including cucumbers, bell peppers, eggplants, and squash, may also be waxed to improve their visual appeal and extend their freshness. Some confectionery items, such as chocolates, candies, and chewing gums, may contain waxes as ingredients to enhance texture, appearance, and shelf stability. They help prevent sticking and improve the overall mouthfeel of these products.

Waxes are produced by a wide range of organisms in the natural world, where they serve various protective and functional roles. Some common organisms that produce waxes include: Many plant species produce waxes as a protective coating on their leaves, stems, fruits, and seeds. These waxes help reduce water loss through transpiration, repel pests and pathogens, and protect against environmental stresses such as UV radiation and extreme temperatures. Examples of wax-producing plants used commercially include the carnauba palm and the candelilla shrub.

Certain animals, particularly insects and mammals, also produce waxes for various purposes. Bees, for example, secrete beeswax to construct their honeycombs and seal their hives, providing structure and protection for their colonies. Beeswax is used in a variety of applications, including cosmetics, candles, and pharmaceuticals. Lanolin, derived from sheep's wool, is valued for its moisturizing properties and is commonly found in skincare products. Some aquatic organisms, such as certain species of fish and marine invertebrates, also produce waxes to maintain buoyancy and protect their surfaces from water damage. Microorganisms of some bacteria and fungi are capable of synthesizing waxes as part of their cell walls or extracellular structures. These microbial waxes may play roles in cell protection, adhesion, and environmental adaptation.

Plant-based waxes, such as Carnauba wax, is extracted from the leaves of the carnauba palm tree native to Brazil. It is renowned for its high melting point and glossy finish. It is commonly used in cosmetics, food products, and car waxes. Candelilla wax is obtained from the leaves of the candelilla shrub found in Mexico and the southwestern United States. It is used in food, pharmaceuticals, and polishes. Soy wax, derived from soybean oil, is a renewable alternative to traditional waxes and is popular in candle making.

Paraffin wax is a mineral wax derived from petroleum. It is widely used in candle making, as well as in coatings, polishes, and industrial applications. Montan wax, extracted from lignite or brown coal, is another mineral wax that is commonly used in polishes, waxes, and coatings. Synthetic waxes are artificially produced through chemical processes and are designed to mimic or enhance the properties of natural waxes. They offer advantages such as consistency, purity, and customizable properties. Some examples include: Polyethylene waxes are produced by polymerizing ethylene gas. They are known for their high melting points, low viscosity, and excellent water repellency. Polyethylene waxes are used in a wide range of applications, including coatings, adhesives, and plastics. Waxes are synthesized through the Fischer-Tropsch process, which converts carbon monoxide and hydrogen into hydrocarbons. These waxes are characterized by their high purity, low odor, and consistent properties. They find applications in cosmetics, coatings, and lubricants.

When comparing natural and synthetic waxes, several factors come into play, including environmental impact, physical properties, and common applications. Natural waxes are generally considered more environmentally friendly than synthetic waxes, as they are derived from renewable resources and biodegradable. Synthetic waxes, on the other hand, may have a higher environmental impact due to their production processes and potential for accumulation in the environment. Natural waxes often have unique physical properties that make them desirable for specific applications. For example, carnauba wax is prized for its high melting point and glossy finish, making it ideal for car waxes and polishes. Synthetic waxes can be engineered to have specific properties tailored to the desired application, offering greater flexibility and consistency. Natural waxes are commonly used in cosmetics, pharmaceuticals, food products, and industrial applications. Synthetic waxes are also widely used in these industries, offering advantages such as purity, consistency, and customization.

The protective waxy barrier around plants may play a role in sending chemical signals to other plants and insects. Plant waxes limit water diffusion, resist drought, control volatile release, deter pest attacks, protect against diseases and insects, or attract pollinating insects. They also produce insect repellents based on wax micro- and nanostructures with specific mechanical and structural properties. Waxes form a protective barrier on the surfaces of plants (such as leaves and stems), animals, and insects, which help prevent water loss and protect against pathogens, insects, and UV radiation. Crystalline waxes can provide defense against herbivory (feeding on plants) by interfering with insect attachment to plants. They also provide protection against bacterial and fungal pathogens and reduce plant-insect interactions.

Cuticular wax, composed of long chain aliphatic, serves as a defense against herbivores, sap-sucking insects, nectar robbers, and insects, contributing to the temporary capture of insect pollinators and preventing the escape of insects. In nature, insects mainly interact with plant surfaces covered by 3D wax structures. Waxes play a crucial role in nature, serving various protective, structural, and energy storage functions for both plants and animals. They form a protective cuticle on leaves, stems, and fruits to prevent water loss and provide a barrier against pathogens, insects, and UV radiation. Waxes can decrease the ability of insects to attach to the plant cuticle surface, and leaves containing waxes and thick cuticles also protect them from insect herbivory.

Insects possess a protective outer layer of wax or grease, crucial for preventing desiccation. During molting, a waxy epicuticle, measuring 0. 1–1 μ in thickness, forms during the shedding of old skin, while wax is also secreted during instars for cuticle repairs. Notable examples of such insects are cockroaches and specific termites, with water insects using similar waxy coatings to repel water, akin to a human raincoat. The wax layer is thicker in females than in nymphs, while crawlers lack this protection.

Chinese wax, or insect wax, is a gelatinous substance secreted by certain insects, utilized in products like candles and polishes, and has properties resembling spermaceti, although it is harder and has a higher melting point. Wax on the cuticle aids insects by preventing dehydration and conserving internal moisture. Insects, particularly bees, secrete beeswax to build honeycombs and seal their hives. The wax-producing dermal glands, modified from epidermal cells, emit mixes of long-chain alcohols and carboxylic acids.

To extract raw wax, insects are harvested and boiled, with the sediment being used as pig feed. Certain waxes also enhance insecticidal properties against pests. Furthermore, crystalline wax structures on many plants hinder insect attachment, demonstrating a dual role in water conservation and pest deterrence. In summary, insect wax is a vital adaptation for survival, functioning primarily as a protective barrier against water loss, while also serving critical ecological roles.

The cuticle is a protective layer on the top and bottom of a leaf and on the surface of non-woody stems. It's waxy and water-repellent. It's produced by the cells in the epidermis, which is the outer cell layer of leaves and non-woody stems.

The cuticle has a complex chemical structure that hasn't been fully deciphered. Its base consists of a substance called cutin. On top of the cutin and interwoven with it are fatty acids, alcohols, hydrocarbons, and other organic (carbon-containing) molecules, which form the wax. The layer overlying the cutin is known as the "cuticle proper" and is the part that is removed during wax collection from a plant.

Small openings called stomata or stomates are located in the epidermis. The cuticle is absent over the surface of a stoma or stomate (the singular term for the opening). Carbon dioxide, oxygen, and other gases move into and out of the leaf through the stomata, which are mostly located on the underside of the leaf. Here, the environment is generally shady and the rate of water evaporation from the leaf is lower than it would be on the upper surface. A stoma is bordered by guard cells that can close the pore when necessary.

The carnauba palm is native to the northeastern part of Brazil. It's also known as the carnauba wax palm and the Brazilian wax palm. The tree grows on the savanna or in open forest. It has the ability to withstand dry periods as well as occasional flooding. It can also withstand moderate salinity. The wax is found on its leaves and leaf stalks (petioles) and is harvested from the upper surface of the leaves. The tree has a single trunk and generally reaches a height of up to 15 meters (49 feet). The attractive leaves are large, deeply divided, and shaped like a fan. They are green, blue-green, or light grey in color. They are borne at the end of a long petiole, which bears spines. The plant needs to be handled carefully in order to prevent injuries from the spines. The lower two-thirds of the trunk bears leaf bases remaining after the loss of older leaves. These remnants are arranged in a spiral pattern around the trunk. The flowers of the carnauba palm are small and yellow. They are grouped in a long and sometimes branched collection known as an inflorescence. The oval fruits of the plant are yellow-green to dark brown in color, depending on their maturity.

The first step in harvesting carnauba wax is to strip leaves from the tree. If this is done carefully, it doesn't damage the plant, which grows new leaves. The best wax comes from young, unopened leaves. According to one Brazilian company involved in the wax extraction, harvesters use a long stick with a knife at the end to reach the leaves. Once the leaves have been removed from the tree, they're dried in the sun. The wax is then removed from the surface of the leaves. A traditional method that is still used is to beat the leaves in order to separate the wax. The material is obtained as flakes or a powder and is then purified in some way. It's often boiled in water. The water is filtered, and the solid that's obtained is pressed. Some companies use solvent extraction to remove the wax from the liquid.

Although there is an overlap in the uses of carnauba and candelilla wax, the plants belong to different groups of flowering plants. Palm trees are monocots, and candelilla is a dicot. Monocot embryos have a single cotyledon (seed leaf), while dicot embryos have two. There are additional differences between the two groups. Carnauba wax is hard and has a high melting point. It's found in polish for cars, floors, furniture, and musical instruments. It's also used to make the shiny coating of candies, the coating of some medicinal tablets, the wax that coats dental floss, and candles. In addition, it's used to coat some specialized paper and cardboard products, including paper plates.

Carnauba wax is sometimes listed as E 903 on ingredient lists. The "E" stands for Europe. The designation is assigned by the European Food Safety Authority. E-designations may be found in countries outside Europe, however, especially on imported food. Carnauba wax is considered safe to eat in the amounts normally added to food. Researchers haven't investigated the effects of eating a large amount of the wax.

The carnauba palm is sometimes known as the "tree of life" because of its many uses. The wax is the most useful product of the plant today. The wood of carnauba palms is used to construct items such as bridges and the beams of roofs. The leaves are used to create thatch for roofs. They are also woven into items such as baskets, bags, hats, and mats. The fruits are edible but don't contain much pulp. They are used as animal feed. Each fruit contains one seed. The seeds are sometimes used as a coffee substitute.

Carnauba palms are often infested by insects that can carry the parasite that causes Chagas disease. Some people use the word "bug" as an alternate name for insect, but according to biological classification, bugs belong to a specific order of insects known as the Hemiptera. The order Hemiptera contains a family known as the Reduviidae. This family contains a subfamily called the Triatominae. The members of the subfamily are referred to as either reduviid bugs or as triatomine bugs. Many triatomine bugs are bloodsuckers. Some—including Rhodnius nasutus, which infests carnauba palms—can transmit Chagas disease. The bugs breed in the palm trees. The disease that they cause is also known as American trypanosomiasis.

American trypanosomiasis is also known as Chagas disease, named after Carlos Chagas (1879–1934), a Brazilian doctor. He discovered the illness in 1909. It is a parasitic illness caused by the parasite Trypanosoma cruzi. It is primarily found in Latin America, but can also be present in the United States, particularly in people who have migrated from endemic areas. The most common mode of transmission is through the bite of infected triatomine bugs (also called kissing bugs or assassin bugs). These bugs often live in cracks and holes in the walls and roofs of houses, especially in poor rural areas. They feed on blood, usually at night, and defecate near the bite wound. The parasite enters the body when the infected feces are rubbed into the bite wound, mucous membranes, or breaks in the skin; infected blood transfusions or organ transplants can transmit the parasite; a pregnant woman can transmit the parasite to her baby during pregnancy or childbirth (congenital transmission); and ingestion of food or drink contaminated with infected triatomine bug feces can also transmit the disease.

The acute phase can be mild or asymptomatic. Symptoms may include fever, fatigue, body aches, rash, swelling around the bite, and swollen lymph nodes. Symptoms may not appear for years or even decades. In severe cases, the chronic phase can cause heart and digestive problems, including an enlarged heart, heart failure, and digestive issues. Treatment with benznidazole or nifurtimox is effective in the early stages of infection. These medications are almost 100% effective in curing the disease if administered soon after infection are also indicated for those with reactivated infection, congenital infection, and during the early chronic phase.

From a distance, candelilla looks as though it consists entirely of thin, blue-green stems growing in an upright bunch. Branches in the stems are uncommon. The plant does produce leaves, but they are small and hard to see. The name of the plant means "little candle" and refers to the appearance of the stems. The mature stems generally range from around one foot to two feet in height but may occasionally be as tall as three feet. The flowers of the plant are beautiful but small. They are white or pink with a red center surrounding yellow or green reproductive structures. They grow all along the stems.

Bundles of candelilla plants are collected by hand. If the root is left, the plant will likely regenerate. If the plant and the root are removed, regeneration isn't possible. The collection and purification of wax from the plants is a multistep, arduous, and time-consuming process. First the candelilla plants are placed in large cauldrons containing water and sulfuric acid; the liquid is heated and boiled. This causes the wax to separate from the plant and rise to the surface in a foam; the foam is removed and placed in a different container. The liquid from the foam is removed, leaving the wax behind; the wax is allowed to cool and solidify; the solid wax is broken into multiple pieces, which are melted to allow debris to separate by sedimentation; and the melted wax is passed through Fuller's Earth or activated charcoal to purify it. Additional refining steps may be performed before the wax is ready to sell. The Fuller's earth is a type of clay known for its ability to absorb materials. Activated charcoal is a form of carbon that does the same thing. Candelilla is sometimes grown as a garden plant. Its flowers attract butterflies. The stems release a milky latex when cut, which may be irritating to the skin. The latex is toxic if ingested and gloves should be worn when handling the plant.

Candelilla wax is used to add a glaze to foods and is found in some brands of chewing gum. It may be listed as E 902 on an ingredient list. Like carnauba wax, it's considered safe to eat in the usual quantities added to food. The wax is used in a variety of cosmetics, including lotions, creams, and lip balm. It's a good vegan substitute for beeswax. Candelilla wax is hard after it has been refined. It's used for some of the same purposes as carnauba wax. It's added to polishes and waxes for floors and furniture and applied to leather. In addition, it's used to coat paper, cardboard, and gramophone records and is added to some lubricants and adhesives.

Though the wax obtained from the carnauba palm and the candelilla plant is useful, some concerns are associated with its collection. In each case, the collection process is labor intensive. In addition, the people collecting the wax sometimes work under unpleasant conditions. Another concern is the status of the plants. If a carnauba palm is stripped of a large quantity of leaves, before they have made carbohydrates by photosynthesis, the tree may be harmed. Collecting too many candelilla shrubs with their roots attached may harm the wild population. A sustainable industry that treats humans well is important with respect to the collection of both types of wax.

Human and other animals have earwax, also known as cerumen, is a natural substance produced by glands in the ear canal. It serves several important functions: For protection, earwax traps dirt, dust, and other debris, preventing them from entering the deeper parts of the ear canal and causing infections; earwax lubricates and keeps the ear canal moist, reducing friction and irritation; as new earwax is produced, it pushes older wax towards the outer ear, where it can fall out or be washed away; earwax contains antimicrobial substances that help trap and kill bacteria, and earwax helps maintain a stable temperature and humidity in the ear canal, protecting the delicate skin and eardrum.

In most cases, earwax is harmless and does not require removal. However, if excessive earwax builds up, it can block the ear canal and lead to discomfort, hearing loss, or infections. Dogs commonly have waxy ears infected with the micro-organism, yeast. I would often show the owner some of the yeast and ask them if they wanted to take it home to use as a starter to make sour dough bread. My wife and I recently had hearing tests. We both had ear wax that made it necessary to consult a healthcare professional for safe removal before they could be performed. Of course, I needed hearing aids and she did not. *Properties, Chemical Composition, Biological Functions & Ecological Importance of Waxes and AI.*

CHAPTER 11

EATING INSECTS

Entomophagy has a long and rich history in human culture. In fact, insects have been a part of human diets for thousands of years, with evidence of their consumption found in prehistoric archaeological sites. Throughout history, entomophagy has been a common practice in many cultures, particularly in parts of Africa, Asia, Latin America, and islands of the Pacific. In some societies, insects were considered a delicacy and were reserved for special occasions, while, in others, they were a staple food source. The roots of entomophagy vary depending on culture and region, but common reasons include the nutritional benefits of insects, their abundance and accessibility, and the cultural and religious significance of certain species. While the practice of entomophagy has declined in some parts of the world due to the influence of Western culture and industrialization, it continues to be important in many societies. Despite its long history and potential benefits, entomophagy has faced cultural and social stigmas in many parts of the world. However, recent efforts have been made to promote entomophagy as a sustainable and nutritious food source and to challenge cultural biases against insect consumption.

There are several references to the consumption of insects in the Bible, particularly in the Old Testament. In *Leviticus 11:20–23*, for example, it is written that any winged insect that walks on "four" legs is considered unclean, while other winged insects, such as locusts, crickets, and grasshoppers are considered clean and can be eaten by the Israelites. "All flying insects that walk on all fours are to be regarded as unclean by you. There are, however, some winged creatures that walk on all fours that you may eat: those that have jointed legs for hopping on the ground. Of these you may eat any kind of locust, katydid, cricket, or grasshopper. But all other winged creatures that have four legs you are to regard as unclean".

Since insects have six legs, it is not entirely clear why insects with "four" legs were singled out as unclean while other winged insects were considered clean. One possibility is that this classification was based on observable characteristics of insects that were known to the ancient Israelites. Insects such as beetles (probably considered unclean) have a different body structure and mode of movement compared to other insects, such as grasshoppers or locusts, which have powerful hind legs and can jump. Another possibility is that the classification of insects with "four" legs as unclean was based on cultural or religious beliefs. In many ancient cultures, insects were associated with death, decay, and impurity; therefore, they were considered unclean. This may have been the case for the ancient Israelites as well. In the end, the reason for the inclusion of these particular insects in the list of unclean animals is not entirely clear, as the text does not provide a specific explanation. However, some scholars suggest that it may have been due to their association with arid and dusty environments, which were considered unclean in ancient Israelite culture. In addition, in the New Testament, John the Baptist is described as having eaten locusts and wild honey in the wilderness (*Matthew 3:4*): "John's clothes were made of camel's hair, and he had a leather belt around his waist. His food was locusts and wild honey."[1]

Brian Fisher, an ant specialist at the California Academy of Sciences, in San Francisco, had been doing fieldwork in Madagascar when he realized that the forests where both he and Sylvain Hugel, an entomologist expert on crickets, conducted much of their research were disappearing. Nearly 80% of Madagascar's forest coverage had been destroyed since the 1950s, and 1-2% of what remains is cut down each year as farmers clear more trees to make room for livestock. The only way to prevent this, Fisher told Hugel in his emails, was to give locals an alternative source of protein. "If you want to be able to keep studying your insects, we need to increase food security, otherwise there will be no forest left," Fisher wrote.[2]

Over 2 billion people are estimated to eat insects on a daily basis. Globally, more than 2,000 insect species are considered edible, though far fewer are discussed for industrialized mass production and regionally authorized for use in food. Many insects are highly nutritious, though nutritional content depends on species and other factors such as diet and age. Insects offer a wide variety of flavors and are commonly consumed whole or pulverized for use in dishes and processed food products such as burger patties, pasta, or snacks. Like other foods, there can be risks associated with consuming insects, such as allergic reactions. As commercial interest in insects as food grows, countries are introducing new regulatory frameworks to oversee their production, processing, marketing, and consumption.

To increase consumer interest in Western markets such as Europe and North America, insects have been processed into a non-recognizable form, such as powders or flour. Policymakers, academics, as well as large-scale insect food producers such as Entomofarms in Canada, Aspire Food Group in the United States, Protifarm and Protix in the Netherlands, and Bühler Group in Switzerland, focus on seven insect species suitable for human consumption as well as industrialized mass production: Mealworms and lesser mealworms, as larvae usually marketed under the term buffalo worms; pancakes made from insect powder; house and tropical crickets; European migratory locust; black soldier fly; housefly; and Cochineal (see Natural Dyes chapter) which is collected to produce carmine, a red dye used for textiles and food.

The nutritional profiles of edible insects are highly variable given the large number of species consumed. In addition to species differences, nutritional content can be affected by geographic origin and production method (wild or farmed), diet, age, development stage, and sex. For instance, female house crickets contain more fat than males, while males contain more protein than females. Some insects (e.g. crickets, mealworms) are a source of complete protein and provide similar essential amino acid levels as soybeans, though less than casein. They have dietary fiber, essential minerals, vitamins such as B12, riboflavin and vitamin A, and include mostly unsaturated fat. Locusts contain between 8 and 20 milligrams of iron for every 100 grams of raw locust, whereas beef contains roughly 6 milligrams of iron in the same amount of meat. Crickets are also very efficient in terms of nutrients. For every 100 grams of substance crickets contain 12.9 grams of protein, 121 calories, and 5.5 grams of fat. Beef contains more protein, containing 23.5 grams in 100 grams of substance, but also has roughly triple the calories and four times the amount of fat as crickets have in 100 grams.

The organoleptic characteristics of edible insects vary between species and are influenced by environment. For instance, aquatic edible insects such as water boatmen and dragonfly larvae have a fish flavor, while diving beetles taste more like clams. Environment is not always a predictor of flavor, as terrestrial edible insects may also exhibit fish-like flavors (e.g. crickets, grasshoppers). Over 400 volatile compounds responsible for the aroma and flavor of edible insects have been identified. Pheromone chemicals contribute to pungent aromas and flavors in some species and the presence of organic acids (like formic acid in ants) makes some species taste sour. Organoleptic characteristics are dependent on the development stage of the insect (egg, larva, pupa, nymph, or adult) and may change significantly as an insect matures. For example, texture can change from soft to crunchy as an insect develops from larva to adult due to increasing exoskeletal chitin. Cooking method is considered the strongest influence on the final flavor of edible insects. Wet-cooking methods such as scalding or steaming remove pheromones and odor compounds, resulting in a milder flavor, while dry-cooking methods such as frying and roasting introduce more complex flavors.

Edible insects are raised as livestock in specialized insect farms and are produced under strict food law and hygiene standards for human consumption. Conditions such as temperature, humidity, feed, water sources, and housing, vary depending on the insect species. The insects are raised from eggs to larvae status or to their mature form in industrialized insect farms and then killed via temperature control. Culled insects may be freeze-dried and packed whole, or pulverized to insect powder (insect flour) to be used in other food products such as baked goods or snacks. In addition to nutritional composition and digestibility, insect species are selected for ease of rearing by the producer based on factors such as disease susceptibility, feed conversion efficiency, rate of development, and generational turnover. *Wikipedia*

In seeking to protect Madagascar's forests, Fisher and Hugel may have found a solution to one of the world's most pressing problems. The United Nation's Food and Agriculture Organization [FAO] says that agricultural production worldwide will have to increase by 70% in order to feed a global population expected to reach 9.1 billion by 2050. Yet agriculture is one of the biggest drivers of natural destruction of insect species that could be developed into a valuable food source.

Decreasing meat production food needs would remove pressure to expand livestock operations while freeing up existing land to restore native ecosystems and increase biodiversity. There is a sustainable alternative to raising and feeding livestock – edible insects. Grasshoppers, crickets and mealworms are rich in protein, and contain significantly higher sources of minerals such as iron, zinc, copper, and magnesium than beef. Yet pound for pound they require less land, water and feed than traditional livestock. Insect farming and processing produces significantly lower greenhouse gas emissions. Not only do insects produce less waste, their excrement, called frass, is an excellent fertilizer and soil amender.

Just as in Madagascar, there are technical and cultural barriers to overcome before bugs compete with beef (or any other meat) for space on the global dinner plate. While two billion people, mostly in Africa, Latin America and Asia, already eat insects; in Europe and North America bugs are more likely to be associated with filth, not food. But attitudes are starting to change.

In 2008, Madagascar's were eating lemurs and other endangered animals to add protein to their otherwise spare diets. In search of sustainable substitutions, residents were canvassed about other meats they liked to eat. Chicken and pork often came up, but so did an unfamiliar item: sakondry. When asked what it was, a few of the locals came back with a plate piled high with plump fried bugs. They were found to have a taste and consistency not unlike cubes of pork belly - crunchy on the outside, with that fatty meatiness of bacon in the middle. The villagers loved sakondry, but the bug wasn't always easy to find. The solution to stopping lemur hunting was how to make something the villagers already wanted to eat easier to get. Sakondry had never been studied, so entomologists and local conservation groups were involved to figure out the insect's life cycle and feeding habits. Once they discovered the ideal host plant, a kind of native bean, the villagers started planting it among their crops and along local pathways. With a ready supply of tasty protein growing just beyond the front door, villagers had less reason to go to the forest to hunt. Two years later, lemur poaching in the area has gone down by 30-50%.

Though he set out to save forests, Fisher's cricket powder is doing more to alleviate famine and improve nutrition in Madagascar. His production facility is in the country's urban center, far from the forested regions where locals struggle to find alternatives to hunting and clear-cutting grazing grounds. To really have an impact, he says, farmed insects not only have to be as good as meat, they also have to be easy to grow, and hyper-local. At the Valala Farms research center, scientists, biodiversity specialists and entomologists are working together to identify the most promising edible insects for each climatic region, and figuring out how to farm them at scale. His goal, he says, is to develop an "insect toolkit" that can be adapted to local needs, whether it's protein powder to address malnutrition, a meat alternative, grubs for a chicken farm, or something that can turn brewery waste into an additive for depleted soils. "We are trying to take advantage of 300 million years of insect evolution," he says. "We want that whole spectrum in our toolkit so that we can go and offer solutions wherever we go, in Madagascar and across Africa—wherever you have poverty combined with malnutrition and biodiversity issues."[2]

When comparing the consumption of insects in the past and today, different points of view offer insights into the changes and developments surrounding insect consumption over time. In the past, even in Western countries, insect consumption was rooted in cultural practices and traditions.

Entomophagy was considered a normal and accepted part of the diet in many contexts (while other insects were consumed out of necessity during times of food scarcity). Today, while insect consumption is gaining traction globally, cultural attitudes toward eating insects still vary significantly. Some cultures embrace entomophagy as a traditional practice, while others may have reservations or consider it unconventional. With the growing recognition of the environmental impact of animal husbandry, there is an increased interest in insects as a more sustainable protein source. In fact, in terms of nutrition, insects are a rich source of protein, vitamins, and minerals and, with a better understanding of nutrition and advancements in food science, insects are being recognized for their nutritional value and potential health benefits.

Moreover, the present era has seen culinary innovations and technological advancements that have transformed how insects are consumed: they are now processed into various forms and incorporated into a wide range of food products, appealing to modern tastes and dietary preferences. This level of innovation and accessibility was likely not present to the same extent in the past. The current global perspective emphasizes the potential of insects to address food shortages and reduce the strain on resources. The cultural and social attitudes towards insect consumption have evolved over time; the consumption of insects was likely more common and acceptable in biblical times and in ancient Rome than it is in modern European culture. They are generally not considered a mainstream food source, and insect consumption is relatively uncommon in many Western cultures, even if they are a sustainable food source for several reasons. Insects produce less waste and pollution and can be produced in a more efficient and environmentally friendly manner than traditional livestock. Insects can also be raised on organic waste, reducing the need for landfills and thus improving waste management. Insects require significantly fewer resources than traditional livestock farming, resulting in a lower carbon footprint. They require less land and feed and produce fewer greenhouse gas emissions. They are highly efficient at converting feed into edible biomass. For example, crickets require six times less feed than cattle to produce the same amount of protein. They can be raised on vertical farms or in small spaces, reducing the need for large amounts of land. Therefore, they may even be produced in urban areas where space is limited, considering they require significantly less water than traditional livestock farming. For example, crickets require 2000 times less water than beef cattle to produce the same amount of protein. Insects are less susceptible to disease and do not require antibiotics or growth hormones. This reduces the use of chemicals in their production, which can harm the environment and human health. The consumption of insects can thus offer a range of benefits for the future, including improved nutrition, environmental sustainability, food security, cultural diversity, and innovation in the food industry.

Insects may be considered comparable in nutritional value to conventional food and may also be digested by most human beings. They are a rich source of protein, vitamins, and minerals. They contain all the essential amino acids required by the human body, making them a high-quality protein source. Insects are also low in fat and have a favorable ratio of omega-3 to omega-6 fatty acids.

As the world population grows, there is an increasing need for sustainable food sources. Insects can provide a reliable and sustainable source of protein. As shown previously, in many cultures around the world, insects are already a traditional food source. Incorporating insects into global food systems, including in Western societies, may help preserve traditional food cultures and promote cultural diversity. In recent years, there has been a renewed interest in the consumption of insects and in novel food products since they are being developed with sustainability in mind, using ingredients that are locally sourced, organic, and/or regeneratively produced; these production methods help to minimize environmental impacts and support sustainable agriculture in the context of a circular economy. Insect production, however, requires expertise, since different factors, including the quality of the diet offered and microbiological assessment, need to be taken into account.

Novel food refers to any food or food ingredient that was not consumed to a significant degree within the European Union (EU) prior to 15 May 1997. This includes either newly developed foods/food ingredients or traditional foods from other parts of the world that are not currently consumed within the EU. The importance of novel food lies in its potential to offer new and innovative food products to consumers while ensuring that they are safe and do not harm human health. Novel food can provide a range of benefits, such as improved nutrition, enhanced flavor, and new culinary experiences. However, the safety of novel food is paramount; therefore, it is subject to a rigorous safety assessment before it can be authorized for sale within the EU. The safety assessment evaluates the potential risks associated with the food, including its composition, toxicity, and any possible allergenic effects. The EU's regulation of novel foods provides a framework for the authorization, safety assessment, labeling, and traceability of novel food products. This ensures that consumers can make informed choices about the food they eat and can have confidence in the safety and quality of novel food products. The development of novel foods is an opportunity to explore more sustainable food sources and production methods. By promoting the use of sustainable and innovative food sources, novel foods have the potential to contribute to a more sustainable and resilient food system because they can help address the problem of malnutrition and improve the overall health of populations. A nutritious diet is essential for good health, and novel food can provide the essential nutrients needed for optimal health.

By exploring the rich history of insect consumption, we can gain a greater appreciation of the important role that insects have played and, probably, will continue to play in human culture and nutrition. Evidence indicates that humans have been consuming insects as a food source for tens of thousands of years. Exploring archaeological and anthropological sources, as well as potential reasons why early humans turned to insects as a food source through a cultural-historical perspective, we noted the nutritional benefits of insects, which were apparently valued by our ancestors, whether as an emergency or luxury food. In Western society, while the cultural acceptance and availability of insects may have been more widespread in ancient Rome, and, to some extent, in the Renaissance period, today's interest in insect consumption is driven by sustainability, innovation, and the evolution of dietary practices. In ancient Rome, insects were consumed as a luxury food, but also as a response to food scarcity, partly due to their availability. They were a readily accessible source of nutrients and were collected during specific seasons or in times of need. Moreover, in ancient times, insect consumption was not governed by specific regulations or commercialized as a mainstream food industry. Today, in many Western societies, including those influenced by Roman culture, insect consumption is not so widespread or culturally accepted. However, interest in eating insects as a sustainable protein source is growing and gaining popularity in some communities and among adventurous eaters. Current interest in insect consumption is driven by sustainability, innovation, and the evolution of dietary practices.[1]

1   Edible Insects: A Historical and Cultural Perspective on Entomophagy with a Focus on Western Societies, Marianna Olivadese et. al, 08/04/2023.

2   They're Healthy. They're Sustainable. So Why Don't Humans Eat More Bugs? Time, Aryn Baker, 02/26/2021.

CHAPTER 12

MUSTARD GAS

The assassination of Archduke Franz Ferdinand by a Serbian nationalist Gavrilo Princip on June 28, 1914, in Sarajevo, acted as the immediate trigger for World War I. Austria-Hungary blamed Serbia and, with German encouragement, declared war on them on July 28, 1914. Due to existing alliances, this declaration of war quickly drew other European powers into the conflict. Austria-Hungary and its ally Germany (the Central Powers) clashed with Great Britain, France, and Russia (the Allied Powers).

The war lasted from 1914 to 1918, resulting in significant loss of life and widespread destruction, making it a pivotal event in 20th-century history. The United States eventually entered the war on the side of the Allied Powers in 1917, after German unrestricted submarine warfare and the Zimmerman Telegram.

The Zimmermann Telegram was a secret coded message from German Foreign Minister Arthur Zimmermann to the German Minister to Mexico, Heinrich von Eckhardt, proposing a military alliance between Germany and Mexico against the United States if the US entered World War I, offering Mexico the return of lost territory. In January

1917, Germany, facing a stalemate in World War I, sent the telegram to Mexico, hoping to draw the US into the war and distract them from the European front. The telegram proposed that if the United States entered the war against Germany, Mexico should declare war on the US and Germany would provide financial support to Mexico to help them reclaim Texas, New Mexico, and Arizona. British intelligence intercepted and decoded the telegram, and shared it with the US government. The American press published the telegram's contents in early March 1917, causing public outrage and fueling anti-German sentiment. The telegram, combined with Germany's unrestricted submarine warfare, significantly contributed to the United States' decision to enter World War I on the side of the Allies.

World War I, also known as the Great War, would leave 17 million people dead or missing in action. Stuck in the squalid conditions of the trenches, it was a living hell for those on the front line. But it was made even worse by the work of industrial chemists. In July 1917, troops based in Ypres, Belgium, reported a shimmering cloud around their feet and a strange peppery smell in the air. Within 24 hours they started to itch uncontrollably and developed horrific blisters and sores. Some started coughing up blood.

They'd been poisoned by mustard gas – one of the more deadly chemical weapons deployed in battle.

And because mustard gas can be absorbed through the skin, gas masks were useless. Even fully clothed soldiers weren't fully protected. It could take up to six weeks to die from mustard gas, and it was a terrible way to die.

Towards the end of the Great War, this gas had not only killed and crippled but instilled terror across the battlefield.

The first use in Ypres alone left up to 10,000 people dead, with many more injured.

Mustard gas was one of a number of weaponized poison gases developed by Fritz Haber, a Professor at the prestigious University of Karlsruhe. Haber was a brilliant chemist, who invented a process for the industrial scale production of ammonia-based fertilizer. This brilliant discovery, known as the Haber process, played a huge role in avoiding worldwide famines and now feeds about a third of the world's population. It won him the Nobel Prize in Chemistry in 1918.

But Haber's role in chemical weapons' development means his legacy will always have its dark side.

Even after the war, Haber enthusiastically promoted the use of poison gas. And his colleagues would go on to make other deadly gases – World War I is known to some as the chemists' war.[1]

World War II formally began on September 1, 1939, when Germany invaded Poland, triggering declarations of war from France and the United Kingdom. However, the war's roots lay in years of international tension and aggressive expansion by Fascist Italy and Nazi Germany. Nazi Germany, led by Adolf Hitler, and Fascist Italy, under Benito Mussolini, pursued aggressive expansionist policies in the 1930s, violating international agreements and treaties. On September 1, 1939, Germany invaded Poland without a formal declaration of war. In support of their mutual defense treaty obligations with Poland, France and Great Britain issued ultimatums to Hitler for the immediate withdrawal of German forces from Poland. The war's origins also stemmed from the unresolved issues of World War I, the Treaty of Versailles, and the Great Depression, which created economic and political instability across Europe.

On December 7, 1941, a date that President Franklin D. Roosevelt claimed would "live in infamy," the Imperial Japanese Navy conducted a surprise aerial assault on Pearl Harbor. This unprovoked attack brought the United States into World War II, as it immediately declared war on Japan. World War II officially ended for America on September 2, 1945 when Japan signed the surrender documents on the USS Missouri, marking "Victory over Japan Day" (VJ Day). While the war in Europe concluded earlier with Germany's surrender, the Pacific theater, where the US primarily fought against Japan, ended on this date.

On the night of December 2, 1943, the Germans bombed a key Allied port in Bari, Italy, sinking 17 ships and killing more than 1,000 American and British servicemen and hundreds of civilians. Caught in the surprise World War II air raid was the John Harvey, an American Liberty ship carrying a secret cargo of 2,000 mustard bombs to be used in retaliation if Hitler resorted to gas warfare. The Luftwaffe's lucky strike, which released a poisonous cloud of sulfur mustard vapor over the harbor—and liquid mustard into the water—prompted an Allied cover-up of the chemical weapons disaster. But it also led to an army doctor's serendipitous discovery of a new treatment for cancer.

In the devastating aftermath of the attack, which the press dubbed a "little Pearl Harbor," U.S. General Dwight D. Eisenhower and British Prime Minister Winston Churchill moved to conceal the truth about the shipment of poison gas, for fear Germany might use it as an excuse to launch an all-out chemical war. As a result of the military secrecy, medical personnel weren't alerted to the danger of contamination from the liquid mustard that spread insidiously over the harbor, mixing with the tons of fuel oil from the damaged ships. In the crush of casualties that first night, hundreds of survivors, who had jumped or been blown overboard and swam to safety, were mistakenly believed to be suffering from only shock and immersion. They were given morphine, wrapped in warm blankets and left to sit in their oil-soaked uniforms for as long as 24 hours, while the seriously wounded were attended to first. It was tantamount to marinating in mustard gas. But all remained ignorant of the peril.

By dawn, the patients had developed red, inflamed skin and blisters on their bodies "the size of balloons." Within one day, the wards were full of men with eyes swollen shut. The doctors suspected some form of chemical irritant, but the patients did not present typical symptoms or respond to standard treatments. The staff's unease only deepened when notification came from headquarters that the hundreds of burn patients with unusual symptomology would be classified "Dermatitis N.Y.D."—Not Yet Diagnosed.

Then without warning, patients in relatively good condition began dying. These sudden, mysterious deaths left the doctors baffled and at a loss as to how to proceed. Rumors spread that the Germans had used an unknown poison gas. With the daily death toll rising, British officials in Bari placed a "red light" call alerting Allied Force Headquarters (AFHQ) in Algiers to the medical crisis. Lieutenant Colonel Stewart Francis Alexander, a young chemical warfare specialist attached to Eisenhower's staff, was dispatched immediately to the scene of the disaster.

Despite the British port authorities' denials, Alexander quickly diagnosed mustard gas exposure. Convinced that preoccupation with military security had compounded the tragedy, he doggedly pursued his own investigation to identify the source of the chemical agent and determine how it had poisoned so many men. After carefully studying the medical charts, he plotted the destroyed cargo ships' positions relative to the gas victims and succeeded in pinpointing the John Harvey as the epicenter of the chemical explosion. When divers pulled up fragments of fractured gas shells, the casings were identified as being from 100-pound American mustard bombs.

On December 11, 1943, Alexander informed headquarters of his initial findings. Not only was the gas from the Allies' own supply, but the victims labeled "Dermatitis N.Y.D." had suffered prolonged exposure as a result of being immersed in a toxic solution of mustard and oil floating on the surface of the harbor.

The response Alexander received was shocking. While Eisenhower accepted his diagnosis, Churchill refused to acknowledge the presence of mustard gas in Bari. With the war in Europe entering a critical phase, the Allies agreed to impose a policy of strict censorship on the chemical disaster: All mention of mustard gas was stricken from the official record, and Alexander's diagnosis deleted from the medical charts.

Alexander's "Final Report of the Bari Mustard Casualties" was immediately classified, but not before his startling discovery of the toxic effects on white blood cells caught the attention of his boss in the Chemical Warfare Service (CWS), Colonel Cornelius P. "Dusty" Rhoads. In civilian life, Rhoads served as head of New York's Memorial Hospital for the Treatment of Cancer and Allied Diseases. Of the more than 617 casualties who suffered from gas exposure at Bari, 83 died, all demonstrating mustard's suppressive effect on cell division—suggesting it might be used to inhibit the fast-multiplying malignant white cells that can invade and destroy healthy tissue. Alexander had extracted invaluable data from the morgue full of case studies, pointing to a chemical that could possibly be used as weapon in the fight against certain types of cancer.[2]

Two decades later, with World War II looming, researchers on the side of the Allied Forces feared a repeat of the mustard gas attacks of the Great War. So, they tried to create antidotes. What they discovered led them into a very different battle. Two doctors at Yale University, Louis Goodman and Alfred Gilman, delved into the medical records of soldiers affected by mustard gas, and noticed that many of them had a surprisingly low number of immune cells in their blood – cells that, if mutated, can go on to develop into leukemia and lymphoma. Goodman and Gilman hypothesized that if mustard gas could destroy normal white blood cells, it seemed likely that it could also destroy cancerous ones.

After successful animal trials, Goodman and Gilman looked for a human volunteer with white blood cell cancer to test mustard gas as a cancer therapy. They found a patient with advanced lymphoma, known today only by his initials: J.D. A massive tumor on J.D.'s jaw meant he couldn't swallow or sleep – he couldn't even fold his arms across his chest because the tumors in the lymph nodes in his armpits were so big. He was encased, front and back, by cancer. His doctors tried everything they could, but his outlook was considered hopeless.

With nowhere else to turn, J.D agreed to try the new experimental drug. At10am on the 27th of August 1942 he was given the first injection of what they called "synthetic lymphocidal chemical". This was in fact nitrogen mustard, the compound used to make mustard gas. Because of the war, J.D.'s treatment was a secret and it was referred to in his records only as "substance X". He received a number of treatments with substance X and with each one he became a little better. He could sleep, he could swallow and he could eat. He was much more comfortable and the pain faded away. This was a monumental moment in the history of medicine. It was the beginning of what we now know as chemotherapy.

After WWII, Professor Alexander Haddow, was working on compounds that could block the growth of tumors and treat cancer. All he needed to make a breakthrough in cancer treatment was a lead – an effective molecule to start from. Mustard gas gave him that much needed and crucial starting point.

In 1948, Haddow published a ground-breaking piece of research in the journal Nature, showing exactly which bits of the nitrogen mustard molecule were needed to kill cancer cells. Perhaps more importantly, he also found out how to make the chemical less toxic, but with more potent cancer-killing activity.

Haddow began by showing that nitrogen mustards could stop the growth of tumors in rats. Then in experiments akin to tinkering with Lego, he altered bits of the molecule, replacing them with different 'bricks'. Replacing certain bits, in particular either of two chlorine atoms, rendered the molecule useless and it no longer blocked tumor growth in his rats. This was an important finding, showing that the molecule needed both chlorine atoms to work. And replacing certain other parts of the molecule altered its activity too. Through this molecular puzzle Haddow worked out which pieces were needed to make a treatment that would benefit cancer patients.

He continued his research, showing how these chemicals actually worked – it was by somehow linking together other molecules inside the cancer cell, ultimately leading the cell on a suicidal path. Other researchers then went on to show that these linked molecules were in fact strands of DNA. This triggered the cell's self-destruct mechanism – causing the cell to shut down and break apart, destroying it.

And so mustard gas went from the very real battleground of the WWI trenches into the frontline of cancer treatment. For J.D, mustard gas gave him an immensely important extra few months with less pain and greater comfort, he lost his life six months after his experimental treatment was started. There is just one entry in his medical records from the 1st of December 1942. It simply says "Died". J.D passed away unaware of the impact that his life and death would go on to have. But Haddow's subsequent work launched the start of a new era of cancer treatment – chemotherapy. All of the drugs that followed worked in the same basic way as Haddow described. And in fact, nitrogen mustard derived chemotherapy is still used to treat some cancers today.

The chemical structure Haddow published is only a few atoms away from the structure of the drug chlorambucil, which is still used to treat a type of leukemia called chronic lymphocytic leukemia and another blood cancer called non-Hodgkin lymphoma (NHL). Survival from NHL has nearly trebled since the early 1970s and now over 60 per cent of people survive for at least 10 years, thanks in part to this drug.[1]

But the story of mustard gas probably doesn't end here. It holds great promise in future cancer survival.

"In the middle of difficulty lies opportunity"- Einstein

1   *Cancer News, Mustard gas – from the Great War to frontline chemotherapy, Sarah Hazell, 08/27/2014.*

2   *The Great Secret: The Classified Chemical Weapons Disaster that Launched the War on Cancer as well as numerous other books on World I, Jennet Conant, 08/12/2020.*

CHAPTER 13

THE TRUMPS

Director and writer Drew Hayden Taylor was living in Dawson City, Yukon when he noticed that there were planes full of German tourists arriving in Canada's westernmost territory. He was surprised to discover that Yukon's biggest tourist market after the United States is Germany. There were German language tour companies and brochures in German at the local tourist information center. There was even a direct flight from Frankfurt to the 25,000 residences of Whitehorse.

Taylore discovered a German obsession with Indigenous North Americans back to a series of novels about a fictional Apache Indian called Winnetou. Written at the end of the 19th Century by an author who'd never been to North America, the series depicts a romanticized ideal of the old West and the Indigenous people who lived there that captured the imaginations of generations of Germans.

Many Germans arrive in Yukon's boreal forest ready for adventure with a Winnetou novel in their pocket. With a population density of 0.1 people per square kilometer, Yukon has all the nature and solitude that German hobbyists crave. German forests, by contrast, are far from wild. They're heavily groomed and extremely orderly. And where there is real forest there is almost never solitude.

You might not be able to get to the Yukon from Toronto without a long stopover in Vancouver stretching your journey up to 20 hours. But if you want to visit from Frankfurt Germany, you can fly direct to Whitehorse on a 767 jumbo jet. It's usually faster to get to Whitehorse from Germany than from Toronto. Really! According to the department of tourism, The Yukon has increased tourism 25 percent in the last decade by targeting German markets. It's a "hip" place for Germans to visit.

As of the 2011 census, 3,203,330 Canadians claim German heritage. German immigrants to Kitchener-Waterloo, (formerly Berlin) Ontario recreated Munich's legendary Oktoberfest festival in their new home. It's now one of the largest Oktoberfest's in the world, pulling in almost a million people every year for beer-soaked, lederhosen-wearing festivities. All the way up in Yukon Territories where German expats run hotels and tour companies, German is one of the largest non-official languages spoken. You'll hear and see it everywhere; in travel brochures, on restaurant menus and at hotels.

The amount of daylight is the same. Although Canada likes to promote itself as "The Great White North," most Canadians actually live in the "Great Multicolored South." Berlin is at 52.5 degrees latitude, just north of Saskatoon at 52.1 degrees. No part of Germany is as far south as Montreal.

Germans are accustomed to long days in summer and short days in winter. The idea of being "north of 60" is perfectly normal for most Germans.

German law limits beer ingredients to barley, hops and water. It prevents brewers from competing with bakers for wheat and rye and keeps the flavor notoriously predictable. Although Canada's two biggest brewers aren't German (in fact, they're not even Canadian anymore either), Molson Pilsner and Labatt Blue Pilsner are available in most parts of the country. The familiar flavor will wash away any homesickness. In the Yukon, the bestselling beer is Yukon Gold, flavored with Saaz hops from Bohemia!

From the Inuvialuit of Tuktoyaktuk to the Mi'kmaq of Halifax the original inhabitants of what is now called Canada are alive and awesome. They might not be anything like the characters from Karl May's Winnetou novels, but if you ask respectfully, they will be happy to explain their culture and share stories.

Teepees, Powwows and Indian camps have long intrigued Germany's fascination with Indigenous Culture. These real people in Canada are a lot more interesting. And what about the delicious Bannock bread washed down with tea? It is a flatbread that originated in Scotland and is a staple food for Indigenous peoples in Canada. It's made from flour, water, and fat, and is often fried in a pan. Oh, most Canadians apologize and appreciate never being asked to say "eh" or "about."

Bennett was built during the Klondike Gold Rush of 1897–1899 at the end of the White Pass and Chilkoot Pass from the nearby ports of Skagway and Dyea in Alaska. During the gold rush, Canadian authorities required miners to have a year's supply of food and equipment to cross the border. This requirement was intended to prevent starvation. The Canadian government required each person to have at least 1,095 pounds of food, or three pounds per day for a year. The total load for a prospector could easily double when including clothes and equipment. Goods purchased in the U.S. were subject to customs duties payable to the North-West Mounted Police and women and men paid $10 for a miner's certificate that allowed them to prospect for gold and other minerals in the Yukon for one year.

Gold prospectors would pack their supplies over the mountains from the ports, then build or purchase rafts in the town of Bennett and use them to take them from Bennett Lake to the Yukon River - where there were gold fields around Dawson City, Yukon. During their travels over White Pass, thousands of horses and mules died while crossing the White Pass Trail in Alaska. The trail became known as the "Dead Horse Trail" due to the number of animals that perished. Causes of death were: Starvation from exhaustion and being under fed; falling off cliffs, drowning in rivers, or smashed against boulders; becoming stuck in mud holes; eating poisonous grasses at the summit; broken legs on slippery rocks; inexperienced Stampeders that had little concern for the animals; and the trail was impassable at times due to mud, rain, and harsh weather conditions.

The stench of rotting carcasses was sickening and sometimes the miner's hunger drove them to eat the bodies of the dead horses, which often made them violently ill. A bronze memorial to the pack horses and mules can be seen at Inspiration Point. Its inscription reads: "The dead are speaking in memory of us."

In 1900, the White Pass and Yukon Route Railroad was completed it bypasses Bennett and went right to White Horse. Bennett soon became a ghost town. What remains are rotted pilings along the lake and river that show where wharves that moored and loaded or unloaded a level quayside area to which a ship may be moored to load and unload cargo, buildings, and even a bridge had been located. Visitors can hike the Chilkoot Trail or ride the White Pass train to get to Bennett. There is a historic Bennett Station House museum and the remains of the Chilkoot Trail National Historic Site.

Due to its remote location, Yukon and Whitehorse itself were some of the last regions of North America to be colonized. The Klondike Gold Rush of the late 1890's saw the Whitehorse area become strategically important due to its location on the Yukon River. It became a popular travel route for prospectors who wanted to sail to Yukon instead of navigating the dangerous Chilkoot Pass. The site of modern Whitehorse became a popular camping ground for migrants heading to Dawson City and was referred to as "White Horse"; the nearby settlement of Canyon City was also a popular destination.

As the Klondike Gold Rush faded, prospectors began looking for other mineral deposits in the area. In 1898 copper was discovered in the hills west of White Horse, a region that was nicknamed the Copper Belt. The first copper claims were made by Jack McIntyre in 1898 and Sam McGee in 1899; McGee would later become famous as the subject of Robert W. Service's poem "The Cremation of Sam McGee." The region saw rapid transportation improvements, most notably the White Pass and Yukon Railway in 1900, which saw Canyon City, located on the Dyea Trail, abandoned due to the railroad directly connecting White Horse with Skagway, Alaska, a popular port of entry for migrants. The name of the town of Bennett and Bennett Lake still has deep roots. *AI*

Richard Bedford Bennett was born in the tiny community of Hopewell Hill, New Brunswick, in July 1870. His family had once prospered in the shipbuilding business, but at the time of his birth they were suffering in poverty. A serious young man and a voracious reader, Bennett was an exceptional student with a prodigious memory. He graduated high school at age 15 and a year later was teaching school. By 18, he was a principal. When school was on break, he worked in law offices. He left education to become a lawyer and moved west in 1897. Bennett excelled at corporate law and his firm included such clients as the Canadian Pacific Railway and the Hudson's Bay Company. He and his childhood friend Max Aitkin (later Lord Beaverbrook) also worked together in a number of successful ventures, including stock purchases, land speculation and the buying and merging of small companies. Bennett became president of a host of companies and served on the boards of many others.

Before he was 40, Bennett was a multi-millionaire. He lived at the Palliser Hotel in Calgary and neither smoked nor drank alcohol. He dated a number of women but never married. He also began a lifelong dedication to philanthropy, giving generously to schools, hospitals, charities and individuals in need.

He seriously entered politics in 1898 and won election to the Assembly of the North-West Territories. His ability to speak quickly, extemporaneously and persuasively earned him the nickname Bonfire Bennett. In 1911, Bennett entered federal politics; he was elected the Conservative Member of Parliament for Calgary. He made a name for himself as a hard worker and persuasive speaker. Among other things, he led an effort that uncovered corruption in the Canadian Northern Railway. However, Bennett was dissatisfied with his role as a backbencher and did not run for re-election in 1917.

In 1921, he was appointed the minister of justice. In 1925, he became the federal member for Calgary West. In 1926, he served as minister of finance; acting minister of the interior and minister of mines; and acting superintendent general of Indian affairs. In 1930 & 1931 his government passed relief acts to provide for more infrastructure construction and direct relief for farmers and the unemployed. Western farmers had been devastated by a collapse in prices, a drought, and a grasshopper plague. Bennett's government made farm loans easier to acquire with the Farmers' Creditors Arrangement Act. In 1935, the Bennett government created the Canadian Wheat Board, which stabilized prices and helped farmers sell their wheat abroad.

Bennett believed that Canada's culture was being swamped by the United States, especially with regards to the dominant cultural force of the day — radio. In 1932, his government created the Canadian Radio Broadcasting Commission, which regulated radio broadcasting to ensure more Canadian content. It also established a publicly owned, national radio network dedicated to telling Canadian stories to Canadians. In 1936, it became the Canadian Broadcasting Corporation.

In 1930, Bennett represented Canada at the imperial conference at which the Statute of Westminster was drafted. The Statute represented a significant step toward Canada's independence by ensuring that Britain could no longer pass legislation applicable to any of its dominions.

In the 1930s, chartered banks controlled interest rates, the value of the Canadian dollar in world markets and the amount of money in circulation. They even printed their own currency. Bennett established a Royal Commission as a step toward creating the Bank of Canada. It would ultimately assume all those powers from the chartered banks. The chartered banks fought the idea, but Bennett persevered. The Bank of Canada Act was passed in 1934 and the Bank opened in 1935. It eventually gained the legal mandate to control Canada's monetary policy at an arm's length from the federal government.

In 2025, CBC reported: "A number of American banks do business in Canada with large lending and commercial and investment banking operations, among other functions, on this side of the 49th parallel. Personal banking in Canada is largely the domain of Canadian-based banks, due to stringent federal regulations designed to protect against bank failures. According to government figures, Canada's large banks hold more than 93 percent of all domestic banking assets. Canadian banks are routinely ranked among the safest in the world." Also, in 2025 the Wall Street Journal reported: "US President Trump said Canada doesn't allow U.S. banks to open or do business in the country. Data from the country's banking supervisor indicates that at least three U.S. banks have operations in Canada. Foreign banks are generally allowed to operate subsidiaries in Canada, so long as they receive approval from the country's finance minister, and in some cases the national bank regulator, known as the Office of the Superintendent of Financial Institutions, or

OSFI. OSFI records show that it regulates Amex Bank of Canada, Citibank Canada, and J.P. Morgan Bank Canada.

After Bennett lost re-election, he suffered a heart attack in March 1935. However, he acted as an effective leader of the Opposition. He attended the House of Commons almost every day and asked blistering questions of the government. He resigned in March 1938 due to health concerns.

Bennett realized a lifelong dream to live in England and moved close to his childhood friend and law partner, Max Aitkin – later to be known as Lord Beaverbook, who had moved to England years before. This was the first home Bennett ever owned. At the outset of the Second World War, Lord Beaverbook was appointed the minister of aircraft production. Bennett worked as his assistant, arranging the building of planes and airfields. For his service in the war effort, British prime minister Winston Churchill appointed him to the House of Lords.

By 1947, Bennett's health was declining and he sold nearly all his investments. He made generous donations to Canadian charities, churches, schools and scholarships. On 26 June 1947, Bennett was enjoying a warm bath when he suffered a fatal heart attack. *Richard Bedford Bennett, Library & Archives Canada.*

Buried in the now ghost town of Bennett in the subarctic are the roots of the family fortune that paved Donald Trump's path to prominence. Only shards of glass bottles remain on the lake shore in Bennett, British Columbia— remnants perhaps of the lively establishment operated by Trump's grandfather that was known for good food, booze and ready women. A church sits further up the slope, its lonely spire peeking out from a thicket of pines.

Bennett was once a thriving transit point for prospectors in the Klondike gold rush at the turn of the 20th century, and Friedrich Trump made a killing running a restaurant and bar. The nest egg he generated in just two years grew into the fortune that has supported his grandson's bid for the U.S. presidency.

The Trump family's gold-rush story began when on October 7, 1885, when Friedrich Trump, a 16-year-old German barber, bought a one-way ticket for America, escaping three years of compulsory German military service. He had been a sickly child, unsuited to hard labor, and feared the effects of the draft. It might have been illegal, but America didn't care about this law-breaking—at that time, Germans were seen as highly desirable migrants—and Trump was welcomed with open arms. Less than two weeks later, he arrived in New York, where he would eventually make a small fortune. Friedrich Trump came to the United States amid a flood of Germans—that year alone, an estimated 1 million made the journey to settle in America. It was, the Times reported, "the start of an adventurous life as a barber, restaurateur, saloonkeeper, hotelier, entrepreneur, gold rush prospector, shipwreck survivor and New York real-estate investor."

He headed to New York to work as a barber before venturing west in search of riches. Following stints in Seattle and now-defunct Monte Cristo, Friedrich Trump departed Seattle for the Yukon in the late winter of 1898, when he was just 29. The gold fever carried him to Bennett, where he and partner Ernest Levin built the Arctic Restaurant, which touted itself as the best-equipped in town. It was open around the clock with "private boxes for ladies and parties," according to an advertisement in the Dec. 9, 1899 edition of the Bennett Sun newspaper. The boxes typically included a bed and scale for weighing gold dust used to pay for "services," according to a three-generational biography by Gwenda Blair, who traced the origins of the Trump family's wealth. Of course, in the rough-and-tumble frontier towns of that era, the Arctic's business model built on food, booze and sex was common.

The Arctic sat a stone's throw from Bennett Lake in the heart of the township, amid a row of similar establishments and a sea of white canvas tents set up by prospectors. It was constructed of milled lumber and stocked fresh oysters, extravagant luxuries in a place where supplies were brought over arduous overland routes.

Trump quickly saw where the real profits lay amid the gold-rush frenzy. An estimated 100,000 prospectors set out for the Klondike, of which only a third actually made it, and a mere 4 percent ever struck gold. Given those odds, Trump's willingness to lay down his pick was "a shrewd move," according to Blair. "He was mining the miners."

Bennett was a key hub for prospectors, who trudged from Alaska across frozen mountains and floated rickety rafts down the treacherous rapids of the Yukon River to Dawson City in search of elusive gold. The town lost its allure with the construction of a railway link from Skagway, Alaska to Whitehorse, allowing miners to bypass Bennett. In response, Trump dismantled the restaurant and its precious lumber and rebuilt it in Whitehorse. A photo in Blair's book shows a mustachioed Fred Trump in a white apron. He's standing at the bar near a wall of drapes behind which women, known as "sporting ladies," entertained miners in privacy.

Trump was a rich man when he left Whitehorse in 1901 to return to his native Kallstadt, where his parents had owned vineyards and married. He later deposited savings of 80,000 marks in the village treasury. But when his draft dodging came to the fore, the couple lost their Bavarian citizenship and were obliged to return to America for good. He returned to New York with his riches that amounted to the equivalent in purchasing power of about half a million euros in 2014. These funds ended up funding the Trump family's first residential real estate investments in the New York area, later carried on by his son Fred and grandson Donald. There, they had three children: Trump's father, Fred, was the middle child. Born in the Bronx borough of New York City in 1905, Fred Trump was an all-American child who spoke no German. Later, he would become one of the city's most successful young businessmen, amassing a fortune even as many around him slumped into financial ruin.

Long before making three consecutive bids for the US presidency, Donald Trump was America's most flamboyant billionaire. The New York real estate mogul's life was splashed all over tabloids and television in the decades leading up to his improbable 2015-16 run for the White House. His household name and unfiltered campaign style helped him defeat seasoned politicians - but a controversy-filled tenure saw him booted from office after a single term. Now 78, the Republican again defied the odds as he made a stunning political comeback placing him back behind the president's desk in the Oval Office.

Trump is the fourth child of New York real estate tycoon Fred Trump. Despite the family's wealth, he was expected to work the lowest-tier jobs within his father's company and was sent off to a military academy at age 13 when he started misbehaving in school. After earning a degree from the University of Pennsylvania's Wharton School, he became favored to succeed his father when his older brother, Fred, chose to become a pilot. Fred Trump died at 43 from alcoholism, something that his brother says led him to avoid alcohol and cigarettes his entire life. He shifted the company's focus from Brooklyn and Queens to glitzy Manhattan. Trump says he got into real estate with a "small" $1m loan from his father before joining the company. He helped manage his father's extensive portfolio of residential housing projects in the New York City boroughs, and took control of the company - which he renamed the Trump Organization - in 1971. His father, who Trump describes as "my inspiration", died in 1999.

Under Trump, the family business shifted from residential units in Brooklyn and Queens to glitzy Manhattan projects. The famed Fifth Avenue became home to Trump Tower, arguably the mogul's most famous property and his home for many years. The rundown Commodore Hotel was restored as the Grand Hyatt. Other properties bearing the Trump brand name - casinos, condominiums, golf courses and hotels - were erected too, from Atlantic City, Chicago and Las Vegas to India, Turkey and the Philippines.

His rise to stardom continued in the entertainment world - first as an owner of the Miss Universe, Miss USA, and Miss Teen USA beauty pageants, then as creator-host of NBC reality show The Apprentice. He hosted 14 seasons of The Apprentice, a reality show that also featured his kids. Apprentice contestants competed for a management contract in his business empire, his trademark "You're fired!" line made "the Donald" a household name.

Trump has written several books, appeared in movies and pro-wrestling programming, and sold everything from beverages to neckties. But his net worth has dropped in recent years, with Forbes estimating he is currently worth around $4bn. Trump has also filed business bankruptcies on six separate occasions, and several of his ventures - including Trump Steaks and Trump University - have collapsed.

He has also shielded his tax information from scrutiny, and reporting in 2020 from The New York Times revealed years of income tax avoidance and chronic financial losses.

His first, and arguably most famous, wife was Ivana Zelnickova, a Czech athlete and model. The couple had three children - Donald Jr, Ivanka and Eric - before their divorce in 1990. Their acrimonious court battle made the front pages of gossip columns, and the late Mrs. Trump's allegations of domestic abuse - which she later downplayed - feature in a new movie about Trump. He married actress Marla Maples in 1993, two months after the birth of their only child Tiffany. They divorced in 1999. His current wife, Melania Trump, is a former Slovenian model Melania Knauss. They married in 2005 and share a son, Barron William Trump.

Allegations of sexual misconduct and extramarital affairs have followed Trump the politician. Two separate juries ruled that Trump defamed writer E Jean Carroll by denying her accusation of sexual assault. He was ordered to pay her $88m in total, but has appealed. Trump was also convicted on 34 felony counts for falsifying business records to cover up a hush money arrangement with adult-film actress Stormy Daniels over an alleged extramarital encounter in 2006.

In a 1980 interview, a 34-year-old Trump describes politics as "a very mean life" and says "the most capable people" instead choose the business world. By 1987 though, he began teasing a presidential bid. He briefly explored entering the 2000 race with the Reform Party, then again in 2012 as a Republican.

Trump was among the most vocal proponents of "birtherism," the conspiracy theory questioning whether Barack Obama had been born in the US. He did not admit it was a lie until 2016 and never apologized.

It was not until June 2015 that Trump formally announced a bid for the White House, declaring the American Dream dead but promising to "bring it back bigger and better." The freewheeling address saw him flaunt his wealth and business success; accuse Mexico of sending drugs, crime and rapists to the US; and, promise to make the country pay for a border wall. Dominating displays on the debate stage and a controversy-riddled policy platform attracted adoring fans and fierce critics in equal measure, as well as a torrent of media attention.

Under the 'Make America Great' in 2015-16 campaign slogan, he easily muscled past rivals in the Republican Party to face off against Democrat Hillary Clinton. The novice campaign was marred by controversy, including a leaked audio tape of him bragging about sexual abuse, and he trailed in opinion polls throughout the general election. But Trump had the last laugh against pundits and pollsters with his stunning victory over a veteran politician. He was sworn in as the country's 45th president on 20 January 2017.

From the very first hours, he brought unrivalled drama to the job, often making formal announcements on Twitter (now X) and clashing openly with foreign leaders. The Trump presidency was an uncertain time for US allies as he withdrew from major climate and trade agreements, banned travel from seven Muslim-majority countries, issued other tough immigration restrictions, launched a trade war with China, implemented record tax cuts, and reshaped Middle Eastern relations.

For nearly two years, a special counsel probed alleged collusion between the 2016 Trump campaign and Russia. Thirty-four people faced criminal charges - on matters such as computer hacking and financial crimes - but not Trump. The investigation did not establish criminal collusion.

Soon after, Trump became just the third US president in history to be impeached, over accusations he pressured a foreign government to dig up dirt on Democratic rival Joe Biden. He was impeached by a Democrat-led House of Representatives but acquitted in a Republican-led Senate.

His 2020 election year was dominated by the coronavirus pandemic. He faced intense criticism for his handling of the crisis as the US led the globe in deaths and infections and for controversial comments, like suggesting research into whether the virus might be treated by injecting disinfectant into the body. He was forced to take a break from the campaign trail in October after he was diagnosed with Covid-19 himself. Though he eventually received 74 million votes - more than any other sitting US president - he lost the race to Mr. Biden by more than seven million votes. From November 2020 to January 2021, he amplified claims of stolen votes and widespread electoral fraud - claims that were knocked down in more than 60 court cases. Refusing to accept the results, Trump rallied supporters in Washington on 6 January, urging them to converge on the Capitol as Mr. Biden's victory was to be formally certified by Congress. That rally devolved into a riot that placed lawmakers and his own vice-president in danger and led to a historic second impeachment. Trump was again acquitted by the Senate, albeit more narrowly. His actions on the day led to the focus of two criminal cases.

Trump's political career appeared as good as dead after the storming of the Capitol. Donors and supporters vowed never to support him again, and even his closest allies publicly disavowed him.

He skipped his successor's inauguration and moved his family to Florida but, with a loyal army of fans still behind him, retained massive influence over the Republican Party. Perhaps the most enduring legacy of his presidency came after it ended - when the three right-wing justices he had nominated to the Supreme Court cemented a conservative majority that helped end nearly 50 years of national abortion rights.

Despite being blamed for poor Republican returns in the 2022 midterm elections, Trump announced another run for president and soon became his party's clear frontrunner. More than a dozen opponents, including his former vice-president, challenged him but fell short as Trump avoided the debate stage and trained his fire on Mr. Biden. Trump began the general election facing 91 felony charges across four criminal cases but his strategy of delaying legal cases has largely succeeded. Three cases will now no longer take place before the election, and his sentencing in New York - on arguably the weakest set of charges - was been delayed until late November.

On 13 July, a 20-year-old gunman attempted to assassinate Trump during a campaign rally in Butler, Pennsylvania. Thomas Matthew Crooks fired eight rounds from an AR-style rifle from atop a nearby roof, wounding Trump in his right ear before the gunman was killed by counter-snipers. Days later, at the Republican National Convention, the party lavished him with praise on him and officially coronated him the Republican presidential candidate for a third consecutive time, setting up an apparent rematch with Mr. Biden.

Mr. Biden was historically an unpopular president, the Democrat's tenure had been marked by post-pandemic economic and infrastructure gains, but also high inflation, surges in illegal immigration and foreign policy chaos. Mr. Biden stepped aside and endorsed his deputy, Kamala Harris. Trump sought to tie her to the administration's failures - with middling success. National polls indicate that, while Miss Harris galvanized liberal voters and raised millions of dollars, the race was deadlocked. Donald Trump told his supporters that 5 November 2024 - the date of the US election - would be "the most important date in the history of our country." His winning the election, was probably the most important day in his life and may also be one of the most, if not the most, important date in the history of the United States of America.

When President Donald Trump returned to the White House, many expected him to target China or address border security with Mexico. Instead, Trump surprised the world by reiterating his plan to expand U.S. territory by acquiring Greenland from Denmark and incorporating Canada as the 51st state. This agenda has naturally drawn criticism from allies, many of whom view it is unfeasible. While Trump's aggressive approach and bombastic rhetoric may be quickly dismissed, it is worth understanding why the United States is expressing such bold geopolitical ambitions. The reasons are a compilation of economics, national security, and global power.

Canada As The 51st State? Canada's vast 9.98 million square kilometers makes it the second-largest country globally and a natural extension of U.S. territory from a geographical perspective. The two nations already share the longest undefended border in the world, but Trump has described this boundary as an artificially drawn line that hinders economic integration and security cooperation.

Economically, Canada is America's second-largest trading partner and number one export market. Trade is governed by the Canada-United States-Mexico Agreement, signed by the first Trump administration. Toronto-Dominion Bank estimates the U.S. is on track to record a trade deficit with Canada of roughly $45 billion (U.S.) in 2024, which is just 5% of the U.S. overall trade deficit. Energy is a significant part of trade between the two countries. Trump argues that annexation would eliminate trade barriers, streamline resource extraction, and strengthen North American energy independence relative to the rest of the world. However, national and economic security interests are a bigger motivation. Control over the border is one issue. For example, Trump has expressed concerns about the flow of fentanyl and illegal immigrants across the U.S.-Canada border. Integrating the two nations would enhance border security. Resource control is another issue. The Trump administration sees access to Canada's large store of natural resources, including oil, minerals, and freshwater, as vital for U.S. economic security. The main prize would be the Arctic. Nearly 40% of Canada's land mass is considered Arctic. By integrating Canada, the U.S. could strengthen its dominance in global trade and Arctic geopolitics. This move would counterbalance the growing Russian and Chinese presence in the Arctic while securing control over critical shipping routes. As one might suspect, Canada is not too receptive to President Trump's overtures. Canadian officials have been quick to reject the idea of annexation. Public sentiment also aligns with this stance; an Angus Reid poll conducted in early January found only 10% of Canadians support a political integration with the United States. Trump is most likely aware that making Canada the 51st state is a long shot. However, his aggressive tactics, which threaten the relationship between the two countries in the short run, could result in a negotiated deal that would allow more integration rather than less.

Greenland, an autonomous region of Denmark, is the world's largest island, spanning 2.16 million square kilometers. It is sparsely populated with just 56,916 residents. Similar to Canada, Greenland's proximity to important Arctic shipping lanes makes it a geopolitical asset. The island also hosts Pituffik Space Base, a key U.S. military installation used for missile defense and surveillance operations.

Economically, Greenland is rich in untapped rare earth elements such as dysprosium, neodymium, europium, and yttrium — critical materials for AI hardware, quantum computing technologies, renewable energy systems, and advanced defense equipment. The Tanbreez project alone contains an estimated 28 million tonnes of rare earth oxides, nearly 30% being heavy rare earth elements. These resources could significantly reduce U.S. reliance on China, which currently controls over 80% of global rare earth element production. The U.S. appears quite serious about gaining control of Greenland, or at minimum, achieving a much closer economic and political alliance. This is not just about Greenland: It is about the Arctic. You have Russia that is trying to become king, this is about critical minerals, this is about natural resources, it's oil and gas, it's our national security. Like Canada, Denmark has fiercely opposed Trump's ambitions to acquire Greenland. But they acknowledged Greenland's need to work closely with the United States on defense and natural resources. This is not the first time the U.S. has expressed an interest in Greenland. In 1946, officials offered Denmark $100 million in gold bars for Greenland. At the time, U.S. officials thought it was a "military necessity." The Arctic has become a focal point of global competition due to its abundance of natural resources, emerging shipping routes, and strategic military significance. The region contains an estimated 13% of undiscovered global oil reserves and 30% of natural gas reserves. Shifting ice patterns are opening new maritime shipping routes, including Canada's Northwest Passage and Russia's Northern Sea Route. These pathways could significantly shorten shipping time by 30% to 50% between Asia, Europe, and North America. Control over these routes would provide an economic and political advantage to the U.S. The Arctic has significant military importance, intersecting North America, Europe and Eurasia. The U.S. military has a presence in Greenland, but so does its adversaries. Russia, which controls 53% of the Arctic coastline, has heavily militarized its territories with airbases and naval forces, while China has declared itself a "near-Arctic state" to justify its growing investments in Greenland's mining sector. It also holds substantial stakes in major Russian Arctic LNG projects. By acquiring Canada and Greenland, the United States would secure dominance over these resources and routes while countering Russian and Chinese ambitions. *Forbes 01/26/2025*

Newly inaugurated U.S. President Donald Trump is pushing to "take back" the Panama Canal, the world's second busiest interoceanic waterway, spurring concerns that the United States could invade the Central American nation. Trump argues that Panama has broken a pledge of neutrality made when the United States transferred the canal to Panama in 1999, claiming that China is operating it. The Panama Canal, an 82-km (51-mile) artificial waterway that connects the Pacific and Atlantic Oceans, saves ships thousands of miles and weeks of travel. Before it was built, ships had to make the long journey around the stormy tip of South America in order to travel by sea between the two oceans. Over two-thirds of all cargo passing through the canal today originates from or is destined for the United States. The U.S. completed construction of the canal in the early 20th century, a project begun by France that cost over 25,000 workers' lives. Following pressure from anti-colonial movements, the U.S. signed treaties in 1977 granting Panama control and full sovereignty over the canal zone and guaranteeing its permanent neutrality. These took effect in 1999. Trump has repeated accusations that Panama has ceded control of the canal to China. He has also said Chinese troops are stationed at the canal. Both Panama's government and the Chinese government have rejected those assertions. However, Hong Kong, U.S., Taiwan, and Singapore operate at either end or both ends of the Pacific and Atlantic entrances. China's economic influence has been growing in Latin America, fueling worries in Washington that the resource-rich region will tilt to Chinese interests rather than those of the United States. Allegations are that American ships are being severely overcharged and not treated fairly in any way and that includes the United States Navy. Between the fiscal years ended in 2020 and 2023, the canal's toll revenue increased almost 26% to $3.35 billion, according to its annual reports. In the fiscal year ended last September, the canal offset less vessel traffic with a water surcharge, which it combined with slot auctions that rose to as much as $4 million per vessel. U.S. military ships enjoy priority of passage. Mulino, who took office last year, has taken a harder line on migration than his predecessor, agreeing to U.S.-funded deportation flights from Panama and installing barbed wire at the Darien Gap, a dangerous jungle route many migrants take crossing on foot out of South America on their way to the U.S. border. *Reuters 02/28/2025*

Others have dreamed the dreams of Trump: In the early 1990s, Walter Russell Mead advocated for a "grand bargain" with the Russian Federation, suggesting that the "United States buy about 3.5 million square miles of Eastern Siberia and the Russian Far East and pay Russia $3 trillion - half of which would be used to purchase goods produced in the United States." At the time, Russian President Boris Yeltsin had offered to sell oil fields, production plants and land to the United States to help pay down some of Russia's then-$70 billion in foreign debt. Times had changed. Russia's gross domestic product was roughly half the size it was in 1991 and nearly half of its people, more than 60 million of them, lived below the poverty line. Russia was a country on the verge of economic implosion. Mead's proposal would fix all that with the stroke of a pen. A $2 trillion purchase of Siberia would pay off Russia's debt, stabilize its currency, upgrade its infrastructure (which would be done by American businesses, thus helping alleviate the U.S. account deficits) and leave more than enough left over to pay all the back wages of every last pensioner. There would even be enough left over for an Alaska-style rebate to every Russian citizen, assuming the kleptocracy didn't skim off more than the usual 33 percent. In return, the United States would acquire a land mass larger than its own with a population of roughly 30 million people. Mead said: "The combination of new territories in Asia and a vast, suddenly solvent market in European Russia would amount, literally, to a new frontier with new opportunities and challenges for generations to come? The deal would double the US's size and put them on the Pacific Rim at the intersection of China, Korea and Japan. Part of the deal would be for cash and part for credits: with, say, half the money, the Russians could place orders in the United States. Fiber optics, consultants, computers, machine tools, whatever they wanted from whomever made the best deal as long as the stuff was American-made. Over, say, a 20-year payment period, we would see something like $75 billion in exports each year to Russia. That would have meant 1 million jobs in the 2015's for 50 states? Even with all the incidental expenses, environmental cleanup, and infrastructure, the deal could help balance the budget." And there's even more than that. Siberia is a land rich in natural resources. By purchasing it from the Russians, America would acquire all the mining rights therein, the great timberlands of the southeast and the warm-water port of Vladivostok. Overnight, the U.S. would become the largest oil producer in the world. Overnight, the U.S. would become the second most important regional player in the Pacific Rim. *For Sale: Siberia, 02/16/2015.*

George Herbert Walker Bush (06/12/1924 – 11/30/2018) was the 41st president of the United States, serving from 1989 to 1993. But by 1992, many conservative Republicans' support of Bush had waned for a variety of reasons, including raising taxes and cutting defense spending. Americans were less concerned with his foreign policy successes than the nation's changing economic situation. Image what could have happened if James A. Baker III, had called his office and said: "Mr. President if you can pull this off by November - You'll get a Peace Prize, another term as president and you won't have to run a campaign. And in 1996, nobody will be interested in Danforth "Mars" Quayle; you'll be the man who balanced the budget, created millions of jobs, canceled the trade deficit and put new stars in our flag. Mr. President Bush, just don't move too slow. Remember, Mount Rushmore is waiting." He didn't take the bait. Neither did the 42nd President William J. Clinton. In 1803, President Thomas Jefferson did just such a deal. Napoleon was caught in a political and financial bind. Jefferson made him an offer. The result was the Louisiana Purchase. The Siberian Purchase made every bit as much sense.

Bennett was once a thriving transit point for prospectors in the Klondike gold rush at the turn of the 20th century, and Friedrich Trump made a killing running a restaurant and bar. The nest egg he generated in just two years grew into the fortune that has supported his grandson's bid for the U.S. presidency. "Who else can say that someone running for president of the United States of America owes his fortune to your home town?" says Scott Etches, 55, a shop owner hawking Trump t-shirts in Whitehorse, Yukon, about 62 miles north of Bennett. "It doesn't matter whether you support or oppose Trump. It's actually a great history."

More than a century after Trump's grandfather left the Yukon, Canadian developers and entrepreneurs are torn over whether to exploit the connection to one of the most recognized surnames on the planet. A luxury wilderness resort is planned for Bennett, complete with a lodge that would look just like Trump's watering hole and maybe a plaque will be placed for Donald John Trump (born June 14, 1946) 45th & 47th President of the United States of America and James Gordon Bennett, Jr. who the lake and town is named after.

No, James Gordon Bennett, Jr. is not related to Richard Bedford Bennett. He was a Scottish-born American journalist and publisher. Richard Bedford Bennett, the Canadian lawyer, businessman and politician, that after a heart attack moved to England. There he received fame when he was appointed by Winston Churchill to the House of Lords for his assistance in arranging the building of planes and airfields during WWII.

It looks like great happenings in Canada's Yukon territory involved a gold rush inspired by impoverished Americans with dreams of riches. At this time, California was mostly witnessing an economy that was limited by a lack of land for farming, missions that were decaying and most economic activity was organized around the ranchos or small farms. The town of Bennett and Lake Bennett was named after an American journalist and publisher, and made possible for a fortune to be made by a man whose grandson was to become the 45th and 47th president of the United States. It just so happened that this man accumulated his riches (not from gold) from the Artic Restaurant & Hotel in Bennett. This venture eventually enabled Donald John Trump to live the dream of trying to "Make America Great."

Maybe Trump's idea of joining Canada and the U.S. as one big happy family just might work out. After all, America helps Canada as they do us: If they became the 51st state both could help "Make North America Greater". "Remember, Mount Rushmore is waiting."

Excerpts from: *The Trumps: Three Generations That Built an Empire, Gwenda Blair, 09/13/2000 and Donald Trump's life story: From real estate to politics, BBC, 09/10/2024, and Trump's Family Fortune Originated in a Canadian Gold-Rush Brothel, Bloomberg, 26/10/2016.*

CHAPTER 14

FAMILIAL NATURAL SHORT SLEEPERS

Trump had comedian Andrew Shulz's "Flagrant" podcast in stitches as he roasted President Biden: "somebody must have convinced him he looks great in a bathing suit. He has an ability to fall asleep while on camera. He has one ability that I don't have — he can sleep! This guy goes on a beach, and he lays down on one of those 6-ounce chairs. They weigh 6 ounces, and he can't lift it. They're meant for children, young people, and old people to lift. They're aluminum, you know, hollow aluminum, they weigh very little, and he can't lift. He can lie down on one of those things, and in minutes, he's stone-cold out, and he's got cameras because he's the president, so they have cameras on him, and then they show him sleeping on the beach. Somebody convinced him he looks good in a bathing suit, and when you're 82, typically bathing suits aren't gonna make you look great. You're not going to be enhanced, alright?" He then looked at the host and declared, "You'll never see me sleeping in front of a camera."

President Donald J. Trump's first 30 days in office have been described as historic. As of May 2, 2025, he has signed 145 executive orders, 37 memoranda, and 45 proclamations in his second presidential term on everything from securing American borders and creating the Department of Government Efficiency (DOGE) to renaming the Gulf of Mexico and eliminating the forced use of paper straws. Since his first presidency, Trump has said he usually gets between four and five hours of sleep per night. In two days, he puts in about as many hours as most Americans do in their entire work week. He's not the only person, or even the only president, who seems to be able to function as a "short sleeper." In January 2018, White House physician Dr. Ronny Jackson said Trump is one of those people who doesn't need a lot of sleep. "I would say he sleeps four to five hours a night. He's probably been like that his whole life. He's just one of those people who just does not require a lot of sleep." In an interview with Fox News' "The O'Reilly Factor" in 2017, Trump said he typically goes to bed at midnight or 1 a.m. and wakes up at 5 a.m. to eat, read newspapers and watch television. "Don't sleep any more than you have to. I usually sleep about four hours per night," he wrote in his 2004 book "Think Like a Billionaire." It is suspected by those in the know that Trump has familial natural short sleep syndrome. *Can you function after 4 hours of sleep...like Trump? Cheryl McCloud, Treasure Coast Newspapers, 02/24/2025.*

Familial natural short sleepers (FNSS) is a rare, genetic, typically inherited trait where an individual sleeps for fewer hours than average without suffering from daytime sleepiness or other consequences of sleep deprivation. This process is entirely natural in this kind of individual and it is caused by certain genetic mutations. A person with this trait is known as a "natural short sleeper". This condition is not to be confused with intentional sleep deprivation, which leaves symptoms such as irritability or temporarily impaired cognitive abilities in people who are predisposed to sleep a normal amount of time but not in people with FNSS. There are no known harmful effects to overall health associated with it and it is considered to be a genetic, benign condition. Individuals with this trait are known for having the life-long ability of being able to sleep for a lesser amount of time than average people, usually 4 to 6 hours (less than the average sleep time of 8 hours) each night while waking up feeling relatively well-rested, they also have a notable absence of any sort of consequence that derives from depriving oneself of sleep. Other common traits among people with familial natural short sleep are an increased ability at recalling memories, they have an outgoing personality, high productiveness, lower body mass index than average (possibly due to faster metabolism), higher resilience and heightened pain tolerance. All of these traits are of slightly better quality in people with natural short sleep than in people with natural normal sleep, essentially making them slightly more efficient than average people.

This condition is life-long, meaning that a natural short sleeper has naturally slept for a shorter time than average for most, if not all, of their lives. This trait is inherited as an autosomal dominant trait, which means that for a person to be a natural short sleeper, they must have at least one copy of a mutation related to this condition. This mutation must have been either inherited or to have arisen from a spontaneous genetic error. A carrier for a mutation associated with FNSS has a 50% chance of transmitting the mutation to one of their offspring. Researchers noted that in the human population this is a rare mutation, with an incidence of 4.028/100,000. There is no specific test, but a good rule of thumb is that, if on the weekend someone's sleep duration does not get longer, despite having the opportunity to sleep in, then they may be a true short sleeper.

A study done in 2001 showed that natural short sleepers are more prone to subclinical hypomania, a temporary mental state most common during adolescence characterized by racing thoughts, abnormally high focus on goal-directed activities, unusually euphoric mood, and a perceptual unnecessity for sleep. Diagnosis is usually not necessary, as this trait is not considered a disorder in and of itself. However, there are various methods that one can use to diagnose the condition including but not limited to the use of questionnaires such as the morningness-eveningness questionnaire, the Munich chronotype questionnaire, etc. Clinical diagnostic methods for the condition include electroencephalograms, delta-power analyses, and genetic testing. There are other conditions similar to this specific trait that share some characteristics between each other, these include: 1-Advanced sleep phase syndrome (ASPS), this is a rare condition affecting the circadian rhythm in which individuals have an early sleep onset and equally early sleep awakening that is part of their regular sleep schedule. While both sleep traits are similar in the sense of early awakening, patients with ASPS typically spend the same amount of time (8 hours) sleeping as an average person, while patients with FNSS do not. Another difference between the two is that early sleep onset is not a feature shown by people with familial natural short sleep. Like FNSS, it has the tendency to be hereditary. 2-Delayed sleep phase syndrome, this is a more common circadian rhythm condition (estimated to affect around 16% of adolescents in the U.S.) characterized by late sleep onset and equally late sleep awakening. While both sleep traits are similar in the sense of late sleep-onset, individuals with FNSS do not suffer from late sleep awakening. Unlike FNSS, this condition is not highly heritable, but it does seem to have at least some genetic component linked to it.

Conditions that may be confused with FNSS include insomnia, which is a common sleep disorder that can be acute or chronic and is characterized by an individual's difficulty to fall asleep. This usually leads to them staying up late involuntarily which shortens their sleep time. While insomnia and FNSS share some common features (late sleep onset, for example), those with insomnia do suffer from the consequences associated with sleep deprivation, something people with FNSS do not experience.

In the U.S., natural short sleepers are a small part of a larger group comprising 30–35% of the population who sleep less than recommended. Individuals with FNSS might be genetically protected against neurodegenerative disorders. Mainly those that cause dementia, such as Alzheimer's disease. Ying-Hui Fu did a study using animal mouse models who were genetically engineered to carry mutations associated with natural short sleep and mutations associated with an increased risk of suffering from dementia. The results showed that mice with both FNSS and dementia mutations did not show as many symptoms of dementia as their dementia-alone predisposed mice counterparts. The same mice who had both Alzheimer's and short sleep gene mutations also had lesser amounts of Aβ plaque depositions in their hippocampus and brain cortexes than those who only carried the Alzheimer's mutations.

According to the Mayo Clinic: "For adults, getting less than seven hours of sleep a night on a regular basis has been linked with poor health, including weight gain, having a body mass index of 30 or higher, diabetes, high blood pressure, heart disease, stroke, and depression." According to the Journal of Clinical Sleep Medicine, sleeping less than 7 hours per night is also associated with impaired immune function, increased pain, impaired performance, increased errors, and greater risk of accidents. *Wikipedia, AI + others.*

Lewis Carroll, author of Alice's Adventures in Wonderland, was a chronic insomniac who often felt the urge to write at night. Living as he did before electric lights were common, he invented what he called a nyctograph, or night-writer, along with a notation system of nyctography for writing without the aid of a light. In a letter to The Lady magazine of October 1891, Carroll reported: "Anyone who has tried, as I have often done, the process of getting out of bed at two a.m. in a winter night, lighting a candle, and recording some happy thought which would probably be otherwise forgotten, will agree with me it entails much discomfort. All I have now to do, if I wake and think of something I wish to record, is to draw from under the pillow a small memorandum book containing my Nyctograph, write a few lines, or even a few pages, without even putting the hands outside the bed-clothes, replace the book, and go to sleep again."

Another writer who commonly wrote at night was the blind poet, John Milton. An early biography of Milton contains many details so striking as to have the aura of utter verisimilitude. One such passage records how he went about composing the ten thousand lines of Paradise Lost. He often worked on his epic in the dead of night or in the early hours of the morning, composing the verses in his head and then memorizing them until a scribe (a friend or family member) came to record them. He normally awakened early, and if the assistant arrived later than usual Milton would "complain that he wanted to be milked." Once the words were on paper, they were read aloud so that the author could edit them. Milton placed a description of this process in Book IX of Paradise Lost, writing that his "heavenly patroness, unbidden, condescends to visit me nightly, and dictates as I sleep or inspires with ease my unpremeditated verse—as she indeed has done since first I chose this epic subject" (prose paraphrase of lines 21-6).

Mikee Mason writes: "myself experience this phenomenon quite commonly. Though not blind, I may as well be at night, and often I wake up with an idea for the book I'm currently working on. In my younger days I used to get up to make notes with a lighted pen, but now I usually just concoct a mnemonic and go back to sleep. To remember an abstract thought, the best sort of mnemonic is a picture. For example, if I happen to have an idea about the Ten Commandments, I may associate it with a mental image of Moses, or of my ten fingers. Before I learned this trick, a thought that came to me in the night was usually lost by morning. But a picture, oddly enough, always sticks, and from the picture I'm able to retrieve the thought. And if, as often happens, the thought comes to me expressed in certain turns of phrase that I wish to preserve, it helps to devise a series of linked images, like a cartoon strip. While this sounds complicated, it really isn't; it can be done spontaneously in a few moments of semi-wakefulness.

A more elaborate version of this experience tends to happen not in the middle of the night but towards morning when my sleep is lighter. Before fully waking up, I'll become half-aware that my mind, all on its own, is at work on a piece of writing, actually composing lines, even editing as I go, rejecting some phrases and substituting others. After all, we dream in moving pictures, often without words: why not in words alone? Upon fully awakening, the first thing I want to do is to write down this new composition. Maybe it's a difficult passage that wouldn't come out right the day before, or maybe it's something brand new. In either case, as I record the lines that were composed in my semi-sleep, often other thoughts flow from these, and first thing in the morning I may find myself writing for an hour. I don't much like doing this; I prefer to get on with my morning routine, and to keep work in its place. But if I'm bursting with some brainwave, I just have to get this fresh matutinal composition onto paper. Like Milton, I have to be milked. People ask me how long I work each day—an impossible question, since any writer worth his salt is basically always working: if not actually writing, then researching, reading, dreaming, thinking, planning—so that even social times or recreation may turn into writing times. Many of my best ideas come in the midst of prayer (and why not?), so I have to put prayer on pause—or, I suppose, continue it in a different way—and get those ideas down. As the monks say, Labore est orare: To work is to pray." *Writing at Night: Lewis Carroll, John Milton, and Me, Mike Mason, posted on 04/01/2022.*

In 2025, Lori Hatcher posted her thoughts on the Gift of Sleeplessness: As I study the Bible, especially the Psalms, I discover that God doesn't clock out at 10 pm. He's just as present in the night as in the day. Psalm 139:11-12 declares, "If I say, 'Surely the darkness shall cover me, and the light about me be night,' even the darkness is not dark to you." Lights on or lights off, God is there. Knowing this helps me feel less lonely when the rest of the world slumbers and I lay awake. Before I studied sleep Scriptures, I considered every sleepless hour a wasted one, but I was wrong. These hours can become some of our most productive ones—if we spend them well.

Psalm 119:148 gives us a peek into one of the psalmist's sleepless nights, "My eyes are awake before the watches of the night, that I may meditate on your promise" (ESV). In the quiet moments between dusk and dawn, he spent his time thinking about God's promises. Perhaps he repeated Deuteronomy 31:8, "The LORD himself goes before you and will be with you; he will never leave you nor forsake you. Do not be afraid; do not be discouraged." Or Psalm 32:8: "I will instruct you and teach you in the way you should go; I will counsel you with my loving eye on you." Some of my favorite promises to think on are James 1:5, "If any of you lacks wisdom, let him ask God, who gives generously to all without reproach, and it will be given him" (ESV), and Philippians 1:6: "He who began a good work in you will bring it to completion at the day of Jesus Christ" (ESV).

The silence of a quiet night invites biblical introspection. David asked the Lord in Psalm 139:23-24, "Search me, O

God, and know my heart! Try me and know my thoughts! And see if there be any grievous way in me, and lead me in the way everlasting (ESV)!" We can (and should) do the same. When God brings to mind a secret (or not so secret) sin, we can confess it, forsake it, and receive God's forgiveness (1 John 1:9). Doing this often brings about the relief and sweet sleep we desire. God disturbed King David's sleep (Psalm 32:4) to lead him to confess his sin and receive forgiveness (Psalm 32:5). Meditating on God's promises in the quiet of the night helps banish our fears and reminds us of truth.

Time alone with our thoughts can also invite the enemy's attack. How do we distinguish between God's voice and Satan's? God reveals our sin (conviction) so He can cleanse and restore us. Satan accuses us to condemn and destroy us. Ask yourself, "Am I feeling condemnation or conviction," then respond appropriately.

David, in Psalm 63:5-7 gives us a blueprint for how to praise and pray to God, "My mouth will praise you with joyful lips, when I remember you upon my bed, and meditate on you in the watches of the night; for you have been my help, and in the shadow of your wings I will sing for joy." Sleepless hours can be powerful hours when we turn our thoughts toward God in prayer and praise. When we recount God's attributes, we gain a proper perspective of our problems in light of who God is. Reminding ourselves that God is mighty, loving, patient, kind, sovereign, generous, just, and all-knowing makes our spirits soar instead of sink. Tears of gratitude replace tears of frustration and laughter banishes languishing.

These night hours can also become holy battle grounds when we wrestle, as Jacob did, for God to bless us and those we love (Genesis 32:22-26). I'm often amazed at who God brings to mind when I ask Him to show me who needs my prayers. I'll think of college friends, church members from years ago, and random people I haven't seen in decades. I receive each name from the Lord and pray as He leads me. Most of us wish we had more time to pray. Perhaps sleepless hours are God's answer to our busy, prayer-deprived lives. I don't often have the luxury of an uninterrupted hour or two (or three) to pray for my family, friends, church members, neighbors, missionaries, and governmental leaders, but my sleepless nights grant me this time. When the world is still, and I'm alone with God, I can pray marvelous blessings into these precious people's lives. Almost every night I pray the prayer John Piper prayed over his children, "Lord, even in their sleep, draw them to you."

What if, instead of lamenting my inability to sleep, I embraced it as a gift—something sent by a loving God for good purposes? I'll be the first to admit that sleepless nights aren't my favorite. But I've chosen to accept them as gifts rather than grief. They've allowed me more opportunities to ponder God's promises, cleanse my heart before Him, and pray His power into our hurting world. As I do, the sweet Spirit of God refreshes me in ways I can't describe. Even when my body wilts with weariness, my spirit stands strong. The next time you toss and turn in sleeplessness, I encourage you to turn your heart toward God. Pillow your head on His chest, whisper into His ear, and feel His arms hold you close. Glory in His presence. Rest in His love.

"Come to me, all who labor and are heavy laden, and I will give you rest. Take my yoke upon you, and learn from me, for I am gentle and lowly in heart, and you will find rest for your souls" (Matthew 11:28-29, ESV). *The Gift of Sleeplessness, Lori Hatcher, 2025.*

President Trump says that to get everything done he works until about midnight or one o'clock in the morning. Then he's back up and at it at 5 am. During particularly busy times, those four to five hours can become as little as three. He's been maintaining this schedule for years, not just as president, his reasons being that he's better able to compete and accomplish more than someone who sleeps double or triple that amount of time. Trump appears to be part of that group called familial natural short sleepers (FNSS) or the "sleepless elite." People who belong in this category can get by and even thrive with a fraction of the sleep that normal people get. It's being attributed to a gene that people refer it to as "the Thatcher gene" or "short sleeper gene" based on Margaret Thatcher's sleeping habits of getting just four hours per night of rest. Though the percentage of the total number of people who fall into this category is small (about 1% of the population), they're at a pretty distinct advantage because they can get by with just four to six hours per night.

During his presidency, Obama was a classic night owl. Often, he'd work for several hours after dinner, up until about 2 am. Then he would rest for five hours. Former president Bill Clinton got more sleep than Trump and Obama, but not by much. He averaged about six hours per night, though often got only four. Like Obama, he did a lot of his work in the middle of the night. But, unlike Barack, instead of emailing his staff, Clinton would phone them in the middle of the night. Also, Clinton almost undoubtedly didn't have the short sleeper gene. We know that sleep deprivation can have devastating health effects, and Clinton had heart surgery in his 50s even though he lived an otherwise healthy lifestyle.

Between naps and an early bedtime, Calvin Coolidge got a whopping 11 hours of sleep per night! However, this habit wasn't entirely due to just being tired or needing extra rest. Instead, historians theorize that his extended sleep schedule was because he suffered from depression. His son died at the tragically young age of 16, and Coolidge likely never recovered, especially since he never sought grief counseling.

George W. Bush slept more than most presidents, getting about nine hours of nightly shuteye. He went to bed at nine o'clock and slept until about 6 am. In defenses of his desire for extra sleep, he said he kept a "tight but efficient" schedule. While George W. Bush got the most sleep, ironically it was his father, George H.W. Bush, president from January 20, 1989 to January 20, 1993, who got the least. It's been reported by live-in White House Staff, that Bush regularly slept just two hours a night, from 2 am until 4 am. However, he did take advantage of napping opportunities throughout the day. If he was traveling, he'd get some rest while in transit. Did George H.W. Bush have the FNSS gene? I highly doubt it. The reason why is Bush's diagnosis of Graves' disease in 1991.

Bush's wife, Barabara, in 1989 was diagnosed with the autoimmune disease, Graves' disease (hyperthyroidism). The odds of two people (not related by blood) developing Graves' disease within two years of each other are long

(Doctor Zebra suggested there is a one-in-three-million odds of it occurring, but thought this answered the wrong question). The Bush dog, Millie, also came down with what was thought to be Graves' disease or maybe lupus. Graves' disease results from the immune system mistakenly attacking the thyroid gland and is not a known disease in dogs or cats. While they can develop hyperthyroidism (an overactive thyroid), this is typically caused by a tumor rather than the autoimmune process seen in Graves' disease in humans. Because of the remarkable thought that there was a coincidence of three cases of auto-immune disease in one household, the Secret Service tested the water in the White House, at Camp David, at the Vice President's residence, and at Walker's Point (Bush's home in Maine) for lithium and iodine, two substances "known to cause thyroid problems."

During Remarks Announcing the Resignation of William H. Webster as Director of the Central Intelligence Agency and a News Conference on May 8, 1991, President H.W. Bush was asked a few questions"

Q. They're saying that possibly you and Mrs. Bush and the dog, having gotten these autoimmune problems, that perhaps it's something to do with the water. The President: Maybe the air. I don't know --

Q. You didn't know about it? The President: No.

Q. Did you know it was being checked? The President: Not checked. I just heard something on the television. I could hardly believe it. The odds against two people in the family having - the doctor told me, the thyroid specialist, one of the classic thyroid men, Colonel Burman, known for his expertise, told me the odds are one in three million. But many people live in the same house together, one of whom has thyroid - so I'm not going to lose confidence in the water at the White House until we know a little more about this.

Q. How about two people and the dog? The President: I feel very comfortable in looking into it. Well, two people and the dog, that's about one in 20 million.

Symptoms of Graves' disease, including those related to hyperthyroidism (overactive thyroid), usually develop gradually over weeks or months. While the disease itself often takes a few months to manifest, certain symptoms, like thyroid eye disease (Graves' ophthalmopathy), can appear at the same time as hyperthyroidism, months before, or even months after. In some cases, the initial symptoms might be so subtle that they are easily missed, leading to a delayed diagnosis. Conversely, some individuals experience a sudden and severe onset of symptoms over a period of a few days or weeks. Symptoms related to thyroid eye disease, such as redness, bulging, or double vision, can appear around the time of the diagnosis or even before.

Midnight strikes, yet your body hums with an electric current of wakefulness, a silent battle waged between overactive thyroid hormones and your desperate desire for slumber. This scenario is all too familiar for those grappling with hyperthyroidism, a condition that can turn the simple act of falling asleep into a nightly ordeal. The intricate dance between our thyroid gland and our sleep patterns is a complex one, with far-reaching implications for our overall health and well-being.

Hyperthyroidism (Graves' disease), affects millions of people worldwide. This condition can manifest in various ways, from unexplained weight loss and increased heart rate to anxiety and, notably, sleep disturbances. The importance of sleep in maintaining our physical and mental health cannot be overstated, making the impact of hyperthyroidism on our nightly rest a critical concern for both patients and healthcare providers.

The connection between hyperthyroidism and sleep disturbances is multifaceted and profound. At its core, hyperthyroidism disrupts the delicate balance of our sleep-wake cycle, leading to a cascade of sleep-related issues. The overproduction of thyroid hormones essentially puts our body into a state of constant alertness, making it difficult to wind down and achieve restful sleep. Patients with hyperthyroidism often report a range of sleep problems; including difficulty falling asleep, frequent nighttime awakenings, and early morning awakenings. These disturbances can lead to chronic sleep deprivation, which in turn exacerbates many of the other symptoms associated with hyperthyroidism, creating a vicious cycle of poor health and impaired quality of life.

Radioactive iodine (I-131) has been commonly used for the treatment of both benign and malignant thyroid conditions since the 1940s. The aim of therapy is to treat hyperthyroidism by destroying sufficient thyroid tissue to render the patient either euthyroid or hypothyroid. Iodine is normally taken up by the thyroid gland to produce thyroid hormones, specifically thyroxine (T4) and triiodothyronine

(T3). These hormones regulate metabolism, growth, development, and other vital bodily functions. I-131, (radioactive iodine), works by targeting and destroying thyroid cells through the radiation it emits. This is because the thyroid gland naturally absorbs iodine, and when radioactive iodine is ingested, the thyroid cells concentrate it, exposing themselves to the radiation's destructive effects. *AI + others.*

With the diagnosis of Graves' disease most likely in April of 1991, George H.W. Bush most likely began treatments with I-131 in May or June of that year. It typically takes between one and three months to see the effects of I-131 therapy on thyroid levels, with the full effect usually occurring within three to six months after treatment. During treatment, many patients develop hypothyroidism (underactive thyroid) within the first six months, and blood tests are recommended to monitor thyroid hormone levels. Hypothyroidism in men can manifest with fatigue, weight gain, constipation, and sensitivity to cold. Men may also experience sexual health issues like low libido and erectile dysfunction, as well as potential fertility problems. Muscle weakness, joint pain, and changes in hair and skin are also common.

The first debate between George H.W. Bush, Bill Clinton, and Ross Perot took place on October 11, 1992. The debate was held at the Field House, Washington University in St. Louis, Missouri. It was the first time three candidates had shared a stage in a televised debate. During the debate, Bush looked at his wristwatch and appeared impatient, possibly setting the stage for losing his bid to a second term as president. "Only 10 more minutes of this crap."— President George H. W. Bush on what he was thinking as he checked his wristwatch on camera in the midst of a 1992 presidential debate with Bill Clinton and Ross Perot. It was the telltale sign of a man made uneasy—or, at least, bored—by an audience member's question about how a deep recession had personally affected him. The then president's display of impatience seemed to speak volumes more than his awkward response. "Of course, you feel it when you are president of the United States; that's why I'm trying to do something about it," Bush said after he'd checked the watch and straightened his suit jacket, "by stimulating the export, vesting more, better education system." Yet as he stood face to face with voters in the nation's first town-hall-style presidential debate, Bush showed himself to be out of touch with ordinary Americans. And simple gestures "became freighted with deeper meaning," says Ellen Fitzpatrick, professor of history at the University of New Hampshire. "Voters were overwhelmed by issues for which there were no easy answers and confused by the rhetorical subterfuge of a political process in which no candidate dared risk alienating voters by taking a stand. And into the void steps this focus on symbolism and gesture.... You can look at the person on TV and size them up on the spot."

Such snap judgments can also work the other way, something Bill Clinton showed with seeming ease when he responded to the same questioner. "Tell me how it's affected you again," he said as he walked up to her and looked straight into her eyes. Where Bush appeared impatient, "Clinton steps in and empathizes, empathizes, empathizes," says University of Pennsylvania political scientist Kathleen Hall Jamieson, coauthor of unSpun: Finding Facts in a World of Disinformation. "So it's declared a victory for Clinton."

Bush later suggested that his gesture may, in fact, have revealed something about his discomfort with the debate. "Was I glad when the damn thing was over?" he said to PBS Newshour anchor Jim Lehrer. "Yeah." *Alex Markels 2008*. Most likely, George H.W. Bush's sleeplessness and behavior can be contributed to the symptoms of Garves' disease, the I-131 treatments side effects and the adjustments of thyroid medication influencing his behavior during his first debate with Ross Perot and Bill Clinton - setting the stage for becoming a one term president.

It is not known whether Trump falls into this group of familial natural short sleepers (FNSS). But there are a few characteristics that most of the short sleepers have been identified with that Trump appears to have: They tend to be more optimistic and upbeat than most people; they tend to wake up early, even on vacation or weekends; since short-sleeping is linked to genetics, the behavior that accompanies it often runs in the family; they tend to be physically active; if they sleep longer than they need, they tend to feel groggy; and, they say they tend to avoid caffeine or don't need it to feel energized.

Am I a member of the elite 1% of the familial short sleepers? "The apparitions that haunt my mind as I'm waiting for sleep to win the battle, the aggregate of dreams replaying life's experiences in bazar ways, the wake ups before any hint of the light of day, and the tossing in bed awake until body heat begins to rise and I'm done with sleep. Pushing me to my computer, I'm desirous to explore the thoughts that are menacing my mind. The complexities of nature that appear so simple, why man does what he does to his fellow man and nature, how God seems to interact in special ways, why the 6,000 to 60,000 thoughts on my thoughts a day (95% repetitive and about 80% negative) seem in an endless stream day and night. Will it ever end? I have my doubts. Near death experiencers and brain probs show organized brain activity during the process of dying and appear to have rapid vivid reviews of life experiences during the process of passing from life or ceasing to exist. I suspect my apparitions of life will follow me into death, becoming my eternal torment, lake of fire and sulfur, where I will eternally suffer from times that I pridefully rejected God's ways and made futile attempts to apply His principles of repentance."

CHAPTER 15

THE AUTOPEN

The autopen has become a modern technological wonder for busy athletes, celebrities, and politicians, but is a headache for autograph collectors. Knowing that autopens exist is not enough. An autograph collector must be able to determine which signatures in his or her collection were written by this mechanical forger. It is not always an easy task. The term "Autopen" designed and manufactured by the International Autopen Company of Arlington, has become the standard term for all machine signed signatures. The machine uses a fabricated matrix to reproduce signatures.

The "Signa Signer" is a popular, more sophisticated version of a signature reproducing machine. It stores information on magnetic media, and can reproduce entire letters. It is about the size of small microwave oven and its "hand" can easily fool the uninformed collector. An autopen with advanced features can reproduce an exact a copy of a person's signature and even an entire letter, thousands of times. It does it with a real pen in a mechanical hand. Each signature is exactly like the previous and knowing the characteristics of these machines can help you to determine genuine signatures from machine-made scribble. Since these machines write the same signature exactly the same way every time, an experienced collector can discover whether the signature in question is real or a fake. You need to compare the unknown signature with known examples of autopens. If the two signatures are exactly the same, it is probably an autopen.

The procedure is fairly simple. Take the signature to be evaluated and place it on top of the known autopen. Hold them both together near a strong light source. (i.e., lay them on my light table.) Align the signatures to see if they match. If they are an exact match, it's an autopen. Some machines can be adjusted to "tighten up" a signature, which may cause a minor change in the height. However, the overall length will usually not change. However, the flaw in this logic is that we have assumed that there is only one autopen pattern per person. Many famous people have many different autopen signatures. John F. Kennedy had eight different patterns. Fred Casoni's book, Best Wishes Richard Nixon, contains 25 different autopen signatures. To definitively identify an "autopen" you need to have all the examples in order to make a proper comparison. There are many excellent references available that illustrate many autopen patterns. Look for autograph experts and ask if they have an autopen file you can use or rent. The International Society of Appraisers is the largest professional association of personal property appraisers. They offer an appraiser referral service.

There are some other characteristics of autopens that should be noted: 1) Autopen signatures have a drawn appearance. They do not 'flow' like genuine signature. 2) The width of the ink line is usually constant from beginning to end. This is because the autopen writes the signature at a constant speed, unlike a "human" signature. 3) Signatures are written with an even pen pressure throughout the signature. The machine cannot vary pen pressure. This too is a good clue of the machine's work. 4) In addition, a noticeable minute wiggle or shake may also be present. Older machine patterns sometimes bind and catch causing a friction shake in the signature. 5) The autopen uses a real pen. The ink will smear and run just like an authentic signature will.

One of the best ways to become familiar with the work of the autopen is to develop a library of its signatures. My autopen file contains over 750 examples of autopens. So, build your own file of patterns and share them with other collectors. Sharing will help you to spot the characteristics described in this article. But just reading is not enough. It takes lots of time, effort, and practice to be a good "Autograph Detective". *Beware the Autopen, Brian Kathenes, 07/05/2017.*

A precursor to the autopen was an instrument called the polygraph (which is not related to the modern device of the same name). While a person using the polygraph wrote an original document on one side of the machine, the device would mechanically facsimile a copy on the opposite side. When President Thomas Jefferson discovered the device, he purchased two: One for the White House, and one for his home at Monticello. John Isaac Hawkins received a patent for the invention of the first autopen in 1803. Although the device could only make copies at the same time that a user was creating an original, a fully automated version was invented in the 1930s. According to National Journal, some sources say that Harry S. Truman was the first U.S. president to use an autopen, though he limited his use of it to signing checks and answering mail. The first president to sign legislation with it was Barack Obama. Others credit Gerald Ford as the first president to openly acknowledge his use of the autopen.

While visiting France, Barack Obama authorized the use of an autopen to create his signature, signing into law an extension of three provisions of the Patriot Act. On January 3, 2013, he signed the extension to the Bush tax cuts, using the autopen while vacationing in Hawaii. In order to sign it by the required deadline, his other alternative would have been to have had the bill flown to him overnight.

Georgia's Republican Representative Tom Graves has questioned whether the President's use of the autopen is constitutional. In fact, Graves wrote to the President demanding "a detailed, written explanation of his Constitutional authority to assign a surrogate the responsibility of signing bills passed by Congress into law." This was after he realized, he said, that the reports of Obama using the autopen were true – according to Graves, when he first heard the reports, he thought they were a joke.

"I thought it was a joke at first, but the president did, in fact, authorize an autopen to sign the Patriot Act extension into law," observed Rep. Graves.

Graves apparently ignored the fact that the White House visited this very issue back in 2005, at which time the legal counsel determined that such use was constitutional. But, says Graves, he is concerned that the use of the autopen to sign legislation could set a "dangerous precedent. Any number of circumstances could arise in the future where the public could question whether or not the president authorized the use of an autopen. For example, Graves stated, "if the president is hospitalized and not fully alert, can a group of aggressive Cabinet members interpret a wink or a squeeze of the hand as approval of an autopen signing?"

What's interesting to us is that the kerfuffle over the President's use of the autopen seems to have eclipsed the discussion about whether or not he should have extended the Patriot Act. *The Internet Patrol, The AutoPen Explained, 06/19/2019.*

President Donald Trump claimed some of former President Joe Biden's pardons are invalid because Biden used an autopen. "The 'Pardons' that Sleepy Joe Biden gave to the Unselect Committee of Political Thugs, and many others, are hereby declared VOID, VACANT, AND OF NO FURTHER FORCE OR EFFECT, because of the fact that they were done by Autopen," Trump wrote March 17 on Truth Social. He referred to Biden's pardons of congressional members who served on the committee that investigated the Jan. 6, 2021, U.S. Capitol attack.

It's uncertain to us whether Biden used an "autopen" — a mechanical device that uses a robotic arm with a pen attached — to sign the pardons. Yet, Trump also claimed that Biden "did not sign" the pardons and "did not know anything about them!" Trump's post followed his statements days earlier criticizing Biden's use of the autopen. Legal scholars agreed that there is no constitutional mechanism to overturn pardons once granted. "Everything was signed by autopen — almost everything," Trump said March 13. "Nobody has ever heard of such a thing."

We found that the Constitution doesn't require a pardon's direct human signing, and subsequent judicial decisions and legal memoranda support an autopen's use for similar purposes. Legal scholars also agreed that there is no constitutional mechanism to overturn pardons once granted. A White House press office spokesperson referred PolitiFact to Press Secretary Karoline Leavitt's March 17 comments, that were in response to a reporter asking whether White House attorneys had told Trump he has the legal authority to reverse Biden's pardons because of the autopen. Leavitt did not directly answer that question but said, "The president was raising the point that, did the president even know about these pardons? Was his legal signature used without his consent or knowledge?"

When we asked the White House was asked whether Trump ever used an autopen, a spokesperson pointed to Trump's comments to reporters the previous night on Air Force One. "I never use it. I mean, we may use it, as an example, to send some young person a letter, because it's nice. ... But to sign pardons and all of the things that he signed with an autopen is disgraceful."

The pardon portion of the Constitution's Article II, Section 2, Clause 1 says the president has the power to grant pardons, but makes no mention of "sign" or "signature." More than a half-dozen constitutional law experts told PolitiFact they see no restriction in the Constitution on the use of an autopen. "The president possesses the power to pardon, but there is no specification (unlike for signing of bills) that this pardon be in writing," said Bernadette Meyler, a Stanford University scholar of British and American constitutional law. "Hence it is not clear that a signature would even be required, as the decision to pardon could be oral rather than written." By comparison, Article I, Section 7 says that bills that pass the House and Senate shall be "presented to the President of the United States; If he approves, he shall sign it."

In 2005, during George W. Bush's presidency, the Justice Department's Office of Legal Counsel wrote a memo to the president's counsel about the legality of using an autopen to sign bills. The department concluded: "The President need not personally perform the physical act of affixing his signature to a bill he approves and decides to sign in order for the bill to become law. Rather, the President may sign a bill within the meaning of Article I, Section 7 by directing a subordinate to affix the President's signature to such a bill, for example by autopen." The Justice Department memo also said there are practical reasons for a president to use an autopen, such as when he is away from Washington, D.C., or wants a law to take effect immediately, for example to avert a government shutdown.

"The DOJ opinion does give Biden cover here," Michigan State University law professor Brian Kalt said. A 1929 Office of the Solicitor General memo, within the Justice Department, said a pardoned man should be given a "token" to show he was pardoned, however, "that need not have the president's autograph. If it shall bear the facsimile signature and be certified by an official having charge of the records as having been issued by the President, or by his direction, that shall be sufficient."

More recently, the U.S. Court of Appeals for the 4th Circuit said in a 2024 ruling that "nothing in the Constitution restricts the President's exercise of the clemency power to commutations that have been rendered through a documented writing." Legal experts agreed that nothing in the Constitution or the law permits pardons to be reversed. "Pardons are final and irrevocable," Kalt said. In an 1869 ruling, a federal court wrote: "The law undoubtedly is, that when a pardon is complete, there is no power to revoke it, any more than there is power to revoke any other completed act."

"Presidents historically have not personally signed grants of pardons for every individual they granted clemency to," notably when granted in large batches such as mass amnesties following wars, said Dan Kobil, a Capital Law School professor. *Fact-checking Trump's claim that Biden pardons are 'void' because he used an autopen, PolitiFact, 03/18/2025.*

Though there were rumblings from the Republican camp, the constitutional right of the president to sign a bill with the autopen has neither been challenged nor tested in court. The constitutionality of a proxy signature has most certainly been challenged, with some legal experts asserting that the problem is not the use of a proxy, but that the principal (in this case, the president) and the proxy (the autopen) are not together at the time of signing.

The three hundred-fifty-year-old proxy law, designed to mitigate fraud or undue influence, has surprising relevance to this new technology. The presidential use of the autopen, or new technology, then, is not only an esoteric interest of collectors, but has very real applications and ramifications that impact the very notion of a well-ordered government. *Wikipedia*

Signatures play a role in the legal system as personal identifiers and methods to authenticate documents. They ensure agreements are binding and enforceable in both personal and professional transactions. As technology evolves, so do the forms that signatures can take, with electronic and digital alternatives becoming more prevalent. Understanding what constitutes a valid signature is essential for compliance and preventing disputes.

A signature, in its legal context, is more than just a scribble; it represents an individual's intent to authenticate a document. The legal definition includes any mark, symbol, or process executed or adopted by a person with the intention to authenticate a writing. This broad definition allows for flexibility in how signatures are applied, accommodating various forms and methods that have evolved over time. The Uniform Commercial Code (UCC), which governs commercial transactions in the United States, provides a framework for understanding signatures. Under the UCC, a signature can be any symbol executed or adopted with the intention to validate a record. This includes traditional handwritten signatures, as well as initials, thumbprints, or even a typed name at the end of an email. The focus is on the intent behind the mark, rather than the form it takes.

In the digital age, the Electronic Signatures in Global and National Commerce Act (E-SIGN Act) recognizes electronic signatures as legally binding. This federal law ensures that electronic signatures hold the same legal weight as handwritten ones, provided they meet certain criteria, such as the signer's intent to sign and consent to do business electronically. The E-SIGN Act has facilitated electronic commerce and streamlined digital transactions.

A valid signature must embody several components. At its core, the signature must be created or adopted with the intention to authenticate a document. This intent transforms a mere mark into a legitimate signature, ensuring it reflects the signer's conscious decision to engage in the transaction or agreement. The underlying intent is often scrutinized in legal disputes, where the authenticity of the signature may be contested.

The context in which the signature is made is equally important. It is essential that the signing process occurs in an environment free from coercion or undue influence. The signer must possess the capacity to understand the consequences of their signature, which implicates considerations of mental competence and legal age. These factors ensure that the signature is a true reflection of the signer's volition and comprehension of the agreement.

A valid signature must adhere to any specific formalities required by applicable laws or contract terms. Certain documents demand additional requirements, such as being witnessed or notarized, to enhance their legitimacy. For instance, wills and real estate transactions often necessitate notarization to confirm the identity of the signer and to prevent fraudulent claims. This procedural adherence safeguards the integrity of the signature and the document it authenticates.

Signatures have evolved significantly, adapting to technological advancements and changing legal landscapes. While traditional handwritten signatures remain prevalent, electronic and digital signatures have emerged as viable alternatives, each with distinct characteristics and legal implications.

Handwritten signatures are the most traditional form, often regarded as the gold standard for authenticity. They involve the physical act of signing one's name or mark on a document, typically using ink on paper. The uniqueness of a handwritten signature lies in its personal characteristics, such as the pressure, flow, and style of the writing, which can be analyzed for authenticity. Despite the rise of digital alternatives, handwritten signatures continue to hold significant legal weight, especially in jurisdictions where electronic signatures are not yet fully embraced. They are often required for documents that necessitate a high level of formality, such as deeds, wills, and certain contracts. The enduring relevance of handwritten signatures underscores their perceived reliability and the trust they inspire in legal and personal transactions.

Electronic signatures, recognized under laws like the E-SIGN Act and the Uniform Electronic Transactions Act (UETA), have become increasingly common in the digital age. These signatures can take various forms, including a typed name, a scanned image of a handwritten signature, or even a click of a button indicating agreement. The primary advantage of electronic signatures is their convenience and efficiency, allowing parties to execute agreements remotely without the need for physical presence. They are particularly useful in e-commerce, where speed and accessibility are paramount. However, to be legally binding, electronic signatures must meet specific criteria, such as demonstrating the signer's intent and ensuring the integrity of the signed document. This often involves using secure platforms that provide audit trails and verification processes to prevent tampering and ensure compliance with legal standards.

Digital signatures represent a more secure form of electronic signatures, employing cryptographic techniques to verify the signer's identity and the document's integrity. Unlike simple electronic signatures, digital signatures use a unique digital certificate issued by a trusted Certificate Authority (CA) to create a secure, encrypted signature. This process ensures that any alteration to the signed document after signing is detectable, providing a higher level of security and authenticity. Digital signatures are particularly favored in industries where data security is paramount, such as finance and healthcare. They comply with international standards, such as those set by the International Telecommunication Union (ITU) and the European Union's eIDAS regulation, which enhances their acceptance across borders. The security features of digital signatures make them an attractive option for organizations seeking to protect sensitive information and maintain trust in digital transactions.

In the evolving landscape of legal documentation, unconventional signatures have introduced both opportunities and challenges. As the boundaries of what constitutes a valid signature broaden, questions arise about the legal implications of such forms. Unconventional signatures, such as biometric and gesture-based signatures, offer innovative ways to authenticate documents but also present unique legal considerations. Biometric signatures, which use physical characteristics like fingerprints or retinal scans, provide a high level of security and personalization. However, they also raise privacy concerns and necessitate compliance with data protection regulations, such as the General Data Protection Regulation (GDPR) in Europe and the California Consumer Privacy Act (CCPA) in the United States. These laws mandate stringent protections for personal data, requiring organizations to implement robust measures to safeguard biometric information.

Gesture-based signatures, which capture the motion of a stylus or finger on a touch screen, offer a more intuitive signing experience. While they can enhance accessibility, particularly for individuals with disabilities, their validity may be questioned due to the potential for variability and replication. Legal systems must grapple with establishing standards that ensure the reliability and enforceability of such signatures. Courts may need to consider expert testimony or advanced forensic analysis to verify their authenticity, adding complexity to legal proceedings.

As the variety of signature forms expands, the need for verification and authentication methods becomes increasingly important to ensure the integrity of signed documents. Verification processes are essential to confirm that a signature is genuine and that the document remains unaltered. Authentication methods vary depending on the type of signature used, but they all aim to establish a reliable link between the signer and the signed document.

For handwritten signatures, authentication often involves forensic analysis. Experts examine the physical characteristics of the signature, such as pressure points and stroke patterns, to determine its authenticity. This process can be complex and time-consuming, but it is crucial in legal disputes where the validity of a signature is contested. In some cases, additional measures, such as witness testimonies or notarization, provide further assurance of authenticity.

In the realm of electronic and digital signatures, technology plays a pivotal role in verification. Electronic signature platforms, such as DocuSign and Adobe Sign, incorporate audit trails and encryption to ensure documents are secure and verifiable. Audit trails provide a detailed history of the signing process, including timestamps and IP addresses, which can be crucial in resolving disputes. Your IP address is a unique number linked to your online activity, somewhat like a return address on a letter. Digital signatures, utilizing cryptographic techniques, offer even greater security by ensuring the document has not been tampered with post-signature. The reliance on third-party verification services, such as Certificate Authorities, adds an extra layer of trust and legitimacy to digital signatures, making them a preferred choice for sensitive transactions.

The notary public's role is to serve as an impartial witness to the signing or authentication of legal documents. Notaries help prevent fraud and ensure that transactions, such as real estate deeds, affidavits, wills, trusts, powers of attorney, and bills of sale, are carried out with the proper documentation and authentication. Notaries are required for many documents, including real estate deeds, affidavits, wills, trusts, and powers of attorney. To become a notary, individuals must be at least 18 years old, reside where they are licensed, and meet specific state requirements. The National Notary Association (NNA) provides resources and information about becoming a notary. *Legal Clarity Team, 10/24/2024.*

The role of a notary public has evolved from ancient scribes to modern-day officials who verify the authenticity of documents. Notaries, originally called scribes, emerged in ancient Rome, recording proceedings and drafting legal documents. Over time, their duties expanded to include certifying affidavits, administering oaths, and authenticating signatures, playing a crucial role in legal and commercial transactions. Marcus Tullius Tiro, Cicero's clerk, developed a shorthand system called "notae tironinae" for recording speeches, and those who used this system were called notarii, the origin of the term notary. As literacy increased, notaries became important for drafting contracts, wills, and other important documents for a fee. Notaries were instrumental in developing commercial law, ensuring the authenticity of contracts and transactions.

In the United States, notaries are appointed by individual states to act as impartial witnesses and deter fraud. They have always been involved in the drafting and authentication of legal documents, including contracts, wills, and deeds; have the authority to administer oaths and affirmations, adding another layer of authenticity to documents; and verifying signatures on various documents, including real estate, court, and financial documents.

A notary public is a public official appointed to deter fraud by witnessing the signing of important documents and verifying the identity of the signer. They ensure the signer is who they claim to be, that they are signing willingly, and that they understand the document. Notaries are impartial witnesses and their role is crucial in various legal and business transactions. Notaries act as a safeguard against fraudulent transactions by verifying the identity of signers and confirming their willingness to sign. They witness the signing of documents, ensuring that the signatures are genuine and not coerced. Notaries confirm the identity of the signer through acceptable forms of identification, like driver's licenses or passports. They ensure the signer understands the document's contents before signing.

Duties of notaries include: Administering oaths and affirmations, which are often required in legal proceedings; certifying copies of documents such as deeds, mortgages, and other documents related to property transfer; wills, powers of attorney, affidavits, and other legal documents; loans, contracts, and other financial documents; and to advance medical directives and other healthcare-related documents that need to be notarized.

To become a Notary Public, meeting eligibility requirements vary by state but often include being at least 18 years old, a legal resident of the state, and having a clean criminal record; filling out an application form provided by their state's notary commission office; submitting the required application fees to the state; completing training and an exam; fingerprinting and a background check; obtaining Surety a surety bond, secure one from an authorized provider (also known as a surety bond, that is a type of financial guarantee where one party (the surety) promises to pay another party (the obligee) if a third party (the principal) fails to fulfill a contractual obligation. It's a three-party agreement designed to protect the obligee from potential losses due to the principal's default); submit an oath of office and bond with the designated state official; and acquire a notary seal (stamp) and journal as required by the state. Some states require continuing education to maintain your notary commission.

To minimize the chances of a will or contract being contested, it's crucial to ensure proper execution, clear communication, and potentially to incorporate specific clauses to deter challenges. Ensure the will is signed and witnessed according to legal requirements and ideally, have it signed in the presence of your lawyer and two independent witnesses not named in the will. Discuss your intentions with potential beneficiaries to avoid surprises and misunderstandings; include a clause that disinherits anyone who challenges the will and is unsuccessful in court; consider using a revocable living trust instead of a will; set aside funds to cover potential legal costs associated with defending the will against challenges; record yourself signing the will and have it certified by a third party to demonstrate your intent; include a clause requiring mediation before a will contest can proceed; include a document outlining your reasons for specific bequests to further demonstrate your intentions; ensure the contract is written in a clear unambiguous language that is easy to understand; have a lawyer review the contract before signing to identify potential loopholes or ambiguities; ensure all parties understand the terms and agree to them before signing; instead of going to court, require disputes to be settled by an arbitrator; and keep records of all communication and negotiations related to the contract. *Google AI*

The issue with using an autopen, particularly for official documents, isn't that people aren't using them at all, but rather concerns around their use in situations where authentication and authorization are critical. A major concern is the risk of the autopen being used without the individual's knowledge or consent, leading to potentially fraudulent activities, especially with sensitive documents. The legal acceptance of autopen signatures can vary depending on the document and jurisdiction. While autopens are accepted in some contexts, others, like documents requiring notarization, often require a witnessed handwritten signature.

Autopen signatures, designed for uniformity, lack the natural variations found in human handwriting. This can make it challenging to definitively prove the authenticity of a single autopen signature without comparing it to other examples. Some perceive autopen signatures as less authentic and lacking the personal touch of a handwritten signature, which can be an issue for personal correspondence or building connections. Using autopens without disclosure, particularly for things like condolences to families of soldiers, can raise ethical concerns and create mistrust.

While autopens can be efficient and convenient for high-volume tasks, concerns about security, legal validity, authenticity, and ethical implications can lead people to question or avoid their use, especially in contexts where a personal and verifiable signature is important.

The use of an autopen by a president is not typically hidden, but the specific individuals who operate the device are not usually disclosed, which can create the appearance of secrecy. This practice is generally accepted as a legitimate way for presidents to handle a large volume of documents requiring their signature. They deal with a massive amount of paperwork, and using an autopen allows them to handle tasks like signing legislation, pardons, and other official documents without being physically present for each signature.

The use of autopens for signing documents is a long-standing practice, with presidents from various administrations utilizing them for various purposes. The Justice Department has issued opinions stating that the president need not personally perform the physical act of signing a bill for it to become law, meaning they can authorize the use of an autopen. The autopen creates a signature that closely resembles the president's actual signature, which can be useful for maintaining a degree of plausible deniability regarding certain actions.

While the use of the autopen is legal, it can be politically sensitive, as evidenced by past criticism of its use. While the practice itself is not secret, the identity of the individuals operating the autopen is often not revealed, which can lead to perceptions of secrecy or even attempts to conceal potential presidential incapacitation. *Google AI*

My question: Since signatures play a role in the legal system as personal identifiers and methods to authenticate documents and they ensure agreements are binding and enforceable in both personal and professional transactions – why can a president have some unidentified person use an autopen to approve legislation, pardons, and other official documents without being present to provide a signature or identify the individual that used the autopen? Why don't they at least have a notary public or other public official appointed to deter fraud by witnessing the signing of these important documents and verifying the identity of the signer? They could ensure the autopen user is who they claim to be, that they are signing for the president, and that they understand his intentions. Notaries are supposed to be impartial witnesses and their role would be crucial to following the president's instructions. They would help safeguard against fraudulent signers by verifying the identity of those using the autopen and confirming their willingness to sign. They would act as a witness by signing the document, placing their notary stamp on it and verifying it in a journal to ensure that the autopen signature of the president is used as he intended. Notaries confirm who the autopen signer is through acceptable forms of identification; like driver's licenses or passports, thumb print &/or a dated video of the transaction, or observing the transaction by a Zoom type service.

I imagined myself as being like the waitress that commented to President Trump that he should consider not taxing tips. He listened and added to his Big Beautiful Bill – no tax on tips. I emailed President Trump directly and News Max, who asks for messages one would like sent to Trump: "Hogepoge, Tue, May 20, 2025: Dear President Trump,

— Whenever I need to sign a legal document, they require me to do it in front of a notary who verifies who I am using my legal ID and they witness me signing the document. They then stamp my document with a registered notary verification and sign it.

— Why doesn't the United States of America require a notary witness and verify who uses an autopen? What is good for the goose should good for the gander. And, the gander has most the big bucks.

— Looks to me like folks in our government don't want to let us know who done it or where our money is spent... Thank You WR Hoge, San Jose, CA Sent from my iPhone

So far, I've not seen a comment concerning my question about using the autopen. He doesn't appear to be like many of the busy athletes, celebrities, and politicians using the autopen and making it a headache for autograph collectors, evaluating value of a document, knowing if a signature came from the hands of a living soul. His presidential proclamations issued on matters of public policy and personally signed were 570 proclamations during his first term (2017-2021), and 70 more during his second term as of June 24, 2025. All of them transparent, lacking of hidden agendas or secrecy, with everything out in the open.

Proverbs 4:23, "Be very careful about what you think. Your thoughts run your life." The heart (or mind) is the origin of our actions. Proverbs 4:23, "Keep your heart with all vigilance, for from it flow the springs of life." Guard one's inner self, as it is the source of thoughts, emotions, and actions. Hopefully it encourages a proactive honest public disclosing approach to maintaining a healthy inner life. Recognizing that our outward behavior is a reflection of our inner state. Your thoughts run your life. Proverbs 23:7, "For what a man thinketh in his heart, so is he." Right or wrong, in the long run – honesty is the best policy.

CHAPTER 16

TOOK A CRUISE

In the 20th century, molasses shipped to Boston primarily originated from the Caribbean Islands; including the islands of Puerto Rico, Cuba and other sugar-producing countries where molasses is a by-product of sugar manufacturing. Molasses played a crucial role in the economy of the Caribbean and New England. It was commonly used in the production of rum, which was a major industry in New England. This trade formed a part of the so-called triangular trade, where molasses from the Caribbean was used to produce rum in New England, and this rum was used to trade for enslaved Africans in the Caribbean. The molasses shipped to Boston was widely utilized industrially during World War I, particularly for producing ethanol for munitions.

Sugarcane undergoes a refining process where the harvested cane stalks are crushed to extract the juice. This juice is boiled to produce sugar crystals, and the liquid left behind becomes molasses. The juice is typically boiled several times to extract as much sugar as possible, and the first boiling yields the most sugar-rich molasses, known as "first syrup" or "cane syrup." Subsequent boiling produces darker, more concentrated forms of molasses, including "blackstrap molasses", which is rich in vitamins and minerals but less sweet than the first syrup.

Sugar beets are processed by washing and slicing them to extract their sugar-laden juice, which is then purified and crystallized similar to cane sugar. The remaining liquid after sugar extraction is also known as molasses. However, beet molasses typically contains a lower concentration of sugar and is often used for animal feed rather than culinary applications. It is generally considered less palatable for human consumption compared to sugarcane molasses. According to various sources, approximately 55-60% of sugar produced in the U.S. comes from sugar beets. Sugarcane not only has a higher sugar content but also yields more palatable molasses. *AI*

The Atlantic slave trade used a system of three-way transatlantic exchanges – known historically as the triangular trade – which operated between Europe, Africa, and the Americas from the 16th to 19th centuries. European workers outfitted slave ships, and they shipped manufactured European goods owned by the trading companies to West Africa to get slaves, which they shipped to the Americas; in particular, to Brazil and the Caribbean islands. First, in West Africa, merchants sold or bartered European manufactured goods to local slavers in exchange for slaves. Then crews transported the slaves, and remaining European manufactured goods, to the Americas where ship merchants sold the slaves and European manufactured goods to plantation owners. Merchants then purchased sugar and molasses from the plantation owners and crews shipped them to North American colonies (later the

US), where the merchants sold the remaining supplies of European manufactured goods and slaves, as well as sugar and molasses from plantations to local buyers, and then purchased North American commodities to sell in Europe, including tobacco, sugar, cotton, rum, rice, lumber, and animal pelts.

This triangular trade route was shorter and more efficient than traditional European routes. It led to a significant increase in rum distilleries in Boston and surrounding areas, becoming a major economic activity. By the mid-18th century, Boston boasted over 25 distilleries, with a total of 51 in Massachusetts by 1770. Massachusetts produced over 40% of the total rum distilled in North America, reaching more than 2 million gallons per year. Rum became a significant export, comprising 80% of New England's exports at its peak.

This booming rum industry, however, was fundamentally dependent on the brutal system of slavery, with rum acting as a key commodity in the transatlantic slave trade. By the late 18th century, the international slave trade was outlawed, impacting the availability of molasses. After the American Revolution, Britain rationed molasses imports to the newly independent American states. Additionally, the rise of domestic grain production in the westward expansion led to the increased popularity of whiskey, displacing rum as the preferred spirit.

These factors led to the decline of Boston's rum distilleries, with only a few remaining by the War of 1812. In essence, Boston's rum production and trade with Europe were a major economic force in colonial New England, tragically fueled by the transatlantic slave trade. While the rum trade eventually declined, its historical impact on the region and its connections to the larger global trade networks remain an important aspect of American history. *Wikipedia*

In 1851, the LDS Church attempted developing the sugar industry in Utah in an official manner through Brigham Young and John Taylor, establishing the Deseret Manufacturing Company in Spring 1851 with $35,000 in capital from the LDS church. The machinery was purchased from Liverpool, arriving in New Orleans, boated to Leavenworth, Kansas, and then by 40 high-end covered wagons to Utah. Troubles with transportation, including heavy snows, caused the company to be nicknamed the "Damn Miserable Company". Some of the equipment was abandoned in the Bear River Valley of Utah, and the original Provo factory location was abandoned by late November 1852. Instead, the machinery was set up in Salt Lake City for a test run in an adobe-construction blacksmith shop. The community it was established in is now known as Sugarhouse, and the test factory ready for first processing by December 1852.

Brigham Young thought John Taylor was a poor businessman, declaring he "knew nothing about transacting business." Young, despite no knowledge of sugar beets or sugar, took over the business. The 1852 effort was a failure, partly because the important vacuum pan never worked correctly, and partly because of a lack of knowledge about the industry. The Deseret Manufacturing Company was out of money, and the LDS church assumed the debts in 1853. The only people who had seen a successful sugar operation, left the company after the takeover.

In 1853, a new full factory design by was called by Young. The project was plagued with delays, in part due to labor and construction materials being needed for construction of the nearby Salt Lake Temple. The factory was scheduled for completion in the fall of 1854, but did not start processing sugar beets until February 1855. The factory ran until March, but didn't successfully produce sugar. The operation closed in fall 1856, never having been successful, though the Church still believed it could be made successful. Later research proved the equipment was manufactured correctly, installed correctly, and similar to later successful factories; the difference was the lack of experienced operators, especially for boiling sugar in the vacuum pan. The two missing steps were an inadequate speed on the vacuum pump, and a missing graining step to produce sugar crystals. The operation was also likely abandoned due to the declining finances of the LDS Church and the Utah War of 1857, as well as Young's poor ability to handle criticism. The expensive equipment, acquired and shipped to Utah at great cost, was reused in other industries around Utah. In the end, the operation was a $50,000 loss. *Wikipedia*

The Utah War, also known as the Utah Expedition or Buchanan's Blunder, was an armed confrontation between Mormon settlers and the U.S. government, primarily driven by tensions over governance and autonomy in the Utah Territory. It occurred from 1857 to 1858 and was rooted in the complex relationships between the Mormon settlers, led by Brigham Young, and the federal government. After the Mormons settled in the Utah Territory to escape religious persecution, tensions arose due to their theocratic governance and practices, particularly polygamy, which were viewed unfavorably by many in the U.S. government and society.

The immediate cause was President James Buchanan's decision to replace Brigham Young as the territorial governor with a non-Mormon Alfred Cumming. This decision was influenced by reports of Mormon resistance to federal authority and fears that the Mormons might establish a separate nation. In response, Buchanan sent a military force to the territory, which the Mormons interpreted as an act of aggression.

Both sides prepared for conflict, with the Mormons declaring martial law and mobilizing their militia, the Nauvoo Legion. The U.S. Military, numbering around 2,500 troops, advanced towards Salt Lake City. One of the most tragic events associated with the Utah War was the Mountain Meadows Massacre in September 1857, where a group of Mormon militia killed approximately 120 settlers travelling to California. This incident significantly tarnished the reputation of the Mormon community and escalated tensions.

The conflict did not result in significant military battles, and after a year of standoffs, negotiations led to peaceful resolution. Federal troops were allowed to enter the territory, and a pardon was granted to the Mormons for any acts of rebellion. This settlement restored federal authority while allowing the Mormons to maintain a degree of autonomy.

The Utah War highlighted the challenges of governance in a diverse and rapidly expanding nation. It also set the stage for ongoing tensions between the federal government and the Mormon community, influencing the latter's quest for statehood and their relationship with the broader American society. It was rooted in cultural, religious, and political tensions, with lasting implications for both the Mormon community and the U.S. government. The conflict is often views as a precursor to the larger national tensions that would culminate in the Civil War.

The concern of supplying sugar to the region was still under discussion. In 1863, Young stated "Importing sugar has been a great drain upon our ... currency. I am satisfied that it is altogether unnecessary to purchase sugar in a foreign market." After years of experimenting with sorghum and deciding sugar beets would work better, Arthur Stayner lobbied the LDS church in 1887, but the church was not interested, due to poor church finances and a committee of the church-owned ZCMI reporting such a venture would be a bad idea. By 1889, Wilford Woodruff was won over to the idea of growing and processing sugar beets, leading to a new enterprise, the Utah-Idaho Sugar Company.

The Utah-Idaho Sugar Company, a major beet sugar producer, was founded in 1907 through the merger of the Utah Sugar Company, the Idaho Sugar Company and the Western Idaho sugar Company with significant involvement from the LDS Church and its leaders who used it as an economic engine for the region. It became a prominent agricultural and industrial force in the Mountain West, expanding to multiple factories and playing a key role in the region's sugar production for decades. The company's roots trace back to the Utah Sugar Company, established in Lehi, Utah, in 1891. This marked the first successful beet sugar production in the Mountain West using American machinery and irrigated beets. *AI*

A hulking 50-foot, tall molasses tank was built by Purity Distilling Company in 1915. The tank measured 50-feet tall by 90 feet wide, and rose over the Boston Elevated Railroad tracks that ran next to it. Tankers delivered shipments of molasses to Copps Hill Wharf, where it was pumped into the tank and stored until it could be sent to distilleries on train cars. The company used the molasses in the tank to make ethanol, which in turn helped create munitions for World War I and alcohol that eventually found its way into beverages like beer, wine, and brandy.

Ethanol played a significant role in World War I munitions production. It was a key ingredient in producing smokeless powder, an important advancement in firearms technology. French chemist Paul Vieille developed the smokeless propellant in 1884 by using ethanol and ether as solvents to make nitrocellulose into a collodion, which was then used to make smokeless propellants adopted by the French military.

By the time January 1919 rolled around, the end of World War I and the coming of Prohibition threatened to dry up Purity's two main sales channels. Months earlier, the abdication of the kaiser in Germany and the signing of the Armistice of November 11 meant the end of World War I. And, in mid-January 1919, the 18th Amendment to the US Constitution was ratified, which would make the making, selling, and transport of alcohol illegal. As the WWI munitions race and the flow of free alcohol was coming to an end, Purity raced to sell all that molasses it held in its tank. And they wanted to do it before Prohibition went into effect in 1920.

At midday on January 15, 1919, Boston's North End was full of workers and residents venturing outdoors to enjoy unseasonably warm weather. At about 1 p.m., they heard a low rumble. At first, many assumed it was a Boston Elevated train approaching. But, within minutes, they realized something was very wrong. The 50-foot tall, tank full of industrial grade molasses had ruptured, sending a wave of 2.3 million gallons of molasses rushing through the crowded North End.

The Boston molasses tank failure in 1919, also known as the Great Molasses Flood, was caused by a combination of factors including a poorly constructed tank, a new shipment of warm molasses, and a subsequent temperature drop. The tank's steel was too thin and brittle, and the tank was not properly inspected. The warm molasses, upon entering the tank, caused a release of gas, which, combined with a temperature drop, increased pressure within the tank and led to a rupture. Though the tank had only been built a few years earlier, local residents knew that it leaked. North End children collected pails of the sticky, sweet molasses. When locals complained that they could see the molasses seeping out at the tank's seams, Purity Distilling painted the tank brown, to disguise the oozing molasses.

The molasses tank was structurally unsound. The steel used was too thin, brittle, and had a flawed chemical composition, making it prone to cracking, according to a study cited by The Boston Globe. Additionally, the tank was not properly inspected, and corners were cut in its construction. A new shipment of warm molasses arrived shortly before the incident. This warm molasses, upon mixing with the colder molasses already in the tank, caused fermentation and the release of carbon dioxide gas. The temperature outside fluctuated from 2°F to 40°F, further impacting the molasses and causing it to expand, increasing pressure inside the tank.

The tank had a vent, but it was not designed to handle the volume of gas produced by the fermentation process in the cold weather. This trapped the gas, leading to a buildup of pressure that the weakened tank could not withstand. The tank's "factor of safety," a measure of its ability to withstand stress, was too low. An engineer later calculated that the tank was subjected to nearly twice the pressure it could safely handle.

The combination of the tank's structural weakness, the warm molasses, and the trapped gases resulted in a rapid build-up of pressure within the tank. This pressure eventually exceeded the tank's capacity, leading to a catastrophic rupture.

By the time January 1919 rolled around, the end of World War I and the coming of Prohibition threatened to dry up Purity's two main sales channels. Months earlier, the abdication of the kaiser in Germany and the signing of the Armistice of November 11 meant the end of World War I. And, in mid-January 1919, the 18th Amendment to the US Constitution was ratified, which would make the making, selling, and transport of alcohol illegal. As the WWI munitions race and the flow of free alcohol was coming to an end, Purity raced to sell all that molasses it held in its tank. And they wanted to do it before Prohibition went into effect in 1920.

When the molasses tank burst, the public wondered whether it had been blown it up. Purity Distilling Company hoped so. Even while the company maintained that the tank failed because it was sabotaged by Italian anarchists, a multi-year investigation involving more than 1,000 witnesses determined the company was at fault. When it turned out that the tank failed as a result of a lot of neglect, victims and their families (21 deaths and 150 injuries) sued. The suits were combined into one of the first U. S. class action lawsuits. It appeared that a lot of corners were cut in building the tank.

Today, the Great Molasses Flood lives on in Boston lore as well as in its construction regulations, which now require licensed architects and civil engineers to be involved in the drafting of project requirements. The legacy of the flood also lives on in the corporate responsibility encouraged by the specter of class action lawsuits. The tank was never rebuilt and the land eventually came under the control of a predecessor for the Massachusetts Bay Transportation Authority. Today, a recreational complex owned by the City of Boston occupies the site. A small, green plaque marks the spot of the disaster. *100 years ago today: Molasses crashes through Boston's North End, NPR.*

Utah-Idaho Sugar Company operated numerous factories, including those in Lehi and Garland, Utah, and Idaho Falls, Sugar City, Blackfoot (my home town), and Nampa, Idaho. It played a significant role in the economic development of the region by providing a valuable cash crop for farmers and creating jobs in the sugar processing industry. The company faced challenges related to fluctuating sugar prices, competition, and agricultural issues like Curly Top disease. In the 1970s, the company shifted its focus to potato processing and eventually ceased sugar production in Utah, with operations continuing in Idaho.

The Amalgamated Sugar Nampa facility is not the only remaining sugar processing operation with roots in the former Utah-Idaho Sugar Company. While the Utah-Idaho Sugar Company, once a major player in the Western beet sugar industry, ceased operations and abandoned sugar production by the late 1970s, it's crucial to understand the intertwined histories of these companies. The Amalgamated Sugar Company, while a separate entity, also had close ties to the LDS Church and its leaders who were instrumental in establishing the sugar beet industry in Utah and Idaho.

Today, Amalgamated Sugar Company continues to operate, headquartered in Boise, Idaho. They are the second-largest beet sugar producer in the United States and have three operating factories in Idaho: Twin Falls, Paul (Mini-Cassia), and Nampa. So, the Nampa facility is one of several remaining from this legacy, although the original Utah-Idaho Sugar Company no longer exists as a sugar producer.

Amalgamated Sugar produces 12% of the total sugar in the United States. While the specific percentage from their Nampa plant isn't detailed, they operate factories in Nampa, Twin Falls, and Paul, Idaho. Amalgamated Sugar is the second-largest beet sugar producer in the US, according to Amalgamated Sugar. They process beets grown on 225,000 acres, including land in Idaho, Oregon, and Washington. The company buys about 6 million tons of beets annually, producing 1.7 billion pounds of sugar, which represents 20% of the beet sugar and 10% of all US sugar. *Wikipedia*

My wife, Shauna's, two children have their birthdays on the 8th and 11th day of June and often celebrate the events on a shared vacation. In 2025 that event involved me and we went on a cruise from New York and into Canada. I left with concerns for three-week old ducklings I had hatched from eight rescued eggs uncovered while mowing our field (see Ducklings anyone). One was unable to walk and I had dreams of helping it survive and observing how it compensated for its handicaps. At our first port of call I was advised that it died.

During a city tour in the center of Boston, we passed by Boston Public Garden where there is an island surrounded by a pond. The announcer mentioned that this was the place Robert McCloskey wrote in 1941 his book "Make Way for Ducklings". Mrs. Mallard was sure that this pond would be a perfect place for her and her eight ducklings to live. The book was inspired by true-life observations and experiences of the author who frequently saw ducks in Boston Public Garden and was aware of the traffic challenges they faced according to Bird Watcher's General Store. This event heightened my concerns about my ducklings back and I spent time on the ship writing about them.

The tour also passed near the area where The Great Molasses Flood in Boston occurred on January 15, 1919, occurred just as the 18th Amendment, which ushered in Prohibition, was being ratified. The flood, caused by a ruptured molasses storage tank, temporarily overshadowed the prohibition news, even though both events were closely related to the demand for industrial alcohol. Molasses was a key ingredient in producing ethanol, a component of munitions and a potential precursor to alcoholic beverages, making its storage crucial as Prohibition approached. My mind reminisced my youth when I would chew on bitter molasses tasting beet pulp, made from sugar beets, fed to milk cows across the street from my home. I also recalled that the LDS Church became involved in the sugar beet industry primarily due to the desire for economic self-sufficiency, the belief that it was divinely inspired and it was mostly an economic disaster for the Mormon. Church leaders saw the industry as a way to provide jobs, decrease sugar prices for members, and foster independence from external economic pressures.

My father-in-law, Nate, and his son, Tim, worked for the Amalgamated Sugar Company in Nampa Idaho. Nate loaned me an interesting book about the production of sugar and Tim gave me a tour throughout the factory. At the time, Tim told me that coal was being used for the energy to extract sugar from sugar beets and was about to switch over to the cleaner fuel natural gas. Currently, the Nampa factory operates four natural gas-fired industrial boilers to provide steam for the sugar production process and to generate electricity. This shift has significantly reduced greenhouse gas emissions at the facility. Amalgamated Sugar completed a new anaerobic digester in 2023 at the Nampa facility. This digester processes wastewater from the sugar manufacturing process, and there's potential to use the biogas produced by the digester to power parts of the factory, including the boilers, in the future.

Have you ever noticed that on the dessert menu on cruise ships they offer both caramel and butterscotch syrupy flavors. On my last cruise I asked the waiter what the differences were. He didn't know and I've never been able to tell the difference. When I got home my troubled mind was satisfied.

The main difference between butterscotch and caramel lies in the type of sugar used and the way the ingredients are combined. Caramel is typically made with white sugar, while butterscotch uses brown sugar. Additionally, butterscotch involves cooking the butter and brown sugar together before adding cream, whereas in caramel, the butter and cream are usually added later in the process. Just so you know: Toffee is made from sugar and butter. Chefs cook toffee longer than caramel so it reaches a hardened, brittle state. Toffee is usually topped with chocolate, nuts or coconut. *AI*

Hopefully, you have found my whimsical journey of interest as I unwound my thoughts on my thoughts mind. The good news is that five of the seven ducklings that were able to hatch are eating an expensive duck food, mealworms, grass sod I've placed in a converted dog run, and lettuce are doing quite well. Two weeks from now their flight feathers should be developed enough to get away from predators and they will be placed in a creek near our home. I'm in hopes that I can see them on a daily basis by taking food to the creek and calling quack, quack, quack.

CHAPTER 17

DUCKLINGS ANYONE

It all started on May 7, 2025. I was mowing the field that leads from McKean Road, San Jose CA. to the bridge that crosses a creek onto our main property. Thankfully, I had raised the mower blade up in hopes of saving some of the wild flowers that were about to go to seed and be low enough to be a fire break for the foliage growing next to the creek. I noticed a duck flying away from the area and several crows, that are always present when mowing, looking for insects and small animals exposed during mowing. The crows began congregating in one area of the field and a California Turkey Vulture began flying over my head and close to the field.

The hen Mallard Duck flew back to the field and landed in the area of the crows. I noticed that her head was held high and her presence caused the crows to back away. Then I lost sight of the duck until I noticed her lying flat against the ground as I mowed near the area. I stopped the tractor, approached her and she flew away revealing eight beautiful light brown eggs. Mallard ducks can have more than one clutch of 8 to 13 eggs in a year. While a hen typically raises one brood per year, if the first clutch is destroyed by predators or other factors, she may attempt to re-nest. This re-nesting can lead to multiple clutches of eggs within the same breeding season. Since she was nesting near the area where, several weeks before, we had been watching a hen duck with ducklings that suddenly disappeared – I suspected that this was the same hen duck.

The hen returned again as I continued to mow the field. Once finished I shut off the tractor and watched the hen laying on the eggs, the crows mingling around the area and the vulture periodically swooping low near the duck. Crows are opportunistic omnivores, meaning they eat a wide variety of food sources, including both plant and animal matter. They consume fruits, nuts, seeds, insects, crustaceans, mollusks, amphibians, reptiles, small mammals, garbage, carrion (dead animals), and even the eggs and young of other birds.

California vultures, specifically Turkey and Black Vultures, primarily feed on the carcasses of dead animals. They also occasionally consume other things like human garbage, some fruits, and on rare occasions, live prey. During the evenings of spring and early summer we often have a smell in the night or early morning that reminds me of the smell of marijuana permeating our yard. It so happens that marijuana and skunks both produce pungent odors, and interestingly, the chemicals responsible for their distinct smells share common characteristics. Both cannabis and skunk spray contain volatile sulfur compounds (VSCs). Specifically, the molecule 3-methyl-2-butene-1-thiol (VSC3), a type of thiol (sulfur-containing compound), that is a significant contributor to the skunky smell in both. This same VSC3 molecule is also responsible for the "skunky" odor found in beer that has been exposed to UV light.

Skunks typically have babies, also known as kittens or kits, in May and June. Mating season occurs in late winter to early spring, with the gestation period lasting about two months. The young are born in a den blind, deaf, and with a fine coat of fur. They stay in a den for several weeks before venturing out with their mother. Young skunks emerge from the den around six to eight weeks of age, typically are weaned around two months of age and mostly seen at night foraging with the mother. Skunks eat both plants and animals and their diet varies by season and location. They commonly consume insects, small mammals, fruits, berries, and carrion. In areas with human activity, they may also scavenge for garbage and pet food. The skunks attracted to our yard appear mostly to be in search or white grubs living in the lawn.

On February 27th 2025 I was able to get a couple of close pictures of two Turkey Vultures consuming something on the grass near our pump house. The Turkey Vulture in California is a large, dark-feathered bird with a distinctive, featherless red head and a long wingspan. They are primarily scavengers, feeding on carrion, and are mostly seen in soaring flight, often gliding with their wings in a shallow "V" shape relying on their keen sense of smell to locate dead animals. They tend to rock and teeter from side to side while soaring and inhabit open areas, grasslands, deserts and woodlands. Turkey vultures are large birds, measuring 25-32 inches in length with a wingspan of around 70 inches. Their plumage is mostly brownish-black, with darker body feathers and paler flight feathers underneath. The head and neck are a reddish color and bare of feathers. A key identification feature is their bare red head and neck, which is thought to help prevent carrion from sticking to their feathers. They also have a pale, hooked beak. Their vocalizations are limited to hisses and grunts.

After the Turkey Vultures left the area, I found a skunk partially consumed with hundreds of blow flies laying eggs in the area. The dentition indicated the skunk was probably born May or June of 2024. The vultures returned several times and a week later I investigated the area and the skunk was completely gone – even the bones and hair. Come to think about it, I didn't even notice a skunk smell.

Had I disrupted the Mallard duck's second chance of raising a family? I sat on the tractor watching the duck tightly covering her brood of exposed eggs. I wondered if she was still laying eggs or had started incubating (brooding) them, if they were near term chicks should I destroy the eggs quickly so they wouldn't suffer the pecks of the crows or vulture, or should I try taking over the task of the mother by attempting to hatch and raise them?

Over seventy years ago my mother built a small box, placed a light bulb inside for warmth, a small pan of water for moisture and several fertile chicken eggs she had purchased from a local poultry producer. My job was to turn the eggs often (like the mother hen) for 21 days until the chicks started pecking a hole in their captive egg. Even though they struggled and I wanted so much to help them, my mother said that if I did the chicks would not build enough strength to survive after being freed by me.

I carefully placed the eight duck eggs in my hoody and took them home. I tried to candle them with a flashlight and could see nothing except an air bubble in the end of each egg. A Mallard egg incubates for 28 days and I had no idea if they were fertile or had started the incubation process. A typical clutch for a Mallard Duck may be up to 13 eggs; the mother lays the eggs at one to two-day intervals, and does not begin the incubation process until all the eggs are laid. Because embryo development doesn't occur until the hen sets on them (brooding), all the ducklings hatch within a couple days of each other. Weather conditions during the laying phase typically doesn't affect the clutch.

I placed a moistened towel in a small plastic storage container, gently placed the eggs on it and a heating pad under the container. The eggs ideally should be incubated at 50% humidity (which I was in hopes the moist towel would provide) and a temperature of 100 degrees Fahrenheit. I monitored the temperature of the eggs with a cool device, called an infrared thermometer, used for cooking that my brother-in-law had introduced to me. I just aimed at each egg, pulled the trigger, a red beam (like a lightsaber in Star Wars or at a store checkout counter) was emitted on an egg and it gave me the temperature of each egg. Depending on the temperature, I would adjust the egg nearer or farther away from the heating pad. I rotated the eggs often during this time. I ordered a chicken incubator that would hold 12 eggs, all stages of development duck food, grit (small rocks that are needed for the gizzard to help digest food), dried mealy worms, and water and food containers. The incubator was lost in the mail and the reorder did not arrive until five days later.

I had no idea if the eggs were fertile or what stage of incubation they were in. However, I soon found out that they were in the 21st day of incubation as they began hatching seven days later (the 28th day). When the eggs started hatching, the egg rotator was removed from the incubator and I raised the moisture to over 60% humidity. The first egg that started to hatch was the third one to release itself from its shell. The seven newly hatched ducklings were left in the incubator until dry and then placed in in an area with a heat source (a 40watt bulb) that was used for several days. At first, they did not show interest in eating and a Google search informed me that the hatchling ducks can live for about 24-48 hours after hatching without food or water because they absorb the remaining yolk sac into their abdomen right before or during hatching. This yolk provides them with essential nutrients during their first day outside the egg. They spend their time resting and gaining enough strength to follow the hen duck to a food and water source. Seven of the eight eggs hatched. Five lived long enough to be released into our creek.

During this time, I recalled a beautiful white duck a client of mine had brought to Camden Pet Hospital. The owner suspected it had been attacked by a predator and was breathing through its severed windpipe (trachea) coming out of its neck. A severed trachea in a bird is a serious injury that disrupts its ability to breathe. The most common causes are injuries, such as those from predator attacks (e.g., dog bites), penetrating wounds (guns, knives etc.), or blunt force (e.g., hit by a car), that can damage or even sever the trachea. It reminded me of a tracheostomy procedure often used in human medicine. A tracheostomy is a surgical procedure that creates an opening, or stoma, in the front of the neck and into the trachea to help a person breathe. A tube, called a tracheostomy tube or trach tube, is inserted into the stoma to maintain an open airway and allow air to enter the lungs.

This tube can be temporary or permanent, depending on the reason for the tracheostomy. The trachea's tissue structure consists of several layers: mucosa, submucosa, cartilage rings, and adventitia. The mucosa, the innermost layer, contains pseudostratified columnar epithelium with cilia and goblet cells that produce mucus to trap debris. The submucosa, beneath the mucosa, is made of connective tissue with blood vessels and nerves. Hyaline cartilage rings provide structural support, keeping the trachea open. The outermost layer, adventitia, anchors the trachea to surrounding tissues.

It is interesting that bird bones, especially in young birds, tend to heal more quickly than in mammals. For example, simple, closed fractures in birds, when properly splinted, can become clinically stable in 2-3 weeks, though a callus may not be radiographically visible for 3-6 weeks. This rapid healing capacity means that sometimes, simple stabilization is all that's required for recovery. Bone healing in mammals generally takes longer, and depending on the severity of the fracture and the species, surgical interventions or implanted supports may be necessary for proper healing. One the other hand, complete healing of soft tissue wounds in birds can take several weeks. Birds have a relatively thin and dry epidermis, with less subcutaneous tissue supplied with blood vessels compared to mammals, which could influence wound healing. Mammals specific healing times vary among the species and the type of surgery. The post-operative monitoring for major surgery is typically recommended for at least 7-10 days. Non-absorbable sutures are usually removed 10-14 days after surgery.

I was able to remove damaged tissues and suture the thin fragile cartilage rings together to reestablish breathing through the duck's mouth. It stayed at the hospital for couple of days before I released it to the owner with instructions that the healing could take weeks and to keep the bird calm and away from the water. We also scheduled a recheck and possible suture removal in a couple of weeks. As I recall, about a week later the owner called and informed me that the duck was doing great until he placed it back into the water and it died a couple of days later. I was devastated. The trachea is narrow, friable, easy to tear and difficult to repair surgically and young ambitious me was starting to feel a little prideful about my abilities. The owner informed me that the duck had been gotten rid of and was not available to do an autopsy. Probably a good thing for my prideful self. Most likely the deep tissues necrosed (died) and pulled away from the sutures placed in the trachea.

I kept the ducklings exclusively in my office until four weeks of age in a plastic storage container and then, during the day, placed them outside in a wire enclosure where they loved being on the lawn during the day and were protected from predators and the rays from the sun. My duties were cleaning the containers used by these very messy smelly animals. They need to drink water to help swallow food and love getting into their water bowl. I was often reminded by my wife that the offensive smell coming out of the office was going to be a short-term event. I also spent, what seemed like endless nights, planning how I was going to help these ducks mature enough to be released in our creek with little risk they would become a predator's easy meal.

Commercial duck food, grit, lettuce and dried meal worms were their diet. Mealworms are the larval form of the yellow mealworm beetle, Tenebrio molitor, a species of darkling beetle. They are edible, commonly consumed in various cultures, and are often praised for their nutritional value - high in protein, healthy fats, vitamins, and minerals. The European Union, for instance, has approved mealworms for human consumption. They can be consumed whole, dried, or processed into flour and incorporated into various dishes. Mealworms can be eaten whole, fried, roasted, or even alive. They can be processed into mealworm powder, which can be added to various foods to increase their protein content. The day may come when there will be wheat and meal flour powder sitting next to the sugar jar in our kitchens.

At six weeks of age, I moved the ducklings permanently outside into a covered dog run with a pond made out of a plastic tarp. Every time I was near the area I made "quack, quack, quack" sounds in hopes that they would know that I was their meal ticket after they were turned loose in our yard near the creek. Ducklings normally stay with their mother for about 8 weeks. During this time, they grow and develop, but are not yet capable of sustained flight. After the fledgling period, which ends around 2 months, the ducklings transition to the juvenile stage and at 7-10 weeks, their wings will fully develop allowing them to fly. Mallards reach full adulthood around 14 months of age. The "drake feather," develops a distinctive curled feather on the tail that appears when the duck transitions to its adult plumage, usually around 2 to 3 months of age. This coincides with the time when they also develop their adult flight feathers and other characteristic drake features. I noticed they were flying for short distances in the dog run and released them into our creek at just over 2 months of age.

Shortly after releasing the five ducklings, I noticed that three stayed close to the area and came on a consistent basis to twice daily feedings. Also, several days after release, I noticed one of the three ducks rapidly swimming across the creek to aggressively chase a duck away. It looked about the age of my ducks and, because it actively swam away from me, I thought the duck was a stranger. I had spent every day standing near the ducklings as they ate, cleaned their plastic crates and dog run, and they knew when I was coming into their area from my quack, quack, quacking. Since their release, the three ducks that stayed close, still came from the creek when I called. They even come to my back door to greet me whenever they thought it was time to eat.

For the first two weeks, after release, one or two of the other ducks showed up. They were much more cautious than the other three and kept their distance. At the time, I used a plastic oil drainage pan filled with food that I took from the house each time I fed the ducks, stayed close to them and took the food pan back in when they were finished. Each occasion, I noticed that when the other ducks showed up, they would not let me close to them and when they tried to eat one of the "three faithful ducks" ducks would chase them away from the food. Suspecting the "three faithful ducks" were hens, I did an AI search and found little about hen ducks being aggressive towards the drakes. One article, without stating male or female stated: "Nature's bird law regulates the peaceful coexistence of the duck flock. The number one bird in the flock can peck or dominate all others. The number two bird can dominate all others except the "top bird" and the number three bird can dominate all others except two." All other Mallard duck articles mentioned that aggressiveness from the drakes during mating season occurs when they have been known to even drown the hen during mating (of course by accident???).

A week later, five showed up for breakfast. I had added two food bowls with the "three faithful ducks" still playing musical chairs as they chased the other two ducks away. Then more ducks began showing up for my morning and evening offerings. So, I began adding four bowls of food. It reminded me of a principle I learned when raising my five children: "When you feed your children, their friends will come." The numbers of ducks arriving and chasing each other around the food bowls increased enough to where the only way I could count them was to take a photo with my phone. Just over two months after their release, (09/23/2025) the count reached 40 young adult looking Mallard ducks (see the photo below) chasing each other at the feeders. The numbers vary from 30 to 40 ducks each feeding and more were usually present in the morning. My dream is that one beautiful spring day a mother duck will show up at our patio with her ducklings all in a row looking for breakfast.

The first egg that started to hatch was the last one to emerge from the shell. It was also the largest duckling, recovered the slowest and couldn't control his feet enough to walk. The large webs of his feet looked frozen closed and could not be used. He mostly dragged his legs underneath him, wiggled his body back and forth to move and was nick named L.D. (Lame Duck). Attempts to teach him to swim was a complete failure. He would turn over like a top and could not right himself. He became weaker and I thought we were going to lose him. However, things improved when we found that he wasn't able to get his head high enough to drink water from the bowl. When held his head up to the water bowl for a few days he learned to drink on his own. To reduce competition, I isolated him from his siblings. He was eating but began constantly chirping from being isolated from the other ducklings. I added one of the siblings that was the smallest in the clutch into his pen and they did well together. Baby duck chirping generally indicates a need for something, such as food, warmth, or comfort. Chirping can also be a way for ducklings to communicate with their mother and siblings, or express excitement. Loud, rapid chirps might signal distress or a desire for attention, while softer peeps could indicate contentment.

The more I worked with the L.D. the more I wanted to help him overcome his diversities. He struggled but did not complain, he could not swim and probably would never fly, he could not survive in the world ducks are accustomed to living in, and the only help I could provide was to take care of his basic needs and protect him from the outside world.

I likened him to Job and Paul in the Bible. They both taught about suffering, faith, and God's plan for us all. Even in the face of immense suffering, one can maintain faith and trust in our Heavenly Father. Hardship doesn't always indicate punishment. It is important to have patience and compassion with ourselves and others when dealing with the limitations of life. There is a plan and we can find joy during all phases of our lives. Was I trying to help the duckling for me or him?

Members of the Church of Jesus Christ of Latter-day Saints believe that animals, like humans, have spirits, in the form of their bodies (D&C 77:2). Like humans and plants, animals were created first as spirits in heaven and then physically on the earth (Moses 3:5). Mortal and subject to death, animals will be saved through the Atonement of Christ (TPJS, pp. 291-92). Humans and animals will eventually live in peace on this earth (Isa. 11:6-9; 2 Ne. 30:12-15; D&C 101:24-26). The Prophet Joseph Smith taught that animals will be found in heaven, in myriad forms, from myriad worlds, enjoying eternal felicity, and praising God in languages God understands (TPJS, pp. 291-92).

Animal spirituality is the idea that animals, like humans, may have a sense of connection to the world beyond their physical existence. It suggests that they can experience emotions, awareness, and a connection to something greater, although not necessarily in a religious sense. Connecting with an animal spiritually involves recognizing and fostering a deep, meaningful relationship that extends beyond mere companionship. It's about appreciating the animal's unique perspective, learning from its behaviors, and acknowledging the spiritual bond that may exist.

This connection can be cultivated through observation, mindful interaction, and even meditation focused on the animal. Connecting with an animal spiritually involves recognizing and fostering a deep, meaningful relationship that extends beyond mere companionship. It's about appreciating the animal's unique perspective, learning from its behaviors, and acknowledging the spiritual bond that may exist. This connection can be cultivated through observation, mindful interaction, and even meditation focused on the animal.

We changed the name L.D. (Lame Duck), given by a friend of ours, to L.D. (Lords Disciple) because of the effect he was having on our lives. He did not live to maturity, but he was a faith-promoting experience in my life that buoyed my spiritual growth and increased my connection to the spirituality of animals I have felt many times during my career practicing veterinary medicine. A recent example occurred while showing the ducklings to a friend of mine, Dan Scudero, who has taught a couple of my grand-kids in school and cares for our swimming pool. He stated: "While cleaning a swimming pool I noticed baby ducklings swimming in the dipping pool that could not get out of the water. I spent time to build a ramp for the ducklings so they wouldn't drown." An often not noticed touching act of kindness, I like to think of as compassionate service, that often touches the giver more than the receiver.

I say to myself, "It's a wonder full world"

CHAPTER 18

ROCKS AND HARD PLACES

"Between a rock and a hard place" is an idiom (a form of figurative language, meaning there meaning goes beyond the literal definition of the words used) that describes a situation where one is faced with two equally difficult options, leaving them with no good choices. The origin of the phrase is often traced to ancient Greek mythology in Homer's Odyssey, where Odysseus had to navigate between the dangerous whirlpool Charybdis and the six-headed monster Scylla.

This phrase originated in the USA in the early part of the 20th century. It is the American manifestation of a phrase that exists in several forms in other cultures. The dilemma of being in a position where one is faced with two equally unwelcome options appears to lie deep in the human psyche. Language always reflects people's preoccupations and there are several phrases that express this predicament. The first of these quite literally conveys the uncomfortable nature of the choice between two lemmas (propositions), that is, "on the horns of a dilemma". Other phrases that compare two less than desirable alternatives are "the lesser of two evils", "between the devil and the deep blue sea", "between Scylla and Charybdis", "an offer you can't refuse" and "Hobson's choice" (a free choice in which only one thing is actually offered). *AI search*

Tom Ray found himself "between a rock and a hard place" in December of 1999. He later wrote: It started as stomach pains, and I thought I might have food poisoning, but then I began to deteriorate at a terrifying pace. I was violently sick, had blinding headaches, my skin grew mottled and pale, I became confused and anxious. It was like being run over by a truck – it was that fast. A later investigation found that the infection had been gained from a trip to the dentist when they nicked my mouth, coupled with a chest infection.

I remember when I first came out of the induced coma, after 5 months, startled and overwhelmed, I found myself in Cambridge, in the UK. I had lost my lower arms, lower legs, and half of my face from sepsis. I didn't know who I was, my memory had gone, I had to be re-introduced to my wife and family. At that point, no-one in the hospital was willing to confirm that I was going to survive – there was this sense that I was some kind of medical freak and that since they'd never had a patient survive sepsis with such severe amputations, I'd probably die of complications and never, ever make it home.

Well, it certainly hasn't been easy. Sepsis has been the challenge of my life, I've spent the last two decades battling to come to terms with radical change in my life, struggling to support my family and coping alone with serious post-traumatic stress.

I had painful surgery to reconstruct my face: They amputated my nose, lips and chin, so the surgeons tried to rebuild my face using grafts from my chest and shoulder.

It was a piecemeal failure. There were repeated attempts to re-line my nostrils and to create a nasal airway. The plastic surgeons did half the job, then gave up, telling me they could not re-instate my lips, or my chin. My nose was half reconstructed, and it's been left blocked. The terror of that facial surgery, much of it with only local anesthetic, stays with me to this day.

I have myoelectric hands provided free by the National Health Service. There are better prosthetics, but these are not available to me, because I cannot pay privately. I wish I could – you can get hands with fingers that articulate separately now, but they're not available to me. My prosthetic legs are painful to wear, ill fitting, and my stumps are often bleeding. I cannot walk very far in them at all.

Added: (Also, recurrent sepsis in amputees is a serious complication stemming from infections around the amputation site or, less commonly, from other sources. These infections can lead to septic shock and potentially require further amputations or other interventions. Preventing and managing these infections is crucial for the amputee's health and well-being. Military personnel are at increased risk of sepsis due to combat-related injuries that can lead to open wounds, severe infections, and trauma. In severe cases, sepsis can cause tissue death and gangrene, requiring amputation to prevent the spread of infection. Approximately 1% of sepsis survivors undergo amputation. The rate of major limb amputation in recent conflicts is reported to be around 5.2% of serious injuries and 7.4% of major limb injuries. This rate is similar to those seen in previous conflicts).

Sepsis (blood poisoning) is the body's extreme reaction to an infection. Sepsis is a twofold condition—first, the infection, and then the body's systemic (whole-body) immune response to the infection. The infection triggers a chain reaction throughout the body, leading to sepsis. The most common cause is bacterial infection. However, sepsis can also be caused by viruses, parasites, or fungal infections. Sepsis is a spectrum of infection. The sequence of severity usually starts as an uncomplicated bacterial infection in the bloodstream (bacteremia), which can lead to inflammation in the body (systemic inflammatory response syndrome). As organ damage and failure starts to occur (severe sepsis), blood pressure falls, decreasing blood flow and oxygen to the organs, leading to septic shock. Septic shock may continue to the point that the body begins to shut down, resulting in multiple organ dysfunction syndrome and death. Sepsis is a medical emergency and should be treated immediately, as it can quickly become life-threatening.

Sepsis is initially caused by an infection that reaches the bloodstream. The most common originating sites of the infection are the gastrointestinal (GI) tract, including the stomach and intestines, where bacteria and viruses can move from the GI tract into the bloodstream. Another possible cause includes a redness and swelling (inflammation) of the lining of the abdomen (peritonitis) caused by stomach or intestinal rupture from ulcers, trauma, or a foreign body causing blockage. Sepsis can also result from: Bacterial, viral, or fungal pneumonia in the respiratory tract; severe dental and periodontal disease can result in significant amounts of bacteria trapped in tartar, which can enter the bloodstream; severe or chronic kidney infection (pyelonephritis) or bladder infection (UTI); and skin wounds or burns that can become severely infected. AI & *Sepsis in Dogs, Veronica Higgs, DVM,03/16/2023.*

Depending on the source of the infection, some cases of sepsis require emergency surgery to correct the underlying condition. During practice as a veterinarian, my experiences with sepsis were mostly from bowel blockage or rupture and pyometra (infection of the uterus). During my first year in practice, I will never forget removing an infected uterus from an unspayed dog with a bloated abdomen resembling a near term pregnancy. During the removal of the enlarged hot friable infected uterus, it seemed to explode in my hands and foul-smelling pus splashed onto my surgical gown, surgical field and the floor. Needless to say, the dog was toxic enough with sepsis that it died under anesthetic before I finished closure of my surgical incision.

When you are in a position that appears to have you firmly stuck, without many options, the phrase that most likely came to your mind was that you were "stuck between a rock and a hard place." Being in a position where you must make a decision, but no matter what decision you make, it will be a painful or difficult one, is how being between a rock and a hard place feels.

Have you ever felt like you had just slipped through the cracks and no one noticed? It feels lonely there. It's hard and isolating. Sometimes, it becomes a way of life, especially if you question the status quo or have a creative mind or a wandering or entrepreneurial spirit. For instance, if you are not concerned about being politically correct because you prefer to have your own opinions, you may find yourself between a rock and a hard place if you are offered a much-needed job which might go against your questioning authority or questioning a culture, or a cultural belief can isolate you in many ways.

Trust me. I've been to this familiar place and finally resigned myself to the fact that this is the place where I live. Conforming to popular opinions has never been something I was known for.

This was a place I despised and cursed, complained and whined about. Living in this isolated place between hard and challenging decisions can be disheartening to those who are focused on how lonely or hard it is. At a time when most people are retiring and enjoying the fruits of their labors, I found myself rebuilding my life and future after several life challenges including divorce, bankruptcy, foreclosure, and betrayal by many who I had trusted more than I should.

What I learned as I healed, is that I had trusted others to determine my identity and worth and had allowed them to make decisions for me in the false hope that they would care for me as much as I cared for them. The lessons learned in a lifetime are many, and if we allow ourselves to be open to new perceptions, a great deal of the richness of life can and will be redeemed. The alternative is to regret and grieve for that which we believe we have lost.

During a season of hating that dreaded place of being in the middle of difficult decisions and desiring to be anywhere but where I was, my oldest son and his wife invited me to come and join them for a fun vacation at an aptly named resort by the name of Fun Valley. Many wonderful memories had been made there with their children and they wanted to include me in their next vacation. Once again, I found myself not being able to fully participate due to a broken toe, and a vehicle that was quickly falling apart and would be unsafe for the long drive. As luck would have it, my mechanic helped me make arrangements with a rental car, and my son purchased a walking stick for me when we arrived.

As I explored the place, I meditated on the many decisions I needed to make, and when there was a break between fishing and other family activities, I wandered down a trail that a family member had pointed me towards. There, in all of its glory, was the most magnificent tree that I've ever seen. Taller than any of the other trees on the mountain, this tree was located at the foot, and was STILL taller than the trees at the top! Its trunk was thick and its roots twisted and gigantic. My grandson, Jake, was with me on my adventure and started climbing up the roots towards the trunk, which he was not able to reach. As my eyes traveled upwards, I was struck with the amazing fact of why this tree was the healthiest tree on the mountain.

Most likely encased in bird excrement, or blown by the wind, a seed had fallen – you guessed it – between the rock and a hard place. All alone, protected from the storms that the other trees endured, this tree grew and grew. Taller and taller, it reached up towards the sky, it's roots and trunk supported on three sides with solid rock. This solid support had provided the tree with an opportunity to grow, unchallenged, in a way that none of the other trees had enjoyed!

A dear friend of mine is another person who stands out among the rest. Her life has been hard and isolating. Born deaf, her parents did not believe in teaching her sign language, but instead, insisted that she learn how to read lips. Her insights, observational skills, and discernment are unlike most people I have ever met. She has a deep curiosity and an ability to focus in order to read lips of those speaking … and in observing other signals, such as body language and vibrations that others never notice.

She enlightened me regarding her unique positioning by saying, "I'm deaf, but do not belong in the deaf community because I do not sign. I am deaf and do not belong in the hearing world." Her rock and a hard place are very real … and her strength, compassion, and wisdom are strong and intuitive.

Not only that, she is a Messianic Jew. Her genetic birth is as a Jew, but because of her faith, she is not accepted among many Jewish people. Among traditional Christians, she is not a part of their community either because she has a deep love for Jewish culture and history that they are curious of, but do not comprehend.

As I watch her interact with people, explore the world around her fearlessly, and ask carefully crafted questions that are succinct and insightful, I am amazed at her strong "root system" and how she stands out among all others because she grew where she was planted. She is an artist too and loves to throw pots on a potter's wheel, as well as creating mosaics and other works of art that visually speak of what she senses in her heart and spirit. I treasure her friendship and am so grateful for her presence in my life.

I dedicate this blog post to her and give her the gift of a new perception of where she was placed on this planet – just as I was given this gift a summer ago. No longer cursing my life among hard places, I'm thrilled that life has challenged me and strengthened me. What a rare gift to have been chosen to grow … between a rock and a hard place so that

I could grow tall and strong, supported by the challenges of life, gifted by their lessons and wisdom. *Are you tired of being stuck between a rock and a hard place? Shannon Parish, 06/06/2017.*

Tom Ray continues: My greatest achievement in the last two decades since I became severely disabled is to have kept my family together. I'm so very proud of this. It's meant that I have had to develop huge reserves of resilience, showing profound understanding of the needs of those close to me, and compromising at every turn. I've not had a single minute of counselling - I've had to manage on my own. My top priority has been to be a good Dad for my beautiful children, and to minimize the impact of my traumatic disability on my wife. I'm a much more considerate person these days. Everything changed for me when I started to appreciate that what had happened to me affected everyone around me, and I had to work hard to mitigate the impact as much as possible. Once I realized that I could control the way I felt, by being very disciplined, I became empowered.

Going back to work was instrumental in this respect. It gave me routine, something external to distract me, and a new network outside of my own situation. I work in a Call Centre, and although the work is low paid and well below my skill level (I have a postgraduate degree), the job has sustained me to some extent. I have also built a business as an inspirational speaker on Resilience & Managing Change, and I give keynote addresses at large events. I love doing this, I get fantastic feedback, and audiences find my story of recovery and resilience inspiring. By spreading the word about sepsis, I feel I am helping to save lives. A feature film has been made about what happened to me. It's called

Starfish (trailer on YouTube), and it's been shown in cinemas right across the world. I wrote a book to accompany it. *Written by Tom Ray & is shared here with his explicit consent, Marvin Zick, 08/20/2019.*

Dr. Seuss, in his infinitely wise and whimsical way, also attested to your better-than-you-know abilities and we don't need to spend our life between a rock and a hard place. He wrote: And when you're alone, there's a very good chance you'll meet things that scare you right out of your pants. There are some, down the road between hither and yon, that can scare you so much you won't want to go on…

So be sure when you step. Step with care and great tact and remember that Life's a Great Balancing Act… And will you succeed? Yes! You will, indeed! (98 and ¾ percent guaranteed.) Kid, you'll move mountains!… Today is your day! Your mountain is waiting. So… get on your way! *Dr. Seuss, Oh, the Places You'll Go!*

CHAPTER 19

JOY AND PEACE

Scottie Scheffler, as of 2025, is the No. 1 golfer in the world who's on the brink of a tournament that could eventually lead the 29-year-old to a career Grand Slam, told reporters at Royal Portrush Golf Club on Tuesday that he, despite his success in the sport, doesn't equate being at the top of his game with a "fulfilling life."

Speaking from The Open Championship in Northern Ireland he stated: "Is it great to be able to win tournaments and to accomplish the things I have in the game of golf? Yeah, it brings tears to my eyes just to think about because I've literally worked my entire life to be good at this sport. But at the end of the day, I'm not out here to inspire the next generation of golfers. I'm not out here to inspire someone to be the best player in the world because what's the point? This is not a fulfilling life. It's fulfilling from the sense of accomplishment, but it's not fulfilling from a sense of the deepest places of your heart."

The man who won two Masters green jackets, the Wanamaker Trophy at the PGA Championship, three Jack Nicklaus Awards as PGA Tour player of the year and the FedEx Cup, was clear in his message: Despite all the winning he's done, the success feels fleeting and isn't truly filling up his cup. "You win it, you celebrate, get to hug my family, my sister's there, it's such an amazing moment. Then it's like, 'OK, what are we going to eat for dinner?' Life goes on. It feels like you work your whole life to celebrate winning a tournament for like a few minutes. It only lasts a few minutes."

That doesn't mean Scheffler embraces losing, however. "It sucks (losing). I hate it, I really do. We work so hard for such little moments. I'm kind of sick, of; I love putting in the work, I love getting to practice, I love getting to live out my dreams. But at the end of the day, sometimes I just don't understand the point.

I love the challenge. I love being able to play this game for a living. It's one of the greatest joys of my life. But does it fill the deepest wants and desires of my heart? Absolutely not."

His soliloquy echoes comments, he's often made in the past, insisting that golf does not define him as a person. He said Tuesday that if it reached the point where the sport ever affected life at home, "that's going to be the last day that I play out here for a living. That's something that I wrestle with on a daily basis about the more unfulfilling aspects of the game. It's like showing up at the Masters every year. Why do I want to win this golf tournament so badly? Why do I want to win The Open Championship so badly? I don't know, because if I win, it's going to be awesome for two minutes."

When the mother of my children was diagnosed with terminal cancer, I found myself in a situation like Scheffler's "what if" of leaving golf if it affected life at home. I also wrestled what I should do on a daily basis concerning how unfulfilling the aspects of veterinarian medicine were compared to spending 24/7 with the last days of my wife. I proposed selling my practice and placing veterinary medicine on hold. She wisely told me that was a really, really stupid idea.

I was able to mostly be with her during her time of need and it would have been a bad idea. My youngest son decided to become a veterinarian, which would have made that choice much more difficult for him to achieve. I never knew if she had discussed our son's intentions with him before she told me not to "sell the ranch" and to continue practice.

During a Brigham Young University graduation devotional on 06/13/1995, W. Mack Lawrence a Second Quorum of the Seventy, made these comments: When first asked if I would accept this invitation to be with you today, the thought rushed through my mind: What could I say that would be helpful, that would cause students to pause and to think? One of my outstanding teachers—an English teacher, once said that the only goal we had all year long was to learn to think.

In this quest, and after prayerful consideration, it came to me that we're all looking for happiness and joy—wherever we are, whatever our past. The pursuit of happiness has been a dream of all people from the time of Adam and Eve. It's a founding principle of this great country of ours. The Declaration of Independence declares that among our inalienable rights are "life, liberty, and the pursuit of happiness."

How would you define happiness?

Dale Carnegie in his book How to Win Friends People said, "Happiness doesn't depend on outward conditions. It depends on inner conditions. It isn't what you have or who you are or where you are or what you are doing that makes you happy or unhappy. It is what you think about." In simple terms, a righteous life is the way—the only way—to happiness, joy, and peace. As one of our hymns reminds us, "Choose the right! There is peace in righteous doing." If there be a theme to my remarks, it is found in the Book of Mormon, 2 Nephi 2:25: "Men are, that they might have joy."1

Happiness is a fleeting, emotional state often described as a feeling of joy, pleasure, or contentment. It is typically a response to a specific event or stimulus and can be triggered by sensory experiences, social interactions, or positive outcomes influenced by external factors. Satisfaction is a more enduring feeling of contentment derived from achieving goals or feeling a sense of fulfillment in one's life. Essentially, happiness is a temporary emotional high, while satisfaction is a deeper, more lasting sense of well-being.

Joy and satisfaction, while related, are distinct emotional experiences. Joy is a deeper, more profound emotion often linked to meaningful experiences, relationships, or a sense of purpose, and it can be a more sustained feeling. Joy is often described as a more profound, lasting emotion that can be tied to a sense of purpose and connection. It can be triggered by meaningful experiences, relationships, or a sense of awe and wonder. Joy is often associated with feelings of inner peace, contentment, and a sense of well-being.

Peace and joy, while both positive emotions, differ in their nature. Joy is often associated with excitement, happiness, and a sense of delight, while peace is linked to calmness, tranquility, and the absence of conflict. Joy is frequently experienced as a more fleeting, reactive emotion, while peace can be a more stable, enduring state. Joy is often triggered by external events, experiences, or achievements. It can be intense and fleeting, like the joy of receiving a gift or achieving a goal. It can be influenced by circumstances, may not be present during difficult times, and may involve a sense of elation, excitement, and happiness. Peace is often described as a deeper, more enduring state of inner calm and tranquility. It can be cultivated through practices like mindfulness, meditation, and spiritual growth. It may be present even during challenging times, providing a sense of stability and resilience. It can involve a sense of harmony, wholeness, and freedom from worry or anxiety. Joy is often a response to something good happening. It's like the spark of excitement when you receive a pleasant surprise. Peace is more like a steady flame, a sense of inner well-being that can be present regardless of external circumstances. It's a state of being rather than a reaction to an event. While distinct, joy and peace can be interconnected. Experiencing joy can contribute to a sense of peace, and cultivating peace can create a foundation for experiencing joy more deeply. *AI*

Elder Joseph B. Wirthlin taught in his general conference address, Running Your Marathon, in October 1989: Our Heavenly Father knows the way for you (and me) to enjoy happiness and peace; the principles of the gospel mark the way. They are (His) gift to (each of us). On the other hand, Satan will try, at every step of the way, to lead (us) off course. His objective is to make you (and me) unhappy and miserable like he is. (2Nephi 2:27) (Maybe that's the source of the oft-heard phrase "Misery loves company.") Vast sums of money are spent each year to package and disguise sin and evil to make them appear enticing, attractive, even harmless. However, regardless of appearances, "wickedness never was happiness" (Alma 41:10) and never will be. Never find yourselves in the position of the Nephites just a few years before the birth of the Savior. They "sought . . . for that which (they) could not obtain; . . . for happiness in doing iniquity, which thing is contrary to the nature of that righteousness which is in our great and Eternal Head." (Hel. 13:38) You cannot find happiness in sin and iniquity. The Lord has given (us) the gift of agency (Moses 7:32) and instructed (us) sufficiently to know good from evil (2 Nephi 2:5). (We) are free to choose (2Nephi 2:27) and (we) are permitted to act (2Nephi 10:23; Hel. 14:30 10), but (we) are not free to choose the consequences. With absolute certainty, choices of good and right lead to happiness and peace, while choices of sin and evil eventually lead to unhappiness, sorrow, and misery.

Another prophet, President Ezra Taft Benson, in 1977 taught: You cannot do wrong and feel right. It is impossible! Years of happiness can be lost in the foolish gratification of a momentary desire for pleasure. Satan would have you believe that happiness comes only as you surrender to his enticements, but one only needs to look at the shattered lives of those who violate God's laws to know why Satan is called the Father of Lies.

My second point of emphasis is to know that enduring happiness comes from what we really are—our thoughts, our deeds of service, the decisions we make—and not from possessions, positions, or prominence. In this world of ours, society places an undue emphasis on the wrong things. As a result, we sometimes seek to measure success—even happiness—by material goods. This is not a true measure! It is so temporary. What matters most is the happiness and joy that comes from living the gospel of Jesus Christ. The laws of God are given for our happiness.

A third point I should like to emphasize is that we should be cheerful in the face of adversity. Just think of these words Joseph Smith wrote to the persecuted and suffering Saints while he himself languished as a prisoner in Liberty Jail: "Therefore, dearly beloved brethren, let us cheerfully do all things that lie in our power" (D&C 123:17). The Saints had been driven from the comforts of their homes and were scattered on the plains of Missouri. The Prophet himself was in jail, facing death—a time in his life when he may have been discouraged, concerned, unhappy. But what did he say? "Therefore, dearly beloved brethren, let us cheerfully do all things that lie in our power."

Happy people are of a cheerful countenance. The Lord has frequently admonished us to "be of good cheer" (John 16:33, D&C 61:36). The Lord has also declared, "Wherefore, lift up thy heart and rejoice, and cleave unto the covenants which thou hast made" (D&C 25:13). Commenting on this verse, President Gordon B. Hinckley said during a talk, "If Thou Art Faithful" in 1984: I believe he is saying to each of us, be happy. The gospel is a thing of joy. It provides us with a reason for gladness. Of course there are times of sorrow. Of course, there are hours of concern and anxiety. We all worry. But the Lord has told us to lift our hearts and rejoice. I see so many people, . . . who seem never to see the sunshine, but who constantly walk with storms under cloudy skies. Cultivate an attitude of happiness. Cultivate a spirit of optimism. Walk with faith, rejoicing in the beauties of nature, in the goodness of those you love, in the testimony which you carry in your heart concerning things divine.

The next point I would like to emphasize is that it is important to distinguish between the pursuit of happiness and the pursuit of pleasure. Sometimes we get so mixed up in our pursuit of happiness that we settle for pleasure. Pleasure is so short-lived. It is here one moment and gone in almost the next breath.

In this respect, consider these observations on the difference between pleasure and happiness by the scholar and apostle Elder James E. Talmage in his book "Jesus the Christ" 1916: The present is an age of pleasure-seeking, and men are losing their sanity in the mad rush for sensations that do but excite and disappoint. In this day of counterfeits, adulterations, and base imitations, the devil is busier than he has ever been in the course of human history, in the manufacture of pleasures, both old and new; and these he offers for sale in most attractive fashion, falsely labeled, Happiness. . . Happiness includes all that is really desirable and of true worth in pleasure, and much beside. Happiness is genuine gold, pleasure but gilded brass. . . Happiness is as the genuine diamond, which, rough or polished, shines with its own inimitable luster; pleasure is as the paste imitation that glows only when artificially embellished. Happiness is as the ruby, red as the heart's blood, hard and enduring; pleasure, as stained glass, soft, brittle, and of but transitory beauty. . . Happiness leaves no bad after-taste, it is followed by no depressing reaction; it calls for no repentance, brings no regret, entails no remorse; pleasure too often makes necessary repentance, contrition, and suffering; and, if indulged to the extreme, it brings degradation and destruction.

Furthermore, there is an even higher level of happiness. Lehi declared, "Men (speaking generically to include women) are, that they might have joy" (2 Nephi 2:25). In 1991, in a talk entitled "Joy and Mercy", Elder Dallin H. Oaks stated: Joy is more than happiness. Joy is the ultimate sensation of well-being. It comes from being complete and in harmony with our Creator and his eternal laws. The opposite of joy is misery. Misery is more than unhappiness, sorrow, or suffering. Misery is the ultimate state of disharmony with God and his laws.1

An unknown author once wrote: "People will not remember you for what you said or what you did. They will remember you because of how you made them feel. Life's travels are your call: First, I was dying to finish my high school and start college. And, then I was dying to finish college and start working. Then, I was dying to marry and have children. And, I was dying for my children to grow old so...I could go back to work. But then I was dying to retire. And, now I am dying. And suddenly I realize I forgot to live.

Please don't let this happen to you. Appreciate your current situation and enjoy each MOMENT...Old Friend.

Arthur Rubinstein, the great pianist, made this observation in his book "My Young Years": Most people, in my opinion, have an unrealistic approach toward happiness because they invariably use the fatal conjunction "if" as a condition. You hear them say: I would be happy if I were rich, or if this girl loved me, or if I had talent, or, their most popular "if": if I had good health. They often attain their goal, but they discover soon some new "ifs." . . . As for myself, I love life for better or for worse, unconditionally." John 14:27 declares, "Peace I leave with you; my peace I give you. I do not give to you as the world gives. Do not let your hearts be troubled and do not be afraid."

CHAPTER 20

MOTHER'S DAY TALK

Did you hear the news last week? It was BIG!! At the age of 94 and after 60 years at the helm, the legendary investor, the Oracle of Ohama, Warren Buffet announced that he is stepping down as CEO of Berkshire Hathaway at the end of this year. The news made headlines everywhere. Now if you don't know, Warren Buffet is considered one of the greatest investors of all time, but I disagree and there is someone better and I'm here to tell you who.

But before we get into why, good morning, brothers and sisters, and happy Mother's Day. I want to say thank you—thank you to every woman here who has nurtured, lifted, and carried someone else's burdens. Whether you are a mother in the traditional sense or you've "mothered" through ministering, teaching, or simply being there for someone in need—you are loved and appreciated. Thank you to our wonderful primary and youth for their singing. And Sister Pieper and Isabella for their inspirational words.

Now getting back to Mr. Buffet. He wasn't always considered the greatest investor. He started as a lowly student, a disciple of Benjamin Graham, an economist and professor at Columbia University who is often called the "father of value investing." Buffet used what he learned about investing to earn a remarkable compound return over his 60-year run—a return of 5,502,284%. To put that into perspective, the broad market earned 39,054% over the same period.

Warren Buffet wasn't just any investor; he used a specific style of investing called value investing. In value investing, you don't chase the flashiest stocks. It's not about short-term profits or quick gains. You look for something overlooked or misunderstood—something with strong fundamentals that, over time, you believe will prove its worth. It's not glamorous. It takes patience. It takes faith in something that's not paying off right away.

Does that not sound like motherhood? We live in a world where people chase immediate rewards. They love the instant validation from likes, shares, comments on their social media posts. In some sense I think it is natural because people crave feedback: we want recognition at work, visible progress in our goals, and that constant sense of movement.

But motherhood doesn't work that way. Motherhood often lacks the instant feedback, those instant returns. There are no performance reviews for diaper changes or bonuses for bedtime stories. No trophies for late-night feedings. No awards for being patient with your teenager. There are years—sometimes decades—where the returns seem invisible. Instead, motherhood is about patiently investing love, effort, and faith, often without visible rewards. And like value investing, the rewards come quietly, steadily, and eventually. It just takes time.

Market investors expect volatility. They understand that even excellent investments experience downturns. Likewise, mothers navigate similar volatility. Children's developmental stages create natural inflections in the mother-child relationship. The toddler who clings adoringly to Mom becomes the teenager who wants to get dropped off two blocks from the school so nobody sees her. The child who once shared everything with Mom suddenly keeps secrets and locks their bedroom door. During these downturns, the world might suggest selling—withdrawing emotional investment to protect against rejection or hurt. But mothers hold steady, recognizing these fluctuations as normal market conditions rather than fundamental failures.

Value investing takes time. Elder Dieter F. Uchtdorf said: "In family relationships, love is really spelled t-i-m-e, time. Mothers invest lots of time in their families, but the time investment rarely pays immediate dividends. The hours spent building block towers with toddlers, attending middle school band concerts, or waiting up for teenagers that are immersed in social media-style dopamine hits. Their investments is in bonds that mature over decades."[2]

A study out of Brigham Young University tracked family religious practices and the correlation with youth faith development: The study found that it wasn't grand spiritual experiences that most predicted children's future religious commitment. Rather, it was consistent family prayer, regular scripture study, and parents who modeled quiet devotion in everyday settings.

The small, cumulative investments—reading a verse or two of scripture with the family, saying a prayer before bedtime with a child after a long day, listening attentively to the fourteenth recounting of playground politics, maintaining composure when a teenager pushes boundaries—may seem insignificant in isolation. But compounded over years, they yield remarkable returns in children's character, resilience, and spiritual depth. And luckily for us, these are the types of time investments mothers make every day.[3]

Unfortunately, they often go unnoticed. When it comes to showing love, mothers put in the t-i-m-e, time!

Value investing requires sacrifice, giving up something today for a greater reward in the future. Mothers know a thing or two about sacrifice and the mother of Moses is a great example. In Exodus 2:3 we read that when Pharaoh commanded all the Hebrew baby boys to be killed, she hid her son for three months. And then she did something unimaginable: "She took for him an ark of bulrushes... and laid it in the flags by the river's brink." That's it. That's all she could do. She couldn't protect him forever. She couldn't raise him under her own roof. But she trusted God enough to release her child into His hands. And what happened? He never forgot his roots and that he was raised briefly by a faithful mother. Years later, that same boy would lead an entire nation out of captivity. This mother's brief, faithful investment yielded deliverance for millions. That is value investing. That is motherhood. And what happened? He never forgot his roots and that he was raised briefly by a faithful mother. Years later, that same boy would lead an entire nation out of captivity. This mother's brief, faithful investment yielded deliverance for millions. That is value investing. That is motherhood.

In value investing, they often talk about the long view; It means ignoring short-term movements. It means not panicking when the price dips. It means sticking with something because you believe in the outcome. Mothers have the ultimate "long view" because motherhood extends beyond mortality. In a social media post President Camille N. Johnson, Relief Society General President, shared that the word motherhood defines women's eternal roles; it describes their nature as nurturers. This eternal perspective helps us see that motherhood isn't just about raising children—it's about participating in God's work of salvation.

When Eve made the courageous choice to partake of the fruit, she did so with an eternal perspective. Were it not for our transgression, she said, "we never should have had seed, and never should have known good and evil, and the joy of our redemption, and the eternal life which God giveth unto all the obedient. Eve's motherhood began not with bearing children, but with choosing a path that would allow all of God's children to progress. Her vision extended beyond her immediate circumstances to encompass the entire plan of salvation. This is the divine pattern of motherhood—seeing beyond the present moment to eternal possibilities. Moses 5:11

This principle of delayed returns isn't new. In Doctrine and Covenants section 64:33, the Lord counsels: Wherefore, be not weary in well-doing, for ye are laying the foundation of a great work. And out of small things proceedeth that which is great. This verse doesn't promise immediate results. Instead, it acknowledges that we're often just laying the foundation—a phase that involves significant effort with little visible progress. The phrase be not weary, suggests this foundation-laying period might be lengthy and potentially discouraging. This passage speaks directly to those seasons when mothering feels like pouring endless love, counsel, and care into an account that shows no immediate growth.

Now, to the mothers who feel like your investment isn't yielding results: don't despair. Maybe your child has wandered. Maybe your home is full of tension. Maybe your offering feels small compared to what others seem to be doing. I want to remind you: Your efforts, no matter how small, matter immensely. The Savior Jesus Christ specializes in turning small offerings into eternal miracles—just ask the boy who shared his five loaves and two small fishes and watched Jesus feed thousands! Small things. Great works. That's the Lord's pattern.

In Warren Buffet's words: "Someone's sitting in the shade today because someone planted a tree a long time ago." For all of us who are sitting in the proverbial shade today because of a tree that was planted long ago and nourished, nurtured, and cared for by loving mothers, let's celebrate mothers everywhere—patient, loving, wise investors whose quiet devotion builds lasting legacies of faith and love.

So, who are the greatest investors of all time, mothers of course because the returns on their investments are infinite. In closing, I bear my testimony that the work of motherhood is holy. That Jesus Christ, the Master Investor in all of us, lives, He knows each of us, and He magnifies your efforts. In the name of Jesus Christ, amen.[1]

Jeffery R. Holland commented: A wonderful young mother recently wrote to me: "How is it that a human being can love a child so deeply that you willingly give up a major portion of your freedom for it? How can mortal love be so strong that you voluntarily subject yourself to responsibility, vulnerability, anxiety, and heartache and just keep coming back for more of the same? What kind of mortal love can make you feel, once you have a child, that your life is never,

ever your own again? Maternal love has to be divine. There is no other explanation for it. What mothers do is an essential element of Christ's work. Knowing that should be enough to tell us the impact of such love will range between unbearable and transcendent, over and over again, until with the safety and salvation of the very last child on earth, we can [then] say with Jesus, '[Father!] I have finished the work which thou gavest me to do.'"4

1 Sheldon McFarland, Almaden Valley Ward, San Jose, CA – Sunday 2025 Mother's Day Talk.

2 Uchtdorf, Dieter F. "Of Things That Matter Most." General Conference, The Church of Jesus Christ of Latter-Day Saints, Oct. 2010.

3 Dollahite, David C., and Jennifer Y. Thatcher. "Talking About Religion: How Highly Religious Youth and Parents Discuss Their Faith."

4 Behold Thy Mother, Elder Jeffrey R. Holland-Quorum of the Twelve Apostles, General Conference, Church of Jesus Christ of Latter-Day Saints, Oct 2015.

CHAPTER 21

TOUCHED BY THE SPIRIT...

Recently attending a Sacrament Meeting the speaker, a hobby airplane pilot - John Tanner, related an experience he had with his oldest son when he reserved an airplane for a pleasure flight in 1998. As I recall, they left for the airport in plenty of time to fill out the required rental paper work, record a flight plan, do a plane visual and "kick the tires." On their way to the airport, three things came up that John had "feelings" they should get done before they got to the airport. One I remember was simply stopping to get some food they could eat on the plane.

Upon arrival, they were informed that the plane they had reserved was given to another party. John was a bit annoyed that the airport had not properly reserved the plane for them and held it for their use. The rest of his story brought to my mind two incidents that have had an effect on my life:

– My five children were mostly still at home and our oldest had two young children. We had assembled to celebrate the fourth of July, had enjoyed a full course meal, were lazily visiting and nearing nap time in our sunken family room. From a mostly restricted view, I happened to glance out our patio's closed sliding door window and noticed a slight ripple on the swimming pool water. My immediate thought was that we hadn't felt an earth quake so the ripple must be from another rat falling into the pool. I would check on it later. Then an indescribable, silent and urgent impulse prompted me to "check out the swimming pool." I challenged the feeling for a short time and then with somewhat irritated effort made my way to the door. To my horror, my grand-daughter Makaila, with a diaper filled with water, was in the pool and about to go off the step into the deeper water. I got to her before she took any water into her lungs and the event became a nonevent that her parents hadn't remembered until years later. She is now 24 and planning a wedding in April of 2025.

— I later had a fence placed around the pool that could be removed for swimming. Removing the fence always reminded me about how we almost lost Makaila and another later event when the pool fence had been left down. My son, Jeremy, and I found our Labrador Retriever, Cinder, floating under the pool cover one fall morning and it took a lot of effort pulling her water drenched body out of the pool. I still try not to imagine how long, a good swimmer like most labs, she had struggled under that pool cover before taking in enough water into her lungs to drown. Why the impulse to save Makaila and not an impulse to check on Cinder before taking out her breakfast the next day?

On the evening of 29 December, 1972 when 163 passengers and 13 crewmembers boarded Eastern Airlines flight 401 to travel from New York's JFK to Florida's Miami International Airport (MIA). For the majority of the time, the flight was an uneventful one, with three members of the flight crew successfully navigating the flight to the skies above Florida. Ready to descend to the runway of MIA, the pilots moved the landing gear into position so they could land safely. But when they did, they realized the green light which indicated the gear was locked into place did not light up. The pilots contracted the control tower at MIA, who instructed them to maintain an altitude of 2,000 feet before attempting to land again once they'd figured out the issue. The three men in charge of the plane engaged its autopilot system and set about trying to figure out why the light was not coming on. And in the dark night, they struggled to determine whether the issue was with the landing gear itself.

In a transcript from the radio, one said: "I can't see it, it's pitch dark and I throw the little light, I get, ah, nothing." A few moments later, the staff at the control tower heard the first officer say: "We did something to the altitude." Loft replied, "What?," before Stockstill asked: "We're still at two thousand right?"

As they'd attempted to figure out why the light was not coming on, the pilots didn't realize that the plane's autopilot feature had disengaged. The plane had dropped rapidly, causing the pilot to say: "Hey, what's happening here?" Seconds later, Flight 401 crashed into swamplands of the Florida Everglades.

Bud Marquis, who was hunting frogs with a friend at the time, witnessed the bright flash as the plane hit the ground, and was the first to arrive at the scene. "I'm one person in the midst of all this," he told NBC News in 2007. "I'm no doctor. I didn't know what to do."

A total of 94 passengers and five crew members died at the scene, while the rest of the survivors struggled in the swamp water, which was now contaminated with jet fuel. Dozens of people were taken to hospital after the crash, with another two people losing their lives in the aftermath. An investigation into the crash determined that the pilots had been preoccupied by the light, and therefore hadn't noticed the plane descending. The investigation determined that the issue was not with the landing gear after all.

Instead, it was simply that the lightbulb used to indicate it was locked in place, which was worth about $12, had burned out.[1]

The airplane John and his son was to be flying in 1998 turned up missing, crashed and recently an updated report was found in the Half Moon Bay Review: "A search has been called off for four people who are believed to have died when their plane crashed in the ocean Friday night after take-off from Half Moon Bay Airport. Robert Beach, 36, of Fremont, who rented a single-engine Piper Arrow plane at Reid-Hillview Airport in San Jose early Friday, has been reported missing. The plane is believed to have been carrying three passengers and the four had reportedly flown from San Jose to Half Moon Bay for dinner.

On Monday, a recently severed foot still wearing a tennis shoe, and an airplane headset washed up near San Gregorio State Beach. The items were discovered by passers-by. Also on Saturday, a fisherman found an airplane seat floating one nautical mile off of Miramontes Point. According to the

Sheriff's Office, at 9:21 p.m. Friday night, it received several reports of a plane in trouble. Callers, whose hometowns were not identified, reported hearing a plane sputtering and seeing lights spiraling into the water. One caller reported that a plane almost hit a restaurant, which was not named.

An airplane rental company located at Reid-Hillview reported one of its airplanes missing on Saturday. Beach did not file a flight plan, but told the plane's owner that he was flying to Half Moon Bay for dinner. The Coast Guard confirmed Beach had a valid pilot's license. An employee at Half Moon Bay Airport told deputies that he flew in earlier in the evening and then taxied over to the Princeton side of the airport. Shortly before 9 p.m. Beach flew out of Half Moon Bay Airport. The Coast Guard initiated helicopter searches Friday night, Saturday, Sunday and part of Monday, before being called off Monday afternoon."[2]

During John's Sacrament Meeting talk, he mentioned that years later his wife introduced him to the Gospel of Jesus Christ. During his study and praying he learned to recognized where those "feelings" came from during his travel to the airport with his son in 1998. Elder Richard G. Scott brings these feelings more to light during a General Conference in October 2009:

Throughout the ages, many have obtained guidance helpful to resolve challenges in their lives by following the example of respected individuals who resolved similar problems. Today, world conditions change so rapidly that such a course of action is often not available to us. Personally, I rejoice in that reality because it creates a condition where we, of necessity, are more dependent upon the Spirit to guide us through the vicissitudes of life. Therefore, we are led to seek personal inspiration in life's important decisions. What can you do to enhance your capacity to be led to correct decisions in your life? What are the principles upon which spiritual communication depends? What are the potential barriers to such communication that you need to avoid?

President John Taylor wrote: "Joseph Smith, upwards of forty years ago, said to me: 'Brother Taylor, you have received the Holy Ghost. Now follow the influence of that Spirit, and it will lead you into all truth, until by and by, it will become in you a principle of revelation.' Then he told me never to arise in the morning without bowing before the Lord, and dedicating myself to him during that day."

Father in Heaven knew that you would face challenges and be required to make some decisions that would be beyond your own ability to decide correctly. In His plan of happiness, He included a provision for you to receive help with such challenges and decisions during your mortal life. That assistance will come to you through the Holy Ghost as spiritual guidance. It is a power, beyond your own capability, that a loving Heavenly Father wants you to use consistently for your peace and happiness.

I am convinced that there is no simple formula or technique that would immediately allow you to master the ability to be guided by the voice of the Spirit. Our Father expects you to learn how to obtain that divine help by exercising faith in Him and His Holy Son, Jesus Christ. Were you to receive inspired guidance just for the asking, you would become weak and ever more dependent on Them. They know that essential personal growth will come as you struggle to learn how to be led by the Spirit.

What may appear initially to be a daunting task will be much easier to manage over time as you consistently strive to recognize and follow feelings prompted by the Spirit. Your confidence in the direction you receive from the Holy Ghost will also become stronger. I witness that as you gain experience and success in being guided by the Spirit, your confidence in the impressions you feel can become more certain than your dependence on what you see or hear.

Spirituality yields two fruits. The first is inspiration to know what to do. The second is power, or the capacity to do it. These two capacities come together. That's why Nephi could say, "I will go and do the things which the Lord hath commanded." He knew the spiritual laws upon which inspiration and power are based. Yes, God answers prayer and gives us spiritual direction when we live obediently and exercise the required faith in Him.

Impressions of the Spirit can come in response to urgent prayer or unsolicited when needed. Sometimes the Lord reveals truth to you when you are not actively seeking it, such as when you are in danger and do not know it. However, the Lord will not force you to learn. You must exercise your agency to authorize the Spirit to teach you. As you make this a practice in your life, you will be more perceptive to the feelings that come with spiritual guidance. Then, when that guidance comes, sometimes when you least expect it, you will recognize it more easily.

The inspiring influence of the Holy Spirit can be overcome or masked by strong emotions, such as anger, hate, passion, fear, or pride. When such influences are present, it is like trying to savor the delicate flavor of a grape while eating a jalapeño pepper. Both flavors are present, but one completely overpowers the other. In like manner, strong emotions overcome the delicate promptings of the Holy Spirit.

Sin is addictive; self-degenerating; conducive to other strains of corruption; deadening to spirituality, conscience, and reason; blinding to reality; contagious; destructive to mind, body, and spirit. Sin is spiritually corrosive. Unrestrained it becomes all-consuming. It is overcome by repentance and righteousness.[3]

The cause 1972 plane crash was reported as 'the failure of the flight crew to monitor the flight instruments during the final 4 minutes of flight, and to detect an unexpected descent soon enough to prevent impact with the ground', according to the National Transportation Safety Board (NTSB). "Preoccupation with a malfunction of the nose landing gear position indicating system distracted the crew's attention from the instruments and allowed the descent to go unnoticed."

The NTSB added that it was possible the altitude hold function on the autopilot had been accidentally disengaged, causing the plane to descend while the pilots were trying to figure out the issue with the light.

A number of safety enhancements were developed after the plane crash, including a system which alerts pilots if an aircraft is in immediate danger of flying into the ground or an obstacle.

Ninety-nine people died in what remains to be one of the worst air disasters in South Florida history, and it all came down to a lightbulb worth just $12. Eastern Airlines continued to operate for almost two decades, eventually ceasing its operations early in 1991. Was the Holy Spirit's inspiration overcome from the strong emotions of the flight crew? Was it there but not heeded?

The flight John and his son were scheduled to take in 1998 was not meant to be. Knowing John's family, I'm sure the Lord had more work for him to do before he is called home. I had the opportunity to attend John's special son's, Matthew Smith, birthday celebration and baptism into the Church of Jesus Christ of Latter-Day Saints on February 8, 2025. The next day, he received the gift of the Holy Ghost during Fast and Testimony Meeting. Matthew is a wonderful story during his first eighteen years of life and I suspect as John and his wife experience Matthew's future it will be obvious why God preserved John and his oldest son from that fatal crash in 1998.

1   One of the worst air disasters in US history was caused by a $12 lightbulb, Emily Brown, 10/16/2023.

2   Plane feared lost at sea, Half Moon Bay Review, Eric Rich, (updated 08/13/2024) 5/28/1998.

3   To Acquire Spiritual Guidance, Elder Richard G. Scott, General Conference, SLC Utah, October 2009.

CHAPTER 22

THE MAN WITH THE GOLDEN ARM

James Christopher Harrison was born on December, 27 1936. In 1951, at the age of 14, he underwent major chest surgery that required a large amount of blood transfusions; despite his fear of needles, he made a pledge to give back by donating blood as soon as he reached the required age of 18. He started donating in 1954. After the first few donations, it was discovered that his blood contained unusually strong and persistent antibodies against the D Rhesus factor (Rh-D) group antigen. Blood which contains a high level of anti-Rh-D antibodies can be processed to create immunoglobulin-based products used to prevent hemolytic disease of the newborn. These products are given to Rh-D negative mothers of unknown or Rh-D positive babies during and after pregnancy to prevent the creation of antibodies to the blood of the Rh-D positive child. This antigen sensitization and subsequent incompatibility phenomenon causes Rh disease, the most common form of Hemolytic Disease of the Newborn (HDN).[1]

The Rhesus factor got its name from the Rhesus macaque monkey, but not because we got it from them! Scientists just happened to first discover this blood type in Rhesus monkeys. It turns out that some forms of Rhesus molecules are found in most life forms … ranging from algae to fish to human. Even a few kinds of bacteria have Rh molecules. Rhesus factor has an even more ancient origin. It's descended from a molecule called Amt. (Amt refers to ammonium transporter proteins which are integral membrane proteins found in every living thing. Its role is in the uptake of ammonium (a form of nitrogen) necessary for biosynthesis within the cell; essentially, they allow organisms to absorb essential nitrogen from their environment by transporting ammonium across the cell membrane). They are found even in Archaea, which is possibly the most ancient life form on Earth. (Archaea refers to a domain of single-celled microorganisms considered ancient or primitive life forms, derived from the Greek word "archaios" meaning "ancient," and signifying their evolutionary lineage as one of the earliest life forms on Earth; originally classified as a type of bacteria, they were later recognized as a separate domain due to distinct genetic and biochemical characteristics. They also have some forms of Rh molecules in their structure). Amt Rh proteins, which refer to the ammonium transporter family, are found in a wide range of species including bacteria, archaea, plants, and animals (particularly mammals).

Scientists found that animals have very similar Rh. But Rh between species varies and is slightly different from the human. When doing these comparisons, scientists also found that Rh is very similar to a different protein: Amt Rh and Amt have similar DNA instructions. In the same way that DNA has instructions for what you might look like, it also has instructions for how your molecules get made. You have a piece of DNA that makes Rh molecules – and that DNA looks very similar to the DNA instructions for Amt.

Blood groups are determined by different groups of antigens present on red blood cells. Similar to antennas on a stereo to catch radio signals, antigens are present on cells to read signals from their environment. So, to have blood type A, B, AB, or O, your red blood cells will have A antigen, B antigen, both A and B antigens, or neither. Cats also have an ABO blood system, though it's not exactly the same as ours. Other animals have entirely different blood groups. Dogs can have type A, B, C, D, F, or Tr blood. Pigs can have Ea, Eb, Ga, Ha, and Ka blood. Horses have groups A, C, D, K, P, Q, and U. Like in humans, blood groups in animals vary by region. And just like in humans, it's necessary to match blood types during a transfusion. In the human Rh antigens are designated as Rh positive and negative if they are not present.

Human Rh factor is an inherited protein found on the surface of red blood cells. If the blood has the protein, you're Rh positive and if it doesn't have the protein, Rh negative. A baby can inherit the Rh factor from either parent. Rh positive is much more common than Rh negative. Having an Rh negative blood type is not an illness, and it usually does not affect your health. But during pregnancy there needs to be special care if the mother is Rh negative and the baby has inherited Rh positive blood from the father. That's called Rh incompatibility.

During pregnancy, problems can happen only if the mother is Rh negative and the baby is Rh positive. Usually, the mother's blood doesn't mix with the baby's blood during pregnancy. However, a small amount of the baby's blood could come in contact with your blood when the baby is born. It can also happen if you have bleeding or trauma to your abdomen during pregnancy. If you're Rh negative and your baby is Rh positive, your body might produce proteins called Rh antibodies if your blood and the baby's blood mix. Those antibodies aren't a problem during the first pregnancy. But problems can happen if you become pregnant again. If your next baby is Rh positive, the Rh antibodies can cross the placenta and damage the baby's red blood cells. This could lead to life-threatening anemia, a condition in which red blood cells are destroyed faster than the baby's body can replace them. Red blood cells are needed to carry oxygen throughout the body. Damaged red blood cells in the newborn from Rh factor disease is the most common form of Hemolytic Disease of the Newborn (HDN).

Harrison was one of the founding donors of the New South Wales Rh Program, one of the first in the world, in 1969; he continuously donated from then onwards. Unlike whole blood, blood plasma can be donated as often as once every two weeks, allowing him to reach his 1,000th donation in May 2011. This had required an average of one donation every three weeks across 57 years. Commenting on his record, he said: "I could say it's the only record that I hope is broken, because if they do, they have donated a thousand donations." On 11 May 2018, he made his 1,173rd and last donation in compliance with Australian policy prohibiting blood donations from those past age 81.

Through their donations, the members of NSW's Rh Program have provided millions of doses of anti-D and helped prevent thousands of deaths and stillbirths, as well as many more instances of sickness and disability caused by hemolytic diseases of the newborn (HDN). Over his lifetime, Harrison's donations amounted to tens of thousands of doses worth of antibodies and had contributed to every batch of anti-D produced in New South Wales. He was awarded the Medal of the Order of Australia (OAM) on 7 June 1999.

In 2007, Harrison was critical of plans to open up Australia's plasma donation to foreign corporations. He believed that opening up the trade would discourage volunteer donations. This opening of trade stemmed from a review of the country's free trade agreement with the United States. In 2011, he was nominated in the New South Wales Local Hero division of the Australian of the Year awards. Research is being done on creating a mixture of monoclonal antibodies, antibodies made by immortalized B cells in bioreactors, that matches what is naturally produced in the bodies of donors such as Harrison. The project has been colloquially called "James in a Jar".[1]

During a BYU Devotional, Kirt R. Saville, Director-of the School of Music shared: My parents, to the best of my knowledge, had never been very active in the Church. They encouraged us children to attend, but their attendance was infrequent. Yet it was from them that I learned how to live a Christian life. My father, in particular, was the kind of person who could never pass by someone who needed help.

I recall a trip that we made from Salt Lake City to Bear Lake, where a weekend of clear blue water, swimming, water skiing, and fun awaited me. Our typical route was to go to Evanston, Wyoming, and then on to Bear Lake. About twenty miles to the southwest of Evanston, my father noticed a man was trying to flag down cars on the other side of the divided highway. My father could never pass by someone who needed help. He drove five miles up our side of the freeway until he found the first turnaround, drove back five miles, picked up the man who had run out of gas, went five miles in the wrong direction, turned around again, drove the twenty-five miles back to Evanston, helped the man get gas, and drove him back to his car. Being an impatient teenager, I was more than irritated at the long delay. After we finally got on our way, I asked my dad why would he go so far out of his way to help someone. Surely someone else would have stopped and given that man assistance. My dad simply responded, "What goes around comes around." After seeing the confused look on my face, he further explained, "I believe that someday maybe you or I will be on the side of the road looking for help, and someone will return the favor." Being ever the optimist, I replied, "I seriously doubt it."

We've heard this saying before in many different forms. The Boy Scout slogan: Do a good turn daily. Pay it back. Do unto others as you would have them do unto you, which is the golden rule. You reap what you sow. These are all well and good, but my dad lived by the mantra "What goes around comes around." He would help anyone anytime and anywhere. But on the other hand, how many times have we heard or said that no good deed goes unpunished? In today's world we see evidence again and again, televised for the world to see, that the world is an ugly place where those who are innocent and who try to do good come out on the short end of the stick.

I often hoped that my father's mantra was true, but I was never quite sure I believed it. Over the years I learned to admire the dedication that my father had to his mantra. But I must say that I never saw it "come around" until years later when we took a trip to Flaming Gorge Reservoir. I remember this trip clearly because it was Friday the thirteenth. Since I was the only child left in the house, I knew it would be a great getaway with my parents. We loved to fish at Flaming Gorge. This happened while I was in high school—which, according to my kids, was shortly after the earth cooled and most likely during the Jurassic period.

We owned a small cabin cruiser that was about fourteen to fifteen feet in length. It was big enough to sleep three if someone was willing to sleep on the floor—and that was always me. We put our boat in at Sheep Creek Marina. Our goal was to go as far north as possible, spend the weekend in our little boat, and fish until we had our limit. As I remember, we joked that it was Friday the thirteenth. What followed later that weekend etched that date forever in my mind.

On Friday, heading toward the Wyoming side of the reservoir, we traveled some distance before we began to fish. Frankly, the fishing wasn't very good, but we loved being out on the boat together in such a beautiful place. I remember my father saying, "Look, there's a man on the far shore who's waving at us."

I looked up but could barely see anyone. Still, I knew that it was time to pull in the lines. We fired up the motor and went toward the other side of the reservoir, where the man was still waving at us. It seemed odd to me that this man was standing on a barren hillside with no other boat in sight, but when he saw that we were coming, he motioned for us to go around a bend into a small hidden cove. When we came around the hill, I was shocked to see a beautiful big yacht pulled onto the shore. It was easily twice the length and width of our little boat. The man thanked us profusely for coming to his assistance. His battery was dead, and he wondered if we could help him. We did, and soon his big motor roared back to life. The man and his family were very grateful. We lost an hour of fishing, but we were soon back out on the reservoir.

The next day the fishing didn't improve. As a matter of fact, it was terrible, so we decided to call it quits and go back to the marina. We were about two miles from the marina where we had launched our boat when we found ourselves fighting a blustering headwind that slowed our progress. The waves were kicking up, and suddenly our engine decided to quit. We tried in vain to get it running, but it simply wouldn't start. My dad was a do-it-yourself kind of guy, and he had built our cabin cruiser from a basic hull. He could always keep our cars and our boat motors running, but not this time. In the midst of trying to pull-start our outboard motor, much to our surprise, the fellow in the big yacht pulled up and asked if he could be of assistance. I had never been so pleased to see someone! Flaming Gorge is a very big reservoir, and we had been out there for two days. I was amazed that of all the people on the reservoir, he would be the person to show up to give us aid. He offered to tow us back to the marina, even though we were still quite a distance out. We happily accepted his kind offer.

All was going well, and we went at a nice and even slow click for some time, being pulled behind this monstrosity of a boat. We could actually see the marina in the distance when suddenly the motor on the yacht died. We checked the gas lines, the fuel filter—everything. But the motor wouldn't start. It was Friday-the-thirteenth-weekend kind of luck. We tried his little trolling motor, but it wouldn't start.

In the meantime, the wind had kicked up into a gale-force wind and was blowing us farther and farther away from the marina. I could barely see the marina in the distance as my dad and Mr. Yacht Guy worked on the engines. Three motors, and not a single one of them would start. What luck!

Out of the blue a little old man and his wife puttered up to us in a little twelve-foot, open-bow, aluminum fishing boat. I remember being shocked to see his wife sitting there all done up pretty with pancake makeup plastered on her windblown face. I thought, "What in the world are these two doing out here in this tiny boat amid all of these winds and waves?"

The old gentleman offered to tow us in. Quite frankly, I looked at him in disbelief. He hooked a line to the big yacht, and with his little twenty-five horsepower outboard motor, he puttered away like a tugboat with a battleship. Soon he and the big yacht faded out of sight as they went toward the marina. Meanwhile, we were being blown ever farther away from our destination. We were still in a pickle. But forty-five minutes later the little old man and his wife came back out to us, tossed us a line, and proceeded to tow us back to the dock. I was amazed that these folks were so willing to go so far out of their way to help us. Their kindness and willingness to give so much time and effort to assist total strangers was a gift that I will never forget.

By now we were fast friends—made so by the events of the day and the weekend. We helped the rich fellow get his yacht loaded onto his trailer, and next we helped load the little aluminum boat. As fate would have it, the old gentleman had left the lights on in his car, so his car battery was dead. My dad pulled out his jumper cables and got the car running. We all helped to get the little boat and ours safely secured onto our trailers. We laughed all the way home about the adventures of that weekend. What goes around really does comes around. I finally had a chance to witness my father's mantra in action. I may be a little slow, but this was a lesson of a lifetime that I couldn't ignore. Thanks, Dad, for being such a great example to me.[2]

One of the most impactful people in the world passed away on 17 February 2025, at the age of 88. Harrison, died in his sleep at the Peninsula Villages nursing home in Umina Beach. The Australian resident had donated his rare blood plasma that saved millions of people since the 1950s. Australian Red Cross Lifeblood announced Harrison's death stating that his blood plasma contained a rare antibody that doctors use to prevent a life-threatening complication in high-risk pregnancies. It's estimated that Harrison's donated plasma saved the lives of over two million children in Australia.

"James was a remarkable, stoically kind, and generous person who was committed to a lifetime of giving and he captured the hearts of many people around the world," said Stephen Cornelissen AM, CEO of Lifeblood, in a statement from the organization. He was known as the "man with the golden arm."

Harrison was married to Barbara Lindbeck, a fellow blood donor from his hometown of Junee, from an unknown date until her death in 2005. They had a daughter named

Tracey, through whom they had two grandsons named Jarrod and Scott. Injections containing Harrison's donations were later used on Tracey when she was pregnant with Scott and again on Jarrod's wife Rebecca during her pregnancies, with Jarrod remarking, "It's pretty cool that part of him went into mum and got me a brother, then protected my kids [and] his great-grandkids."[1]

"Because I have been given much, I too must give; Because of thy great bounty, Lord, each day I live; I shall divide my gifts from thee; With ev'ry brother that I see; Who has the need of help from me.

Because I have been sheltered, fed by thy good care, I cannot see another's lack and I not share; My glowing fire, my loaf of bread; My roof's safe shelter overhead; That he too may be comforted.

Because I have been blessed by thy great love, dear Lord, I'll share thy love again, according to thy word. I shall give love to those in need; I'll show that love by word and deed: Thus, shall my thanks be thanks indeed. *"Because I Have Been Given Much", Hymns, Pg 219*

What goes around comes around. "The wind blows to the south and goes around to the north; around and around goes the wind, and on its circuits the wind returns." *Ecclesiastes 1:6-7*

1   James Harrison (Blood Donor).
2   *Living a Life of Service and Love: What Goes Around Comes Around, Kirt R. Saville, BYU Director-School of Music, 08/01/2017.*

CHAPTER 23

COMPASSIONATE SERVICE

Of the nearly 3,000 people who were killed on Sept. 11, 2001, the greatest single loss was suffered by one company that was located on the top five floors above where American Airlines Flight 11 crashed into the North Tower of the World Trade Center. None of the 658 employees who came to work that day at the financial trading firm of Cantor Fitzgerald survived.

By a twist of fate, the company's CEO, Howard Lutnick, was scheduled to come in late that morning because he was taking his 5-year-old son to his first day in kindergarten. Faced with such unbearable losses, including his brother, his best friend, and 200 of the employees he personally hired, he initially felt there was no choice but to shut the company down, a company that went from earning a million dollars a day to losing a million a day. Lutnick admits that he felt survivor's guilt.[1]

Survivor's guilt (or survivor guilt) is the experience of psychological distress due to surviving or escaping a situation relatively unharmed or unaffected, as compared to others. When one emerges relatively unharmed from an accident, conflict, or pandemic, for example, while others have died or experienced significant loss, a person may experience survivor's guilt, despite bearing no responsibility for the outcomes that occurred.

Disasters are arbitrary. A tornado can destroy one family's home and leave another across the street intact. A mass shooting can leave one person critically injured and someone next to them unscathed. A layoff could wipe out a department but still leave a few workers standing. Such scenarios are difficult for people to make sense of, and their empathy or underlying personality states or traits may make them feel like they did not deserve to be spared.

Survivor guilt is not a recognized clinical diagnosis, but the experience is common and often requires treatment. Someone living with survivor's guilt may feel the same things as people facing other forms of guilt: numbness, disconnection, shame, sadness, headaches, trouble sleeping, and social disconnection.

Some research suggests that people with a history of depression or low self-esteem may be more prone to survivor guilt than others. An individual may feel that they can never do enough to help others who were touched by a disaster, thereby compounding their guilt. Sometimes, instead of helping at all, their guild leads them to withdraw from their community and even their close social circle.

In everyday life, someone carrying feelings of survivor guilt may feel badly about advancing at their job while their spouse or sibling is unemployed, or riding in a bike race while their closest friend has to give up riding because of a serious injury. But research suggests that not talking about one's victories, big or small, because of guilt or a sense that they are undeserved, jeopardizes both one's own mental health and one's close relationships; the reality is that most people close to us do want to share in our achievements and that doing so enhances connections.[2]

Lutnick did not dwell on his survivor's guilt. Instead, he rallied workers at other branches and decided to keep the company alive, to work harder than ever and to take care of the families who lost loved ones by offering them 25% of the company's profits, and providing for health care for 10 years. The families eventually shared $180 million.[1]

Steven A. Smith relates: One evening, when I was about eight or nine, I was asleep in the top bunk bed in the upstairs bedroom I shared with my brother. Perhaps while having a particularly vivid dream, I rolled over in my sleep, slipped off the edge of the bunk bed, and crashed to the floor. Thales was in a downstairs room immediately below my room, having arrived home from a date. He heard the crash, rushed upstairs, and found me winded and tearful on the floor. I do not remember what he said, but I remember him lifting me and gently putting me back into bed. I wish everyone had an older brother like mine, someone on whom you can always depend when you fall. Sadly, my professional experience as a psychologist teaches me that many do not enjoy this privilege. The brave individuals with whom I work often face life alone, trying to understand their struggles in life and the sadness that consequently besets them. They often have no one to lift or help them. Even those who have intact families, kind and loving parents, and good friends often fight to find happiness and purpose in life or to feel connected to others. At times the perceived isolation clients experience is incapacitating, intensifying the struggles they face. They need others!

In the parable of the good Samaritan, the Savior drew our focus from the wounded man to two figures, a priest and a Levite: And by chance there came down a certain priest that way: and when he saw [the wounded man], he passed by on the other side. And likewise, a Levite, when he was at the place, came and looked on him, and passed by on the other side.

As I have read this parable over the years, I have previously been inclined to condemn the inaction of the priest and the Levite. After all, they were in positions of authority and might rightly be expected to provide comfort, solace, and care for the wounded man. In recent readings, however, I have begun to consider what the priest and the Levite may have been thinking when they passed the wounded, suffering man. I suspect that their thinking may have paralleled that of many in contemporary society who witness suffering while passing "that way": "I can't help...I don't know what to do...I feel awkward...I don't know this guy...He shouldn't have been walking here at night... Someone else with greater expertise will show up to help."

As Elder Gerrit W. Gong suggested in his most recent conference address, "Though we should help each other, too often we pass to the other side of the road, for whatever reason." There are many reasons why we may pass by when friends or acquaintances experience intense spiritual difficulties or psychic isolation. Those in their immediate sphere may feel inadequate, not knowing what to do. At times the suffering of our acquaintances and loved ones seems quite beyond our help and understanding. We may feel justified in "passing by on the other side."

The call to alleviate suffering in others can be one of our more challenging Christian duties. We may perceive ourselves as being inadequate and thus excuse ourselves for not helping. However, as difficult as this duty may appear to be, it can paradoxically prove to be one of the most satisfying. Stopping to help, giving what we can—even when we feel inadequate—may not only alleviate the suffering of one of Heavenly Father's children but can also, through our choices to help those in need, actually engender small changes in our character and give us greater confidence in our ability to be a compassionate disciple.

By sharing as best we can in the sufferings and sicknesses of others, we too can develop our empathy—that everlasting and vital virtue. We can also further develop our submissiveness to God's will, so that amid our lesser but genuinely vexing moments we too can say, "Nevertheless not my will, but thine, be done" (Luke 22:42).[4]

One of the most common reasons we may fail to offer aid and help is our tendency to judge others or ourselves as being inadequate. One of the most common and debilitating irrational beliefs is a tendency to engage in human rating. Human rating is the belief that we can somehow accurately rate human beings as adequate or inadequate. We are hampered by human rating. Individuals and organizations in our society use this natural human tendency in many ways. Some of the most obvious examples can be seen in advertising. Advertising emphasizes the human tendency to compare ourselves with others and pushes the message that we can be better through the purchase of the right kind of car, chewing gum, or dish detergent. Interestingly, part of our economy is driven by human rating and individuals' tendency to purchase goods to help them "be better." Another—and even more subversive—trigger of human rating has in recent years taken center stage in the lives of many individuals. My clinical experience suggests that social media can be even more misleading and destructive than advertising. Social media platforms of every stripe routinely but falsely suggest that others' lives are happier, more glamorous, and more exciting than our own. Consciously or unconsciously rating ourselves based on misleading or altogether false images or information can lead to frustration, anger, or depression. Both advertising and social media heighten our own natural tendency to see ourselves as "less than" others. In summary, human rating stops us from being who we truly are and who Heavenly Father intends us to become.

And if men [and women will] come unto me I will show unto them their weakness. I give unto [women and] men weakness that they may be humble; and my grace is sufficient for all [women and] men that humble themselves before me; for if they humble themselves before me, and have faith in me, then will I make weak things become strong unto them. *Moroni 27* The truth is that we are weak, just like every other human on the face of the planet. However, the greater truth is that our efforts to love and lift, though given by a fallible human, will be enhanced through Heavenly Father's loving guidance and influence.

Dr. Kristin Neff, a psychologist studying self-compassion, has stated, "Compassion is, by definition, relational. Compassion literally means 'to suffer with,' which implies a basic mutuality in the experience of suffering." Thus, compassion is more than a recognition of an individual's negative experience and feeling badly about it. It implies an ability to "suffer with" an individual who is struggling. Like Dr. Gilbert, Dr. Neff stresses developing compassion for self. Self-compassion requires a willingness and ability to develop compassion and empathy for self. A synonym of compassion is empathy. As a beginning therapist, I spent a great deal of time learning to reflect clients' words and feelings, hoping that I could establish what my professor called "accurate empathy." I still find it very satisfying when a client says, "That is exactly what I mean!"

Compassion and empathy require real work. It can be difficult to understand oneself or another person. It is even more difficult to enter suffering with oneself or another. Perhaps this difficulty is one of the things that leads us to the other side of the road, wanting to help but struggling to find the ability to enter suffering with self or with another. Yet a willingness to enter and understand suffering can be one of the most healing things we can do.

The point of my address today is simply this: a humbling duty we have as disciples of Christ is to be His hands in helping make this happen. We can be there to pick others up, dry their tears, and even heal their wounds. In the words of the hymn, "I would be my brother's keeper; I would learn the healer's art." *Steven A. Smith is the director of Student Development Services.*[3]

Cantor Fitzgerald, L.P. is an American financial services firm that was founded in 1945. It specializes in institutional equity, fixed-income sales and trading, and serving the middle market with investment banking services, prime brokerage, and commercial real estate financing. It is also active in new businesses, including advisory and asset management services, gaming technology, and e-commerce. It has more than 5,000 institutional clients. Cantor Fitzgerald is one of 24 that are authorized to trade US government securities with the Federal Reserve Bank of New York. Their 1,600 employees work in more than 30 locations, including financial centers in the Americas, Europe, Asia-Pacific, and the Middle East. Together with its affiliates, Cantor Fitzgerald operates in more than 60 offices in 20 countries and has more than 12,500 employees.

Before 2001, the company's headquarters were located between the 101st and 105th floors of the North Tower of the World Trade Center in New York City, just above the impact site of American Airlines Flight 11 during the September 11 attacks. 658 Cantor Fitzgerald employees who were present that day were killed, representing the largest loss of life among any single organization in the attacks.

An Unbroken Bond book was written by Edie Lutnick about the 658 Cantor Fitzgerald employees who died in the 9/11 attacks. It tells the story of the victims, their families, and how they came together in the face of tragedy. All proceeds from the book's sale benefit the Cantor Fitzgerald Relief Fund and the charities it assists. The Cantor Fitzgerald Relief Fund provided $10 million to families affected by Hurricane Sandy. Howard Lutnick and the Relief Fund "adopted" 19 elementary schools in impacted areas by distributing $1,000 prepaid debit cards to each family from the schools. A total of $10 million in funds was given to families affected by the storm.

Two days after the 2013 Moore tornado struck Moore, Oklahoma, killing 24 people and injuring hundreds, Lutnick pledged to donate $2 million to families affected by the tornado. The donation was given to families in the form of $1,000 debit cards.

Each year, on September 11, Cantor Fitzgerald and its affiliate, BGC Partners, donate 100% of their revenue to charitable causes on their annual Charity Day, which was initially established to raise money to assist the families of the Cantor employees who died in the World Trade Center attacks. Since its inception, Charity Day has raised $192 million for charities globally. *Wikipedia*

Howard Lutnick, the CEO of Cantor Fitzgerald, was chosen to be commerce secretary in 2025 by the 47th President of the United States. The United States Secretary of Commerce is responsible for leading the Department of Commerce and advising the president on commerce issues. The secretary reports directly to President Donald J. Trump and is a statutory member of the Cabinet of the United States. The secretary was appointed by the president, with the advice and consent of the United States Senate.

His responsibilities include: 1-International trade: Negotiate trade agreements, reduce barriers to international travel, and represent the US's interests to foreign governments; 2-Economic growth: Promote job creation, economic growth, and sustainable development; 3-Innovation: Support entrepreneurship and innovation; 4-Fair trade: Ensure fair trade practices; 5-Data: Oversee the collection of economic data; 6-Travel and tourism: Coordinate the implementation of national travel; 7-Congressional inquiries: Respond to congressional inquiries on a variety of topics; and 8-Award grants and make payments to support international advertising and promotional campaigns.

"Put on then, as God's chosen ones, holy and beloved, compassionate hearts, kindness, humility, meekness, and patience, bearing with one another and, if one has a complaint against another, forgiving each other; as the Lord has forgiven you, so you also must forgive." *Ephesians 4:32*

1   A CEO took his son to school on 9/11; the decision saved his life, Marvin Scott, 09/03/2021.
2   Survivor Guilt, Reviewed by Psychology Today Staff.
3   Being Christ's Compassionate Hands, BYU Devotional, Steven A. Smith, 06/29/2021.

CHAPTER 24

MUSK'S MAGA HAT

Yesterday, Elon Musk showed up to the Madison Square Garden rally of former President Donald Trump in a curious hat. It was black and embroidered with "Make America Great Again," rendered in blackletter, the jagged letterform style often found in the logos of heavy-metal bands. "I'm dark gothic MAGA," Musk told the crowd.

But people had other ideas for what he was trying to evoke with his look. In no time, the internet erupted with opinions about the hat and its lettering. Some on X argued that Musk's hat displayed Fraktur, a gothic font once used by the Nazis in Germany. But the reality is even more complicated than that. According to type and calligraphy experts, the blackletter on Musk's hat wasn't Fraktur, or any other Nazi-associated font—but it didn't have to be to have the same effect.

Cheryl Jacobsen, an adjunct professor of lettering at the University of Iowa, explains that blackletter was established in Germany as a folk style tied to the Bible. Flavors of blackletter were used throughout medieval Europe and have been used ever since by many other cultures and in many other contexts.

Blackletter has a long history of use in Germany, though it was eventually replaced by Roman letterforms. During the rise of Adolf Hitler in pre-WW II Germany, the Nazi party re-embraced blackletter—specifically Fraktur and Textura letterforms—as a nod to its ardent nationalism. It showed up on propaganda, in newspapers, and on the cover of Hitler's Mein Kampf.

But "the relationship between Nazis and blackletter typefaces is complicated," says Florian Hardwig, managing editor of Fonts In Use typography archive. "In January 1941, with the war in full swing, they did a 180-degree turn and banned all broken script—commonly known as blackletter—from official communications." Hitler claimed blackletter was invented by a Jew, although the reality was that the letterforms were simply too hard to read for most people.

Still, blackletter has persisted as a visual marker of Nazi ideology thanks to film and TV, as well as its use by Neo-Nazi groups in Germany and elsewhere. Jacobsen cites the book Blackletter: Type and National Identity, which states: "Fraktur is now perceived worldwide as Nazi script, even after its interdiction by the Nazis themselves."

Hardwig says the typeface on Musk's hat was not Fraktur. "I would characterize the style used on Musk's cap as a modernized Old English," Hardwig says. "It is not in the style most commonly associated with Nazism." He adds that "members of the general public associate all sorts of blackletter with Nazi Germany, but strictly speaking, the font on the cap is not a Nazi font per se."

Internet sleuths believe that the hat uses Anemouth, developed in 2021. "It's such a weird bastardized version of [blackletter]," Jacobsen says.

Why did Musk wear the hat? Of course, for the 99.9% of people on this planet who are not typeface experts, the differences in blackletter font families are impossible to distinguish. For most Johns, Joes, and Elons out there, the typefaces look so similar that, in our brains, they are interchangeable. Which is why Musk's choice to wear one on his hat feels so rife with meaning.

Hardwig says that blackletter typefaces are often associated with toughness or even aggressiveness, regardless of their origins. "Choosing such a style for an application outside specific fields such as newspaper mastheads or beer logos is typically done for the sake of provocation," he says.

Musk is a known provocateur—to put it kindly. For him to wear this hat at this rally, especially after wearing other, less semantically loaded MAGA hats during previous campaign trail appearances, is not exactly a coincidence.

Before the event, Trump's increasingly vitriolic language led many media outlets to draw a parallel between the MSG rally and a rally held in the same location in 1939, where the pro-Hitler organization German American Bund preached its Nazi ideals camouflaged as pro-American rhetoric. Twenty thousand people attended that rally—with another 100,000 waiting outside—where people spoke against the backdrop of a colossal full-body portrait of George Washington flanked by swastikas.

Could Musk have been oblivious to this connection? Perhaps. Was he aware and simply wearing the hat as a proverbial middle finger to his detractors? More likely. The truth is, it doesn't really matter if the hat's lettering is set in the official Nazi brand-book typeface or a variation of it. What matters is the message. Even if Musk was simply being daft and felt like dressing up as a MAGA goth on this particular day, he forgot a cardinal rule of design: Objects do not exist without context. *Fast Company, Did Elon Musk really wear a MAGA hat with Nazi front to Trump's rally? Jesus Diaz, 10/28/2024*

CHAPTER 25

HOW WE FEEL ABOUT OUR POSSESSIONS

George M. Pullman introduced luxury to the nation's rail lines. He even created a model company town for his workers—a feat that prompted some to proclaim him the "Messiah of a new age" and helped raise Chicago from the mud.

He began his career lifting buildings. Taking over a business started by his father, he moved warehouses and barns to allow a widening of the Erie Canal. During the 1850s, officials in Chicago decided to raise their whole city ten feet to allow for drainage of its mud-clogged streets. Pullman jumped at the opportunity. Directing hundreds of men armed with screw jacks and cribbing, he lifted houses and hotels, even an entire city block, without breaking a single pane of glass.

More than anything, Pullman wanted to raise himself. The word "businessman" had recently been coined—a man who was neither merchant nor manufacturer but a mobilizer of capital, an entrepreneur. Pullman was a businessman by instinct—shrewd, gifted at calculating value, and always open to the new.

Lifting and moving buildings was an exacting operation—hesitation or a lapse of control could mean disaster. It required careful planning, a commanding presence, and steady nerves. These were the qualities on which George Pullman built his success.

Railroads had begun to dominate the landscape before the Civil War, and those who could look beyond that terrible conflict could see opportunity approaching. Pullman hired a substitute to take his place in the Union army and set to work fashioning a high-quality sleeping car. It was ready before the war was over. When the first transcontinental rail line opened in 1869, his business took off.

George Pullman did not invent the sleeping car—most of the credit went to Theodore T. Woodruff, an upstate New York wagon maker whose car debuted in 1857. But Pullman contributed his share of innovations. He based his success on two ideas: luxury and revenue. Employing both traditional craftsmen and an early version of the assembly line, he created cars that appealed to the Victorian taste for ornamentation—lush carpeting, brocade upholstery, and chandeliers. He installed double-glazed windows and an improved suspension for a quieter, more comfortable ride.

Rather than sell the cars, he retained ownership and contracted with the various railroads to add them to passenger trains as an enticement to customers. Pullman then pocketed the extra fare each passenger paid for an upgrade to Pullman luxury. This arrangement gave him a steady stream of revenue. It also meant that he kept complete control over the operation and maintenance of the cars.

And those cars proved irresistible. Business travelers could sleep while they rode to the next day's meeting.

Middle-class customers could bask in tony amenities and attentive service. Hungry passengers could feast on gourmet fare in an ornate dining car, another Pullman innovation. For the very wealthy, he offered absurdly opulent private cars. Through buyouts and mergers, Pullman's company gained a monopoly in the business. The name Pullman came to stand for quality and class.

A staunch Republican, George Pullman followed the spirit of Lincoln when he offered jobs to freed slaves. The men served as porters on the cars. They catered to passenger needs and performed the intricate task of transforming a coach car into a rolling dormitory for the night. The Pullman Company soon became the largest employer of African Americans in the country.

Concerned about the tenements and squalor that had accompanied industrialization and about the trouble that unrest might bring to capitalists, Pullman constructed a model town adjacent to his huge factory on Chicago's outskirts. Pullman, Illinois featured the Midwest's first indoor shopping mall and an elegant library, along with parks, playing fields, and neat brick homes for the workers. A local clergyman said it was "how cities should be built." Of George Pullman, the Chicago Times predicted that "future generations will bless his memory.[1]

Pullman, Illinois, developed in the 1880s just outside the Chicago city limits, was one of the largest and most substantial early company towns in the United States. Entirely company-owned, the town provided housing, stores, a library, churches, and entertainment for 6,000 company employees and many dependents.

After the United States experienced the Great Railroad Strike in 1877, its legacy included more powerful unions and a tendency for employers to consider the broader well-being of their employees. Pullman's objective in building a company town was to attract a superior type of employee and further elevate these individuals by excluding adverse influences.

Demand for Pullman cars and a growing workforce led Pullman to the development of his company town. In late April 1880, George Pullman announced his plans to build the town and a new factory. The Pullman Palace Car Company purchased 4,000 acres of undeveloped prairie land in the Village of Hyde Park. It was 14 miles south of Chicago between Lake Calumet and the Illinois Central rail line south of Chicago. Architect Solon Spencer Beman and Landscape Architect Nathan Barret were hired to design the town's layout, buildings, and factories. Desiring buildings that would be both practical and aesthetically pleasing, the homes were designed in a simple yet elegant Queen Anne style. Buildings that housed shops and services included Romanesque arches. The town's layout was planned to include Arcade Park and Lake Vista in a curvilinear fashion to avoid monotony.

Groundbreaking for the "first all-brick city" began on April 24, 1880, and work proceeded at a furious pace, with over 100 railroad supply cars unloaded per week over the summer. By fall, several factory shops were completed to refine the building materials, including painting, iron, and woodworking, and a brickyard was built south of the site. The brick was manufactured from clay found on the site.

These shops would be employed to contribute to continuing construction.

By January 1, 1881, residents began moving into the dwellings. Housing for workers was separated from the industrial areas. It comprised mostly row houses erected in long blocks but with many floor areas, detailing, and elevations. Some apartment structures, duplex buildings, and a few single-family houses were also built. All dwellings included gas, running water, indoor plumbing, sewers, and regular garbage removal. Using mass production methods, by 1884, some 1,400 dwellings had been completed.

The building's exteriors were red brick with limestone trim. The interiors featured high ceilings and large windows. Interior walls were purposefully painted in light colors to provide a cheerful environment. The town's streets were paved, swept, and watered daily, and the sewage from the town was converted into fertilizer and sold at a profit. These features, along with the relative spaciousness of the homes, placed Pullman's accommodations well above the day's standards.

Two rooms in the cheaper apartment buildings built for the lower-income workers were rented for $4.00 a month, and the two-story rowhouses from $14.00 to $100.00 a month. Rent for dwellings was deducted from employees' paychecks. The rent charged for the buildings was planned to ensure a six percent return on the company's investment. Pullman also established behavioral standards that workers had to meet to live in the area. Employees were not required to live in Pullman, although workers tended to get better treatment if they lived there.

The company also provided the residents with physician medicines and fire protection. Before long, work began on the first non-industrial building in town — The Hotel Florence, a church, the Midwest's first indoor shopping mall, offices, an elegant library, and a theater. The bar in the Florence Hotel was the only place within the town limits where alcohol could be served and consumed. These buildings were grouped near 111th Street, facing the railroad station. The town also included parks and playing fields, and the streets were lined with flowers and greenery.

The factories at Pullman attracted thousands of people, the majority of whom were skilled workers. These workers commanded a higher salary than unskilled workers, and Pullman intended to attract and retain these employees. The company also employed women in "appropriate" jobs such as sewing. The *Hour Week Journal* of New York quoted Pullman on August 5, 1882 as saying: The "Capital will not invest in sentiment, nor for sentimental considerations for the laboring class. But let it once be proved that enterprises of this kind are safe and profitable, and we shall see great manufacturing companies develop similar enterprises, and thus, a new era will be introduced in the history of labor."

Pullman attracted wide attention as a model community. In the fall of 1884, representatives of the labor bureaus of 13 states visited and studied the town. Though their report was generally favorable, they found the rentals a bit higher than in nearby Chicago. They also noted that Pullman's residents enjoyed broad avenues, parks, prompt garbage collection, and many other advantages that working men could not obtain in Chicago. The most serious criticism was that the residents had little or no voice in the conduct of community affairs. They could not own property in the town, they had no say in its government, the company controlled all media of opinion, and they lived under the strict paternalistic guardianship of George M. Pullman. By July 1885, Pullman's population exceeded 8,600. Ethnically diverse, less than half of Pullman residents were native-born, most being immigrants from Scandinavia, Germany, England, and Ireland.[2]

"I am not a destroyer of companies. I am a liberator of them! The point is, ladies and gentleman, that greed, for lack of a better word, is good. Greed is right, greed works. Greed clarifies, cuts through and captures the essence of the evolutionary spirit." These are the words of Gordon Gekko, played by Michael Douglas in the 1987 film Wall Street. The poster boy for unharnessed greed echoes the sentiment of rational free-market economists, who view greed as not only an inevitable aspect of human nature but ultimately a desirable one.

As the prevailing (yet simplistic) economic theory goes, greed motivates competition, and competition is essential for growth in a functioning market. By focusing on personal gains, people directly contribute to the greater good. The late American economist Milton Friedman espoused this ideology of greed when he said, "The world runs on individuals pursuing their separate interests." He asked, "Is there some society you know that doesn't run on greed?" Homo economicus, the rational self-interested being that represents standard economic theory, benefits society only to the extent that he maximizes his own utility.

Yet greed has historically had a bad reputation. Even today the overwhelming majority of people shun greedy behavior. When we consider the situations in which financial self-interest benefits individuals and society and when it impedes, there are few of the former and many of the latter. The belief that greed allows markets to flourish is more likely a reflection of the ability of Homo sapiens to justify our selfish motivations than it is a prescription for economic success. Understanding this fact, along with a greater appreciation of greed's harm, can go a long way toward curtailing selfish behavior.

In ancient times, the idea of greed as a sin is planted throughout history. Philosophers from Socrates and Plato to David Hume and Immanuel Kant viewed greed as a moral violation, to be avoided and denounced. Roman Christian poet Prudentius depicted greed in the Early Middle Ages as the most frightening of all vices. And in its itemized treatment of this sin, among others, the Bible set forth the 10th commandment: "Thou shalt not covet thy neighbor's house, thou shalt not covet thy neighbor's wife, nor his manservant, nor his maidservant, nor his ox, nor his ass, nor any thing that is thy neighbor's."[3]

Then President James E. Foust in October 2002 commented during a General Conference of the Church of Jesus Christ of Latter-day Saints: I have learned that selfishness has more to do with how we feel about our possessions than how much we have. The poet Wordsworth said, "The world is too much with us; late and soon, getting and spending, we lay waste our powers." A poor man can be selfish and a rich man generous, but a person obsessed only with getting will have a hard time finding peace in this life. Elder William R. Bradford once said: "Of all influences that cause men to choose wrong, selfishness is undoubtedly the strongest. Where there is selfishness, the Spirit of the Lord is absent. Talents go unshared, the needs of the poor unfulfilled, the weak unstrengthened, the ignorant untaught, and the lost unrecovered."

I recently spoke with one of the most generous people I have ever known. I asked him to describe the feelings of fulfillment that have come because of his generosity. He spoke about the feeling of joy and happiness in one's heart from sharing with others less fortunate. He stated that nothing is really his—it all comes from the Lord—we are only the custodians of what He has given us. As the Lord said to the Prophet Joseph Smith, "All these things are mine, and ye are my stewards."

Sometimes it is easy for us to forget that "the earth is the Lord's, and the fulness thereof." The Savior warned us, as recorded in the book of Luke: "Take heed, and beware of covetousness: for a man's life consisteth not in the abundance of the things which he possesseth. "And he spake a parable unto them, saying, the ground of a certain rich man brought forth plentifully: "And he thought within himself, saying, What shall I do, because I have no room where to bestow my fruits? "And he said, This will I do: I will pull down my barns, and build greater; and there will I bestow all my fruits and my goods. "And I will say to my soul, Soul, thou hast much goods laid up for many years; take thine ease, eat, drink, and be merry. "But God said unto him, Thou fool, this night thy soul shall be required of thee: then whose shall those things be, which thou hast provided? "So is he that layeth up treasure for himself, and is not rich toward God." Luke 12:15-21 "Lay not up for yourselves treasures upon earth, where neither moth nor rust doth corrupt, and where thieves do not break through nor steal: But lay up for yourselves treasures in heaven, where neither moth nor rust doth corrupt, and where thieves do not break through nor steal: For where your treasure is, there will your heart be also" (Mathew 6: 19-21)

Some years ago, Elder ElRay L. Christiansen told about one of his distant Scandinavian relatives who joined the Church. He was quite well-to-do and sold his lands and stock in Denmark to come to Utah with his family. For a while he did well as far as the Church and its activities were concerned, and he prospered financially. However, he became so caught up in his possessions that he forgot about his purpose in coming to America. The bishop visited him and implored him to become active as he used to be. The years passed and some of his brethren visited him and said: "Now, Lars, the Lord was good to you when you were in Denmark. He has been good to you since you have come here. … We think now, since you are growing a little older, that it would be well for you to spend some of your time in the interests of the Church. After all, you can't take these things with you when you go." Jolted by this remark, the man replied, "Vell, den, I vill not go." But he did! And so will all of us! It is so easy for some to become obsessed with what they possess and to lose eternal perspective.[4]

Today, rather than taking a purely moral approach, much of the opposition to greed appears to stem from its negative effects on others. When people prosper at the expense of others, for example, observers are repulsed. In a study published in 1986 psychologist Daniel Kahneman, now emeritus professor at Princeton University, and his colleagues showed that consumers refuse to support companies that take advantage of their customers for the sake of profit (through price gouging, for example). More recently, in unpublished work, Amit Bhattacharjee, now at the Tuck School of Business at Dartmouth, and his colleagues at the University of Pennsylvania reported that people judge even the mere act of profit seeking as harmful to society. The researchers found that more profitable firms were regarded as less deserving of their winnings, less subject to competition and more motivated to make money regardless of the consequences. Furthermore, when asked to compare two hypothetical organizations that were identical aside from their "for-profit" or "nonprofit" status, people perceived for-profit firms as less valuable and more socially damaging than the nonprofits. Thus, the perception of greed as harmful extends to the mere act of profiting, which is of course the only way that capitalist markets can function.

This aversion to greed-driven, profit-seeking behavior may be based on a fundamental desire for fairness, including, for example, more equal wealth distribution. In a study published in 2013 sociology graduate student Esra Burak of Stanford University showed that 61 percent of Americans claim that they would support a cap on compensation for extremely high earners, regardless of how hard they have worked or what they have achieved. In addition, in laboratory games in which people are asked to contribute to a public pool of money that will later be split among all participants, players readily penalize those who greedily hold on to their resources. They keep defectors in check and will do so even when restoring fairness comes at a personal financial cost.

Despite this capacity to rationalize selfishness, people do not always avail themselves of it. They can often be quite selfless, sacrificing their own welfare to benefit others.

People help those in need, donate money to charities and volunteer their time. In scenarios such as the dictator game, most participants reliably share some of their wealth—despite the fact that the rational economic decision is to keep it all.

All in all, humans are part Scrooge and part Robin Hood. We are more likely to be selfish when we can easily explain our choices or when we fail to consider the people who could suffer from them. Yet when we think about the people whom we can hurt and help, we behave more considerately. The lessons are straightforward: we must not let rational economic theory eclipse the fact that greed can be damaging.

Next, we should work to make the consequences of our actions clearer, with the hope that our cooperative spirit will be boosted by concrete examples of those who might bear the brunt of our actions. And finally, we must combat the rationalizations of self-interest, including the simplistic mantra that greedy behavior propels society forward.[3]

I used to have a lunch meeting with a management consultant, Don Dooley, on a monthly basis concerning the economics and staffing of my veterinary practice, Camden Pet Hospital. His experience, advice and positive attitude was most appreciated especially when I was an inexperienced solo practice owner.

On a yearly basis, he would look over my corporation's profit and loss statements. One year he told me that my business had "no value." This startled me because I was earning enough to be sufficient for my family needs and was quite pleased with my staff's performance and their income. Don told me that I was becoming complacent and not keeping up my corporate income with inflation. If I were to sell Camden Pet Hospital, a buyer would evaluate the practice income needed to make payments on a loan and what was needed to care for his private needs. The practice was caring for my family; but there was not enough income to support a purchase unless I lowered the asking price.

I asked him what should be done? He said that he worked with a veterinarian who was divorced two times and his personal debt load encouraged him to always be looking for creative ways to increase income. He also told me that he was not suggesting I try that route – maybe I should buy an expensive car.

His serious advice was: "The clients visiting my practice were not looking for me to under value my services or not offer the best available medicine in order to buy their friendship. They were looking to not be taken advantage of and offered the best veterinary care available for their companion animals."

I helped resolve my self-imposed feelings of lack of value for services offered guilt feelings and fear of pushing expenses on my client by: When cost of medical care became an issue to the client, I offered three choices of care and left it up to the owner to determine a course of action a:

One: Discussing the procedures and tests I would recommend in hopes of getting an accurate diagnosis and proper course of treatment. Offering that a referral to a specialist might be necessary for diagnosis and follow up care.

Two: Following my experience, observations and the results of what testing procedures were within the client's economic restraints - treating in accordance with our findings in hopes that the patient would respond.

Three: Not go further with diagnostics or treatment. Advising the owner as to some of the things they might "try at home" and reminding them that I was more than willing to visit with them by phone if they had questions.

In the conflict between George Pullman's idealism and his instinct for making money, money usually won. He hired African American porters in need of work, but he paid them starvation wages—they had to rely on tips and endure the scorn of racist passengers. He created a town replete with flowers and greenery, but he charged exorbitant rents, posted demeaning rules, and allowed no town government. The company ran the show and Pullman's spies invaded employees' privacy.

The patriotic Pullman was stung when economist Richard Ely criticized his model town as "well-wishing feudalism" that was ultimately "un-American." The human aspect of affairs did not come naturally to Pullman. One of his office workers noted that "I never knew a man so reserved." His boss, he felt, would have liked to have treated people as friends, "but he couldn't. He just didn't know how."

Still, his company prospered and Pullman reveled in his position as one of the grandees of Chicago society. His sumptuous mansion on Prairie Avenue, "the sunny street that held the sifted few," was the scene of gala parties. Pullman and his wife spent a week with President Grant at the White House, and the sleeping car magnate hired Lincoln's son Robert as his personal lawyer.

Then came trouble. In 1893 a financial panic plunged the nation into the worst depression that American citizens had yet seen. Pullman laid off workers and cut wages, but he didn't lower rents in the model town. Men and women worked in his factory for two weeks and received only a few dollars pay after deducting rent. Fed up, his employees walked off the job on May 12, 1894.

The Pullman strike might have attracted little notice—desperate workers struck against hundreds of companies during the depression. But the Pullman employees were members of the American Railway Union, the massive labor organization founded just a year earlier by labor leader Eugene V. Debs. At their June convention, delegates of the ARU, a union open to all white railroad employees, voted to boycott Pullman cars until the strike was settled.

At the convention, Debs advised members to include in their ranks the porters who were essential to the Pullman operation. But it was a time of intense racial animosity, and the white workers refused to "brother" the African Americans who manned on the trains. It was a serious mistake.

The boycott shut down many of the nation's rail lines, particularly in the West. The workers' remarkable show of solidarity brought on a national crisis. Passengers were stranded; rioting broke out in rail yards. Across the country, the price of food, ice, and coal soared. Mines and lumber mills had to close for lack of transportation. Power plants and factories ran out of fuel and resources.

George Pullman refused to accede to his employees' demand, which was to assign a neutral arbitrator to decide the merits of their complaints. The company, he proclaimed, had "nothing to arbitrate." It was a phrase that he would repeat endlessly, and one that would haunt him to his grave.

Railroad corporations cheered him on and fired employees who refused to handle Pullman cars. The railroad managers, determined to break the ARU, had a secret weapon in the fight. U.S. Attorney General Richard Olney, a practicing railroad lawyer even while in office, declared that the country had reached "the ragged edge of anarchy." He asked courts for injunctions making the strike illegal, and he convinced President Grover Cleveland to send federal troops to Chicago and other hot spots to face down strikers.

Although state governors had not requested federal intervention, U.S. cavalry troops and soldiers with bayonets were soon confronting rioters. Several dozen citizens were shot dead. Debs and other union leaders were arrested. Nonunion workers began to operate trains. The strike was soon over.

That summer, the Pullman workers returned to their jobs on George Pullman's terms. But their 63-year-old boss had little to celebrate. Many thought the nation's distress could have been avoided if Pullman had shown more humanity. He was scorned even by some of his fellow tycoons—one thought a man who wouldn't meet his employees halfway was a "God-damned fool."

Eugene Debs, although he had lost the strike, was lionized. One hundred thousand cheering supporters welcomed him when he emerged from a six-month jail term for defying the injunction. Frustrated by government intervention on the railroads' side, Debs turned to socialism as the only way to rectify the nation's industrial ills. He led the Socialist Party for almost a quarter century, running for president five times under its banner.

George Pullman's public image never recovered. The federal commission that investigated the strike judged that his company's paternalism was "behind the age." A court soon ordered the company to sell off the model town. When Pullman died three years after the strike, he left instructions that his body be encased in reinforced concrete out of fear it would be desecrated.

A clergyman exclaimed at Pullman's funeral, "What plans he had!" But most remembered only how his plans had gone awry. Eugene Debs offered the simplest eulogy for his pompous antagonist: "He is on equality with toilers now."[1]

On September 11, 2001, the twin towers of the World Trade Center in New York City were hit by terrorist-controlled airliners that caused both towers to collapse. Thousands of people were killed. Out of this tragedy have come hundreds of stories of courageous, unselfish acts. One very poignant and heroic account is the Washington Post's story of retired army Colonel Cyril "Rick" Rescorla, who was working as vice president for corporate security of Morgan Stanley Dean Witter.

Rick was a very experienced ex-military combat leader. He was in his office when "the first plane struck the north tower at 8:48 a.m. ... He took a call from the 71st floor reporting the fireball in One World Trade Center, and he immediately ordered an evacuation of all 2,700 employees in Building Two," as well as 1,000 more in Building Five. Using his bullhorn, he moved up the floors, working through a bottleneck on the 44th and going as high as the 72nd, helping to evacuate the people from each floor. One friend who saw Rick reassuring people in the 10th-floor stairwell told him, "Rick, you've got to get out, too."

"As soon as I make sure everyone else is out," he replied. "He was not rattled at all. He was putting the lives of his colleagues ahead of his own." He called headquarters to say he was going back up to search for stragglers.

His wife had watched the United Airlines jet go through his tower. "After a while, her phone rang. It was Rick. "'I don't want you to cry,' he said. 'I have to evacuate my people now.' "She kept sobbing.

"'If something happens to me, I want you to know that you made my life.' "The phone went dead." Rick did not make it out.

"Morgan Stanley lost only six of its 2,700 employees in the south tower on Sept. 11, an isolated miracle amid the carnage. And company officials say Rescorla deserves most of the credit. He drew up the evacuation plan. He hustled his colleagues to safety. And then he apparently went back into the inferno to search for stragglers. He was the last man out of the south tower after the World Trade Center bombing in 1993, and no one seems to doubt that he would've been again last month if the skyscraper hadn't collapsed on him first."

Amid the great evil and carnage of September 11, 2001, Rick was not looking for what might be in it for him; instead, he was unselfishly thinking about others and the danger they were in. Rick Rescorla was the "right man in the right place at the right time." Rick, "a 62-year-old mountain of a man cooly [sacrificed] his life for others." As the Savior Himself said, "Greater love hath no man than this, that a man lay down his life for his friends."

Most of us don't demonstrate our unselfishness in such a dramatic way, but for each of us unselfishness can mean being the right person at the right time in the right place to render service. Almost every day brings opportunities to perform unselfish acts for others. Such acts are unlimited and can be as simple as a kind word, a helping hand, or a gracious smile.

The Savior reminds us, "He that findeth his life shall lose it: and he that loseth his life for my sake shall find it." John 15:13 One of life's paradoxes is that a person who approaches everything with a what's-in-it-for-me attitude may acquire money, property, and land, but in the end will lose the fulfillment and the happiness that a person enjoys who shares his talents and gifts generously with others.

I wish to testify that the greatest fulfilling service to be rendered by any of us is in the service of the Master. In the various pursuits of my life, none has been as rewarding or beneficial as responding to the calls for service in this Church. Each has been different. Each one has brought a separate blessing. The greatest fulfillment in life comes by rendering service to others, and not being obsessed with "what's in it for me." Of this I bear witness in the name of Jesus Christ, amen.[4]

---

1 *The Rise and Fall of the Sleeping Car King, Smithsonian, Jack Kelly, 01/11/2019.*

2 *Kathy Alexander/Legends of America, Pullman Illinois, updated March 2024.*

3 Greed: How Economic Selfishness Harms Us All, Scientific American, D. Ariely & A. Gruneisen, Nov 2013.

4 *What's in It for Me? President James E. Foust, General Conference, October 2002.*

CHAPTER 26

MYTHOLOGY AND MAN

There are numerous similarities between the Greek myths of how the world was created, and the Maori mythological creation account. This is a fascinating fact, given the disparity between the time periods of Greek civilization and Maori civilization and the geographical distance between these parts of the world:

The Titans were the Greek mythological deities that preceded the Olympians. The world of the twelve Titans was carnage. Although bigger than gods, the gods were more powerful and defeated them. Zeus, a god, was the son of Cronus, a Titan, and ruled the Earth from Olympus once the action had occurred.

The Maori stories of Creation, the first period was in darkness. Rangi and Papa, out of whom all beings grew, were locked together, the sky flat down on the earth. The gods were their sons: Tane of the forest, Haumia of uncultivated things, Tumatuaenga of war and mankind, Rongo of peace, Tangaroa of the sea and Tawhirimatea of the wind. All creatures grew tired of living in the constant darkness and the brothers decided that they had to find a solution. Tu thought killing them was the answer. However, it was decided to separate them. Each god in turn tried his best to push them apart. Tane, the last to attempt it, succeeded where the rest had failed. This brought about Te Ao Turoa (the natural world).

There was no shortage of conflict, war and fighting in both cultures' creation myths. In Greek mythology, the Trojan Horse was a wooden horse said to have been used by the Greeks during the Trojan War to enter the city of Troy and win the war. After a fruitless 10-year siege, the Greeks constructed a huge wooden horse at the behest of Odysseus, and hid a select force of men inside, including Odysseus himself. The Greeks pretended to sail away, and the Trojans pulled the horse into their city as a victory trophy. That night, the Greek force crept out of the horse and opened the gates for the rest of the Greek army, which had sailed back under the cover of darkness. The Greeks entered and destroyed the city, ending the war.

In Maori mythology, the god of war is also the god of mankind. The oral histories of war and noble fighting were passed down through generations of Maori before the time of James Cook. Much like the fables of the gods, the Trojan Horse and women were contributing factors in the story and victory for the Greeks over the city of Troy, successful warfare between Maori tribes was influenced by European settlements of New Zealand, the introduction of the potato (taewa), the interwoven Maori fables of the creation story and women.[1]

Māori warfare traditionally involved hand-to-hand combat, with weapons designed to kill. It occurred between tribal groups for both practical and cultural reasons. Practical causes included population pressure, competition for land – particularly horticultural land, competition for natural resources and the need to protect stored food supplies. Cultural reasons were linked to the concepts of mana (power of the elemental forces or moral authority or prestige) and utu (reciprocation or balance). Tribal groups might seek to fight others to increase tribal or personal mana. Additionally, utu might require a group to make reprisals for insult, injury or trespass. A well-known saying about warfare states, 'He wāhine, he whenua, e ngaro ai te tangata' (Through women and land do men die).

Pā (village or hillforts) seem to have first appeared in New Zealand around the 1500s. There are thousands of pā around New Zealand. The fact that 98% of pā are located in horticultural areas suited to Polynesian crops suggests that there was a relationship between horticulture and war. It was common for pā to have areas for storage of the harvest.

Traditionally the mana or prestige of a tribe and its members was all important. Tribes and their chief could increase mana (power of the elemental forces or moral authority or prestige) by triumphing over other tribal groups. Insults, slander, theft, murder, assault and adultery by other tribal groups could negatively affect mana. To restore the tribal mana it was often believed necessary to seek utu. A common translation of utu is revenge; however, culturally it refers to returning balance. Any reason for waging war on another tribe was known as a 'take'. The preferred time for an attack was around dawn.

At the conclusion of a war, it was vital to make peace. Women often had a role in sealing the peace. Arranged marriages between victors and high-ranking women of defeated tribes was common. If a peace is concluded in time of war by men, it will not be a firm or lasting one. It is termed a male peace, and stands for treachery, deceit, trouble. But if women assume the function of making peace, that is known as a female peace, and it will be a firm, durable one.

A peace arrangement known as a tatau pounamu (greenstone door) was a metaphorical reference to an enduring peace. The door represented safe passage between the territories of two tribal groups. Pounamu referred to the enduring nature of the peace, and in some cases a pounamu weapon would be handed over to signify the peace. A saying suggested that this, and peace made by women, were the two enduring types of peace. A peace secured by a woman is as lasting as a peace from tatau pounamu.

The Maori people of Chatham Islands were able to forge a continuous period of peace. According to Maori tradition, after a series of wars an important chief declared an end to war, putting a permanent restriction on murder and cannibalism. 'From now and forever, never again let there be war as this day has seen!' This became known as Nunuku's law. It is likely that the ability to hold to Nunuku's law was assisted by the wealth of food resources on the Chatham Islands.

Māori weaponry) was designed for hand-to-hand combat. In battle it was common for toa (warriors) to take a weapon such as a long-handled fighting staff and a short weapon such as a club tucked into a belt. Māori wore little into battle apart from a kilt or a belt. In some cases, a cloak to shield spear thrusts was worn. Māori did not use bows and arrows, so fighting was almost entirely hand-to-hand.

Famous weapons were given names and handed down from generation to generation.

The war party was called a taua. It usually involved toa (warriors), rangatira (leaders) and a tohunga (ritual expert). A large war party would often travel to battle in a waka taua (literally a war party canoe). The size of a taua was small groups up to a few hundred people.

Trickery and deception were common strategies to win a battle. Because combat was hand-to-hand, surprise could have a vital effect on the outcome of a battle. The two places that these strategies were commonly put into place were when visitors arrived at a marae (meeting grounds), or attempted to get into a pā during a siege. At a welcome onto a marae either visitors or hosts might suddenly fall upon the other in a pre-meditated attack. A number of strategies were devised to get into pā, which, if properly constructed and defended, could be virtually unassailable.

Beached whales were a valued resource, as they were used for meat, and their teeth and bones used for weapons and ornamentation. Strategies were used that tricked people safe in a pā into going to the seashore to investigate whale strandings. One tribe made a fake whale from the skins of numerous kurī (Polynesian dogs). A hundred warriors were concealed in the 'whale' and when the villagers left the pā to harvest the whale they were overcome by the warriors.

In Hawke's Bay, Taraia ordered his warriors to lie on a beach covered in black mats to resemble pilot whales. In the pre-dawn the inhabitants looked down and saw what they thought was a row of pilot whales, but when they went down to harvest them, they were attacked by the warriors.

The Te Aupōuri tribe were formerly known as Ngāti Te Awa. While under siege in Makora pā, the people lit a huge fire which covered Whangapē Harbor with dark smoke. They were able to escape under cover of the smoke.

Following a battle the victors would take prisoners of the defeated people, particularly women and children, who would become slaves. In some cases, some of the defeated enemy would be killed and eaten. The consequences for the defeated would depend on the closeness of the relationship and degree of enmity between the parties. In some cases, some of the victors would marry women from the defeated group and merge the groups. The taua (war party) would return home and undergo ritual cleansing, which involved lifting of tapu (spiritual restriction).

In some cases a hapū (political unit) would seek assistance from an ally prior to the battle. One method of asking for this assistance was to send a valued weapon or taonga (treasure) to a neighboring tribe as a gift to invite them to take part in a battle. Accepting the gift implied agreement. Take-kai-kīnaki involved a gift of food. Acceptance of the food indicated a willingness to join.

The role of a tohunga was to act as a medium for the war god. The tohunga was relied on to interpret signs and inform the chief as to whether they would be successful in war. Their role was also to say the appropriate karakia (ritual chants for spiritual guidance) and put the war party under tapu (sacred – not to be touched) prior to leaving for battle. The fighting season was usually the summer months once the harvest had been completed. This was the time when food was plentiful and warriors had time for fighting.[2]

New Zealand is a chain of two large islands plus 890 smaller islands. It lies between the Pacific Ocean in the east and the Tasman Sea in the west, beyond which 2000 km away is Australia. Eighty million years ago, the land that later became NZ separated from the southern landmass of Gondwanaland, starting a long period of biogeographic isolation. This isolation resulted in the elevated presence in NZ of fauna and flora, and when humans arrived, there were no terrestrial mammals except for three species of bat. All vertebrate browsers and predators were birds, and some large invertebrates evolved ecological roles filled by rodents elsewhere.

Then followed two waves of human colonization, the first by Polynesians in the late 13th century and the second by Europeans, beginning with Captain James Cook's 1769 voyage. Both settler groups cleared forests, hunted native fauna for food, and introduced mammal species that became widespread. Forest cover was reduced from 82% to 24% after human arrival. Thirty-two mammal species have become resident in forests and other habitats. Of these, 14 are currently widespread, including the marsupial brushtail possum, three rodents (black, brown and Pacific rat, house mouse, and the stoat from the weasel family).

The endemicity (remaining native) of terrestrial species in NZ remains high, being 84% of vascular plants, 72% of birds, 89% of reptiles and frogs, all bats, 81% of insects, and 88% of freshwater fishes. Numerous extinctions occurred since human arrival, including an estimated 41% of endemic birds. Other species, including the little spotted kiwi and the ancient reptile tuatara, were extirpated from the two main islands but survived on mammal-free offshore islands.[3]

The environment was neither untouched nor pristine when organized European settlement began in the 19th century. The Maori also had a significant impact on New Zealand's forests, albeit over a much longer period of time (centuries as opposed to years). Between the beginning of Polynesian settlement in New Zealand around the fourteenth century and the beginning of organized European colonization in the nineteenth century, it is estimated that forest cover was reduced by about half, largely through fire.

It is believed that virtually all the forests of the eastern South Island were destroyed during a relatively brief period of burning from AD 1300 – 1450, leaving only isolated areas of forest. Forest was also burnt out in the lower east coast of the North Island and in the Hawke's Bay. In the more northern regions, it is believed that forested areas were subjected to periodic localized burning to maintain fern lands (which were an important source of food).

Maori also had a significant impact on islands fauna: nearly forty species of birds, a bat, three to five species of frogs and numerous lizard taxa became extinct during the pre-European Maori era. Factors leading to the extinction of these species were direct hunting, predation by or competition with introduced dogs and rats, human disturbance of nesting sites, and habitat destruction (mainly through burning). Bird species in particular were extremely vulnerable to any kind of human disturbance owing to their inability to fly, low breeding rates and ground-nesting habit.[4]

Before European arrival in New Zealand, carbohydrates were hard to find. Māori placed great value on the kūmara, a sweet potato they had brought from Polynesia. The remains of their early gardens and storage pits can still be seen around the country. The Polynesian ancestors of Māori brought kumara with them as a food plant when they arrived in New Zealand in the 13th century. It is believed that early Polynesians had voyaged to South America, and took kūmara from there to Polynesia.

The climate in New Zealand was much cooler than the tropical islands of Polynesia. Kūmara would not grow in the winter – instead, it had to be stored and planted out again when the weather warmed up. Some areas were too cold to grow it at all. The other food plants that people brought from Polynesia did not grow well in the new, cooler country. So kūmara became very important. The red and yellow sweet potato currently eaten are a different variety from traditional Māori kūmara – they came to New Zealand later, from North America.

Māori developed large kūmara gardens, often on sloping, sunny land. They grew the plants in mounds of soil, adding sand and gravel to make it drain better. Fences protected the gardens from wind and pūkeko birds. The plants were sometimes attacked by caterpillars of the kūmara moth, and Māori kept tame seagulls to eat the caterpillars. Eventually, suitable land for kūmara gardens became harder to find.

Kūmara tubers were harvested around March. They were stored in underground pits over winter, so some could be eaten and the rest planted out in the next spring. Kūmara were cooked in hāngī (earth ovens), boiled, or steamed. Small tubers were sometimes dried in the sun.

Much of the activity to produce kūmara became ritualized – it was even associated with Rongo, a high-ranking atua (god). Rongo was also the god of peace, which may reflect the importance placed on kūmara gardening compared to fighting and warfare. Before planting the main crop, there was a ceremonial kūmara planting known as the māra tautāne. This took place away from the main crop, and the tubers were set apart for the atua. When the main crop was planted, karakia (prayers) were said, and an offering was made to placate the gods – usually a bird. Tapu (spiritual restriction) was invoked by the tohunga (priest), and remained in force until harvest. This kept people away from the gardens.

The harvest of the kūmara was highly ritualized. The tapu was lifted in a ceremony called the pure. The first fruits were set aside for the gods, usually Rongo, and a hākari (feast) was held. The mauri (life force) of the kūmara crop was often protected by certain talismans. These included taumata atua – stone images representing atua, Rongo in particular. There were also atua kiato – wooden pegs with carved heads, which were inserted into the ground. Sometimes skulls or preserved heads were put on a post to preserve the mauri of a kūmara crop.[5]

The potato also originated in South America at least 2,000 years ago. It was introduced to Europe and the United Kingdom in the 16th century. Potatoes (taewa) were first brought to New Zealand by European explorers in the late 18th century. Māori, the first settlers in New Zealand, gave the traditional cultivars Māori names and have continued to grow them ever since.

The introduction of potatoes had a really positive impact on Māori society. Before potatoes were introduced, Māori grew kūmara, taro, yams and gourds brought with them from Polynesia, but they didn't grow well in New Zealand's cooler climate. Māori rapidly included potatoes as a main crop because they were so easy to grow and higher yielding than kūmara. They grew in all areas of New Zealand, whereas kumara only grew in warmer northern areas.

Potatoes became a staple Māori food crop and also a valuable form of currency for trading. By the time Europeans settled in New Zealand in the mid-19th century, Māori were growing taewa extensively. They were a vital food crop for the European settlers and were also exported to Australia. The commercial production of taewa by Māori peaked in the late 1850s and rapidly declined after the land wars that ended in 1872. Many of the traditional varieties are still grown by Māori today – mostly in rural areas and for their own consumption.

Taewa are considered a taonga (treasure) by Māori. They treasure them because of their historical and cultural significance. They are a link to their cultural heritage and early lifestyle in New Zealand and are particularly precious because they have been passed down from their ancestors through many generations. Their value as a taonga is likely to be a key factor in Māori continuing to grow taewa despite the plants' lower yield compared to modern potatoes. It can also be argued that they taste better![6]

The musket wars (most took place between 1818-1840) were preceded by traditional warfare between tribes, involving hand-to-hand fighting with traditional stone or wood weapons. The introduction of muskets meant fighting could be done at a distance. The change in weaponry and strategy was not immediate, but developed over a few decades. The musket wars were followed by the New Zealand wars. Rather than intertribal warfare, fighting was now between tribal groups against the Crown and, at times, the Crown's tribal allies.

The death toll from the musket wars was significant, although the actual number of casualties is not known. It is likely that there were around 20,000 deaths from direct and indirect causes. The high numbers reflect the decades of war and the fact that warfare affected all parts of the population, civilian and combatants. While the toll from the wars was considerable, the Māori population was to be affected much more by disease in the following decades.

Traditionally men had been both warriors and cultivators of the soil, and warfare was confined to summer months. The ritual aspects (see above) of growing kūmara (sweet potato) meant it had to be cultivated by men. Taewa (potatoes) did not have the same ritual needs and could be grown by slaves and women, allowing men more time for warfare. Potatoes also provided more food per hectare than kūmara. Surplus potatoes were used to purchase muskets, or could be carried by travelling war parties. Better economic production and surplus food allowed taua (war parties) to travel much greater distances. Also, a number of significant battles saw Māori using ships to travel to distant places.

Historians suggest "Potato Wars" as a more accurate name for these battles.[7]

A friend of mine, Richard Hunter, served the Church of Jesus Christ of Latter-Day Saints as a mission president with the Maori people in New Zealand during the early 2000s. He told me stories of how the people seemed to "just know" about upcoming events that were to happen or decisions that needed to be made (a spiritual attribute?). Māori spirituality is based on the belief in the interconnectedness of all things, and a deep respect for nature. It is rooted in the concept of tapu, which means sacredness, and noa, which means commonness.

He also told me about how the Maori would go to war during the summer months on a regular basis and stopped only when the food supplies began to ran out. The sweet potato did not store well and when it was gone – the war ended until the next summer. He also told me that the potato stored longer and when it was brought to the islands wars became longer, they were used to buy muskets, death rates increased and the Maori people were approaching extinction.

These discussions about people hating one another, reminded me of the book of Ether recorded in the Book of Mormon that covers over 1,700 years of history from 2200 B.C. down to the time of Coriantumr and Shiz who assemble all the people to mortal combat. Millions are slain and the Spirit of the Lord ceases to strive with them. The Jaredite nation is utterly destroyed and only Coriantumr remains. Ether's writings: "And it came to pass that when they were all gathered together, every one to the army which he would, with their wives and their children—both men, women and children being armed with weapons of war, having shields, and breastplates, and head-plates, and being clothed after the manner of war—they did march forth one against another to battle; and they fought all that day, and conquered not. And it came to pass that when it was night they were weary, and retired to their camps; and after they had retired to their camps they took up a howling and a lamentation for the loss of the slain of their people; and so great were their cries, their howlings and lamentations, that they did rend the air exceedingly.

And it came to pass that on the morrow they did go again to battle, and great and terrible was that day; nevertheless, they conquered not, and when the night came again they did rend the air with their cries, and their howlings, and their mournings, for the loss of the slain of their people.

And it came to pass that Coriantumr wrote again an epistle unto Shiz, desiring that he would not come again to battle, but that he would take the kingdom, and spare the lives of the people. But behold, the Spirit of the Lord had ceased striving with them, and Satan had full power over the hearts of the people; for they were given up unto the hardness of their hearts, and the blindness of their minds that they might be destroyed; wherefore they went again to battle. And it came to pass that they fought all that day, and when the night came they slept upon their swords. And on the morrow they fought even until the night came.

And when the night came they were drunken with anger, even as a man who is drunken with wine; and they slept again upon their swords. And on the morrow they fought again; and when the night came they had all fallen by the sword save it were fifty and two of the people of Coriantumr, and sixty and nine of the people of Shiz. And it came to pass that they slept upon their swords that night, and on the morrow they fought again, and they contended in their might with their swords and with their shields, all that day. And when the night came there were thirty and two of the people of Shiz, and twenty and seven of the people of Coriantumr.

And it came to pass that they ate and slept, and prepared for death on the morrow. And they were large and mighty men as to the strength of men. And it came to pass that they fought for the space of three hours, and they fainted with the loss of blood. And it came to pass that when the men of Coriantumr had received sufficient strength that they could walk, they were about to flee for their lives; but behold, Shiz arose, and also his men, and he swore in his wrath that he would slay Coriantumr or he would perish by the sword. Wherefore, he did pursue them, and on the morrow he did overtake them; and they fought again with the sword. And it came to pass that when they had all fallen by the sword, save it were Coriantumr and Shiz, behold Shiz had fainted with the loss of blood. And it came to pass that when Coriantumr had leaned upon his sword, that he rested a little, he smote off the head of Shiz. And it came to pass that after he had smitten off the head of Shiz, that Shiz raised up on his hands and fell; and after that he had struggled for breath, he died. And it came to pass that Coriantumr fell to the earth, and became as if he had no life." Ether15:15-32

The Maori Potato (Musket) Wars largely came to an end in the late 1830s due to a combination of factors including: the widespread availability of muskets among all tribes, creating a balance of power, the exhaustion from constant warfare, the increasing influence of Christian missionaries, and the growing unease of British authorities regarding the conflicts, which eventually led to the signing of the Treaty of Waitangi in 1840; essentially, once everyone had access to muskets, large-scale, decisive battles became less feasible, leading to a gradual decline in fighting and a search for peace.

1   General _hello@aotea.co._
2   Traditional Māori warfare – Riri, by Basil Keane.
3   Rodent management in Aotearoa New Zealand: approaches and challenges to landscape-scale control, John G. Innes et al, 03/15/2023.
4   Impacts of the Maori on the environment, Envirohistory NZ, 12/15/2009.
5   TEARA, The Encyclopedia of New Zealand, Story: Kumara (Sweet Potato).
6   The cultural value of taewa (Māori potatoes), Dr Jaspreet Singh/ Riddett Institute.
7   Story: Musket wars, Encyclopedia of New Zealand.

CHAPTER 27

MAIDEN TRIP, KON-TIKI AND THE SWEET POTATO

Recently I watched a movie called *Maiden Trip* about a Dutch sailor named Laura Dekker. I remembered the event more from the court case arguments as to why she should or should not be allowed to make an attempt at sailing around the world.

Dutch sailor Laura Dekker went further than most to become the youngest person to solo circumnavigate the world. She faced the scrutiny of a critical media, court battles with the Dutch state, psychological testing, the confiscation of her boat and the threat of being removed from her parents.

"I clung onto hope and just kept going, hoping something would change," she recalled. "I am quite a positive thinking person so I like to keep going, but I definitely had low moments."

Laura Dekker and her parents were surprised by the Dutch state's fierce opposition to her plans. Born in Whangarei, New Zealand while her parents were sailing around the globe, Dekker grew up on the water and on boats. Sailing was just a normal part of her life. Dekker explained: "To us, it wasn't as crazy as it seemed to so many other people, especially for me, because sailing was literally all I knew. I really couldn't understand what the fuss was about, which is part of the reason why I really wanted to keep fighting. It seemed really unfair that three judges, who had no idea about boats or sailing, needed to decide whether I was capable of doing such a thing or not."

The police were alerted after a friend's mother reported her to the authorities, and her father, Dick, had to fly to England and sail with her back home. This was just the start of unwanted state intervention in her plans, and she was placed under a guardianship order. She upgraded her boat to a Hurley 800, but this was confiscated by the courts.

"To us, it wasn't as crazy as it seemed to so many other people, especially for me, because sailing was literally all I knew. I really couldn't understand what the fuss was about, which is part of the reason why I really wanted to keep fighting. It seemed really unfair that three judges, who had no idea about boats or sailing, needed to decide whether I was capable of doing such a thing or not," explained Dekker.

Frustrated, she wrote a note for her father, cleared out her savings account and flew on her New Zealand passport from Paris to Saint Martin to buy a 30ft Dufour Arpège. By now a worldwide search warrant had been issued for her, and she was picked up by the island police, and returned to the Netherlands.

Undeterred, Dekker continued to search for the right boat. It was her father who pointed out the extended Jeanneau Gin Fizz advertised in the paper. Having spent seven years on the yard, Guppy was covered in plants and mold. Dekker's initial reaction was, "Really? Yuk! It looked gross and neglected but Dad and I could see the potential in it. The courts had decided that I needed a bigger boat so there was not much of a choice, plus she was a ketch so the sails are comparatively a little bit smaller and easier to handle, and was a really strong boat."

They had just a few months to get the boat ready if Dekker wanted to start her circumnavigation in the summer. In May 2010, Guppy, with a newly fitted windvane, was back in the water, and Dekker began sailing the boat in home waters before a passage to England and back. By July, the courts had lifted the guardianship order and she was finally free to leave.

A few weeks later, with her father on board, Dekker left the Netherlands and sailed to Portimão, Portugal to give Guppy a proper shakedown sail. On 21 August 2010, aged 14, she left Gibraltar to sail around the world singlehanded.

"I think I was experiencing every single emotion that you can have at the same time. I was just so nervous, but also super-happy, super-excited; I barely slept. But I was missing my family, so I was sad too," explained Dekker.

She and Guppy followed the trade winds, sailing to the Canary Islands, Cape Verde Islands, across the Atlantic to Saint Martin, through the Panama Canal, across the Pacific Ocean, through the Torres Strait, across the Indian Ocean, around the Cape of Good Hope and then back to Saint Martin via the South Atlantic.

She made stops along the way; Customs and Immigration officials never questioned her. Meeting new people was one of the highlights of her 17-month voyage, and saying goodbye to return to sea was often hard. "At the beginning,

I remember I would count the days until I was on shore again. I enjoyed sailing, but I enjoyed being on land more. Halfway through the trip that just changed. I really started to love being on the ocean.

I always just kept going. I always opted to keep going downwind, and then when it got really bad I hand steered because I felt that was the safest option, as the boat surfed really well. I finally accepted that I wasn't going to be able to change the weather or the winds, and I was sometimes just going to float backwards for a few days."

Dekker arrived in Saint Martin on 21 January 2012. She was 16, and had just sailed her last leg from South Africa to the Caribbean in 41 days. It was the end of her circumnavigation of the world, but she didn't feel excited; the voyage had been about exploring the world and challenging herself and she had done that along the way.

She mentioned that it was really South Africa where she felt she had achieved everything she wanted to, where she felt she had sailed through storms and calms and had really faced herself and seen the world. To her arriving in Saint Martin felt like "just another stop."[1]

Born on October 6, 1914, in Larvik, Norway, Thor Heyerdahl was no armchair anthropologist. He gained worldwide fame in 1947 when he crossed the Pacific Ocean on a primitive balsawood raft to prove his theory that South Americans could have originally populated Polynesia. In 1937, fledgling Norwegian zoological researcher Thor traveled to the South Pacific with his newlywed wife to study the flora and fauna of the isolated Marquesas Islands. As he collected a menagerie of specimens on the tiny Polynesian island of Fatu Hiva, however, Heyerdahl's curious mind drifted from thoughts of living creatures to those of ancient civilizations. Aware of the prevailing scholarly wisdom that people from Southeast Asia had arrived from the west to first populate Polynesia, the Norwegian couldn't help but notice the trade winds and breakers rolling across the Pacific Ocean from the east. Heyerdahl noted the presence of South American plants such as the sweet potato in Polynesia and the similarities between stone figures on Fatu Hiva and the monoliths erected by ancient South American civilizations. He saw parallels in the physical appearances, rituals and myths of Polynesians and South Americans, and around the glow of a fire, he listened as an elder spoke of a demigod named Tiki who brought his ancestors to the island from a big country beyond the eastern horizon.

Heyerdahl returned to Norway with fish, jars of beetles and a new dream—to challenge conventional wisdom and demonstrate that the first people who settled Polynesia came from the east, not the west. He abandoned his zoology studies and developed an ethnological theory that two waves of people from the Americas populated the South Pacific. The first wave, Heyerdahl said, arrived around A.D. 500 from pre-Incan Peru by way of Easter Island on rafts that drifted on the currents of the Pacific Ocean; the second came approximately 500 years later from the coast of British Columbia by way of Hawaii. Critics thought the theory impossible and said the open rafts of South America's pre-Incan civilizations were hardly seaworthy enough to make an oceanic crossing.

Heyerdahl, however, was determined to prove that such a voyage was possible—even if it meant risking his life. Although the Norwegian had no sailing experience and couldn't even swim, he announced plans to make the perilous crossing on a log raft built only with tools available to pre-Columbian South Americans. "Your mother and father will be very grieved when they hear of your death," one skeptical diplomat told Heyerdahl when hearing of his plan. Promising "nothing but a free trip to Peru and the South Sea islands and back," Heyerdahl recruited a five-man crew who built a 30-by-15-foot raft made of nine balsawood logs harvested from the Ecuadorian jungle lashed together with hemp ropes. An open bamboo cabin with overlapping banana leaves covering the roof provided the only protection from the elements.

With a smash of a coconut against the bow, the vessel was christened Kon-Tiki after the legendary Peruvian sun god who had vanished westward across the sea, a mythical figure who served as the mirror image to the Polynesian demigod Tiki who had arrived from the east. On April 28, 1947, Kon-Tiki departed Callao, Peru, with six men and a Spanish-speaking green parrot aboard. Borne along by the northeast-east trade winds that billowed the massive square sail bearing the image of the bearded Kon-Tiki, the raft groaned and creaked as it drifted across the vast blue desert of water. Although the vessel carried a radio that the crew used to provide daily meteorological and oceanographic observations, a rescue would have been nearly impossible given their remote location in the ocean. They navigated with just the sun, stars, currents and winds as their guides. They maneuvered the raft with only the sail, paddles and a temperamental steering oar as they beat against waves that in stormy conditions towered higher than their masts.

Each morning the cook collected the flying fish that flopped onto the deck overnight. The seaweed and shellfish that grew on Kon-Tiki's underside lured sardines, tuna, dolphins and at least one unwelcome visitor. One day when crewmember Knut Haugland leaned over to wash his hands, he came face-to-face with a 30-foot whale shark, the world's largest fish species. "Its body rose to the surface like a small mountain," he recalled in his diary. After circling the vessel for an hour, the enormous sea monster thankfully found other ocean prey.

On the voyage's 93rd day, Heyerdahl and his crew finally spotted palm trees on the horizon. The winds and currents, however, kept the vessel out at sea. More than a week later, as dawn broke on August 7, they spotted a reef on the starboard side. As the fragile timber raft approached the jagged reef, the cresting waves grew and sent tons of water splashing over Kon-Tiki. The crew clung to whatever they could as the mast snapped and the swells heaved them onto the Raroia atoll in the Tuamotu Archipelago near Tahiti.

All arrived safely—except for the parrot that had vanished during a storm out at sea—after covering 4,300 nautical miles in 101 days, an average speed of 42.5 miles per day. Heyerdahl had proved that an ancient voyage from South America to Polynesia was possible. However, he could not prove that it had actually occurred, and most scholars continue to dismiss his theory and believe the first Polynesian settlers arrived from Southeast Asia.

Heyerdahl recounted the epic voyage in the bestselling 1950 book "*Kon-Tiki: Across the Pacific by Raft*" and in a documentary the following year that won the Academy Award. He continued to conduct research expeditions to

Easter Island, the Galapagos Islands and South America until his death in 2002, and he led voyages across the Atlantic and Indian Oceans in primitive vessels similar to Kon-Tiki to prove how other ancient civilizations may have been interconnected. The raft he sailed across the Pacific Ocean in 1947 is now on display at the Kon-Tiki Museum in Oslo.[2]

In the April General Conference of 1962, Elder Mark E. Petersen of the Council of the Twelve said, "As Latter-day Saints, we have always believed that the Polynesians are descendants of Lehi and blood relatives of the American Indians, despite the contrary theories of other men."

Surprisingly, one of the most tangible evidence of the influence of Lehi's descendants on the Polynesian culture may be the humble sweet potato. Botanists accept the fact that the sweet potato (Ipomoea batatas) is of Central or South American origin, and many scholars have attempted to satisfactorily explain its presence in Polynesia, where it is important to the people, both dietarily and culturally. Over the years, three controversial theories have been presented to account for the sweet potato's presence in Polynesia, where it bears the South American name of kumara or kumal.

The first theory, generally accepted as most logical for about 150 years, was that the sweet potato was introduced from South America into Polynesia by Spanish explorers during the 16th and 17th centuries.

Even though early explorers did not record seeing the sweet potato, another theory claims the potato was introduced during pre-Columbian times by Polynesians who visited South America and then sailed back home. This theory gains support from the fact that the sweet potato is referred to in most archaic chants and myths throughout Polynesia. It also has a close association with Maori gods, and its planting, cultivation, and storage were traditionally accompanied by elaborate rituals. Similarly, a number of Hawaiian chants and sacred charms used in connection with the sweet potato are in an archaic form of speech. And Dutch admiral Jacob Reggeween, who discovered Easter Island in 1772, reported that sweet potatoes were part of the native diet there.

In addition, Maori tradition says a fleet of five outriggers and a canoe brought people from Tahiti to New Zealand in the middle of the 14th century, and those people carried sweet potatoes with them. Other traditions indicate that Polynesian travelers found descendants of other Polynesians who had migrated some 200 years earlier, and that they ate sweet potatoes.

Another possible area of association between South America and Polynesia is the similarity of names for the same food. In Peru, the sweet potato is known as kumara and kumal, while natives of New Zealand and the Easter Island know it as kumara.

The question arising from the second theory is that although there is plenty of evidence for the sweet potato's existence in Polynesia long before the Spaniards came, was it really introduced by voyaging Polynesians who visited South America?

Writing in 1935 (long before Thor Heyerdahl's Kon-Tiki balsawood raft expedition from Peru to Polynesia), Dr. Roland B. Dixon rejected any idea that the South Americans could have traveled to Polynesia because they had neither the skill nor the crafts for such a long voyage. The Peruvian balsawood vessels would not survive long immersed in water, he said. However, knowing that Tahitians had made the journey to New Zealand, he believed it possible for them to have sailed east to South America, learned of the sweet potato with its South American name, and returned home with it. (See "The Problem of the Sweet Potato in Polynesia," American Anthropology, vol. 34, pp. 40–59.)

The theory that Polynesians, not South Americans, made the round trip has been challenged recently by Dr. James Hornell, who contends that such an event would have survived in the Polynesian legends like stories of voyages to and from Central Polynesia, New Zealand, Hawaii, and the Easter Island did. ("How Did the Sweet Potato Reach Oceania?" Journal of the Linnean Society, vol. 53, pp. 41–62.)

Dr. Hornell concludes: "... there remains the possibility and even the probability that transmission of the sweet potato may have resulted from an involuntary drift voyage from Peru, consequent upon the miss mating and crippling of a balsa raft when on a coastwise voyage. When such an occurrence happened, the northbound Peru current would take charge until a position was reached where the northward current merges into the South Equatorial Drift. This in turn would take charge and carry the helpless craft westward to the Marquesas (and other Polynesian) Islands, where, granted a friendly reception, any tubers uneaten would be taken ashore and planted, the quichuan (Peruvian) names going with them."

In line with Dr. Hornell's thinking is the report found in the Book of Mormon: "And it came to pass that Hagoth, he being an exceedingly curious man, therefore he went forth and built him an exceedingly large ship, ... and launched it forth into the west sea…And behold, there were many of the Nephites who did enter therein and did sail forth with much provisions, and also many women and children; and they took their course northward…And ... this man built other ships. And the first ship did also return, and many more people did enter into it; and they also took much provisions, and set out again to the land northward. And it came to pass that they were never heard of more. And we suppose that they were drowned in the depths of the sea. And it came to pass that one other ship also did sail forth; and whither she did go we know not." (Alma 63:5–8 app 56 B.C.)[3]

The people who lived in Polynesia hundreds of years ago were known for their voyaging capability. They practiced wayfinding, or navigating, by using careful observations of the natural world including the stars, the Sun, and ocean waves. We know they sailed between clusters of islands that includes Marquesas, Mangareva, and Rapa Nui using their sturdy double-hulled canoes, but did they travel all the way to South America? Until recently, the strongest evidence to answer this question was the presence of the sweet potato, a crop native to South America, in Polynesia. However, recent research analyzing human DNA from Polynesians and South and Central American groups sheds new light on the mystery.

The sweet potato is native to South America. It is also found in Polynesia. How did it make its way to Polynesia? There are only a couple of ways for people to travel long distances separated by water—either by airplane or boat. But how did a plant travel from South America to Polynesia? Birds could have flown and carried plant material with them. Another possible theory is the plant's shoots floating in the water and surviving the long journey. Or people carried the sweet potato to Polynesia.

The theory that shoots of the sweet potato floated to Polynesia in the water is supported by research as recent as 2018 (Muñoz-Rodríguez et al., 2018) finding evidence that the most recent common ancestor between the South American crops and Polynesian crops lived 100,000 years ago. However, since the Polynesians were exceptionally known for their voyaging capabilities, it is thought they could have made their way from Rapa Nui, the closest island to the South American coast, to Peru and back with the crop.

To further expand the mystery, in 1947 Norwegian explorer Thor Heyerdahl proved singlehandedly that he could make a 7,000-mile trip starting in Peru and going toward Polynesia on a raft far less equipped for the 101-day voyage than the Polynesians' impressive double-hulled canoes. So, who made the first voyage, or did anyone? Until recently, the enigmatic sweet potato was the only link between Polynesia and South America.

According to research from Ioannidis et al. (2020), human DNA now supports another link between Polynesia and South America. These researchers analyzed genetic data from over 800 individuals from the Polynesian population and Indigenous South and Central American groups and found that people in eastern Polynesian populations have DNA showing a combination of Polynesian and South American ancestry. This DNA link supports the theory that people from the two cultures connected. What's more surprising is that the DNA can estimate how far back to contact occurred. The results indicate that despite the proximity of Rapa Nui to South America, the DNA of South American offspring first appeared on islands farther west around 1200 CE (AD). This ancestral DNA mixture of Polynesian and South American first occurred among people inhabiting the South Marquesas Islands and took just over 200 more years to spread to Rapa Nui (Ioannidis et al., 2020). When new evidence is found, scientific ideas can change.

The human DNA gives more support than before to theories regarding human migration between Polynesia and South America but in which direction? The Polynesians may have sailed farther than initially thought. Did they return with South American persons? Did the South Americans make the journey west? The human DNA evidence also does not completely refute the hypothesis for the sweet potato's presence in Polynesia from natural dispersal. What we do know is a more precise time for when humans from the two cultures connected. But new evidence doesn't answer every question and can sometimes raise new questions to be investigated.[4]

Some thoughts from Robert H. Daines, professor & research specialist of plant biology at Rutgers University, about three early Polynesian plants from the book Kon-Tiki. These facts appear to give further evidence that the Polynesian people are related to ancient civilizations in Central and South America:

…In the South Seas islands the sweet potato will grow only if carefully tended by man, and, as it cannot withstand sea water, it is idle to explain its wide distribution over these scattered islands by declaring that it could have drifted over 4,000 miles with ocean currents from Peru. (pg 103) …the bottle gourd…which again cannot propagate itself in a wild state by drifting across the sea alone…the Polynesians dried (it) over a fire and used (it) to hold water… (they are also) found in prehistoric desert graves on the coast of Peru and were used by the fishing population. (Pg 103)

…We had two hundred coconuts, and…Several of the nuts soon began to sprout, and we had been just ten weeks at sea, we had half a dozen baby palms a foot high, which had already opened their shoots and formed thick green leaves… The nuts we had in baskets on deck remained eatable and capable of germinating…but we laid about half among the special provisions below deck, with the waves washing around them. Every single one of these was ruined by the sea water. (pages 103-104)[5]

- Laura Dekker arrived in Saint Martin on 21 January 2012. She was 16, and had just sailed her last leg from South Africa to the Caribbean in 41 days. It was the end of her circumnavigation of the world, but she didn't feel excited; the voyage had been about exploring the world and challenging herself and she had done that along the way.

She mentioned that it was really South Africa where she felt she had achieved everything she wanted to, where she felt she had sailed through storms and calms and had really faced herself and seen the world. To her arriving in Saint Martin felt like "just another stop."

At 27, and a mother, would Dekker allow her children to circumnavigate the world solo at the age of 14? She replied: "I can't really say no, but it does depend upon the child. The only thing I can say is that I will definitely raise them to follow their dreams and their goals, and let them fall on their noses and do as much as possible themselves while I'm still able to catch them if they don't manage. If it doesn't challenge you, it won't change you."

- In 1947 Norwegian explorer Thor Heyerdahl proved singlehandedly that he could make a 7,000-mile trip starting in Peru and going toward Polynesia on a raft far less equipped for the 101-day voyage than the Polynesians' impressive double-hulled canoes.

- Thoughts from Professor Robert H. Daines about three early Polynesian plants from the book Kon-Tiki: The sweet potato will grow only if carefully tended by man and cannot withstand sea water, the bottle gourd cannot propagate itself in the wild by drifting across the sea alone, and the coconuts stored blow deck where the ocean waves washed around them were ruined by the sea water.

- Human DNA gives more support than before to theories regarding human migration between Polynesia and South America but in which direction? The Polynesians may have sailed farther than initially thought. Did they return with South American persons? Did the South Americans make the journey west?

- Hagoth the ship builder had at least two ships that were lost at sea. "And the first ship did also return, and many more people did enter into it; and they also took much provisions, and set out again to the land northward. And it came to pass that they were never heard of more. And we suppose that they were drowned in the depths of the sea. And it came to pass that one other ship also did sail forth; and whither she did go we know not." (Alma 63:5–8 app 56 B.C.) Were they lost at sea or did they drift to the Polynesian coast with a load of sweet potatoes from somewhere in the Americas?

1   *Laura Dekker: 10 years on after becoming the youngest person to sail solo around the world, Katy Stickland, 11/17/2022.*

2   *Thor Heyerdahl's Kon-Tiki Voyage, Christopher Klein, History. com, 2014.*

3   *Hagoth and the Polynesians, written by Robert E. Parsons - from Robert E. Petersen's 1962 Conference talk. Hagoth and the Polynesians.*

4   *From Sweet Potatoes to DNA: New Evidence Supports Links Between South American and Polynesian Cultures, Smithsonian Science Education Center.*

5   *Robert H. Daines, president of the Brunswick New Jersey East Stake, is a professor and research specialist of plant biology at Rutgers University.*

CHAPTER 28

WILDFIRES AND NATE

Sugar was farmed on a relatively small scale in the islands until the U.S. Civil War. But the conflict cut off the North from sugar grown in Louisiana, leading to a surge in imports from Hawaii. In the 1870s, the U.S. and what was then the Hawaiian Kingdom signed a treaty that eliminated U.S. tariffs on sugar and rice and Hawaiian tariffs on cotton and other products. Plantation profits almost doubled. Sugar cane growing expanded further after the U.S. annexed Hawaii and property rights for plantation owners became more secure. Acres planted with sugar cane exploded from 15,000 in 1876 to 238,000 in 1941.

Entrepreneurs from the U.S., Britain and beyond - including several descendants of Protestant missionaries to Hawaii - got into the business. They brought in laborers from China, Japan, Portugal, Puerto Rico and elsewhere for the crushing work of plowing, planting and cutting cane. A distinct language, Hawaiian pidgin or Hawaiian Creole English, emerged as immigrants and Native Hawaiians looked for ways to communicate. Sugar growers began diverting vast quantities of water from wetter parts of the islands to drier areas with arable land. The last sugar company in production, Hawaiian Commercial & Sugar, which ran the plantation harvested its last cane in 2016. It had been diverting water from 19 streams in east Maui and several others in central Maui to irrigate its 36,000 acres. Some of the old plantation irrigation infrastructure today supports housing subdivisions and golf courses on arid land.

Plantations started to close in the 1950s. The pace accelerated in the 1980s and 1990s. U.S. tariff and quota protections for sugar began declining in the decades after World War II amid broader trade liberalization. Plantation workers first began to organize effective unions in the 1930s, which helped build Hawaii's middle class but also made the industry less competitive compared with other countries. Then Hawaii's land values began to spike as the introduction of passenger jets reduced travel times to Hawaii and launched a tourism boom. Many landowners found they could make more money building hotels and homes than growing cane. The last Maui plantation's parent company lost $30 million on its agriculture business in 2015. The end of the sugar industry brought many changes for Hawaii but was not a surprise.[1]

Wildfires were regarded as uncommon in Hawaii until relatively recently, with those that did break out usually attributed to eruptions from one of the archipelago's six active volcanoes or to lightning strikes. On the other islands with less volcanic activity, fires did occur, but very, very rarely. The Maui situation is an Anthropocene phenomenon, referring to the epoch defined by humanity's influence over the planet. The last time Hawaii suffered a major burst of wildfires was in August 2018, when 70mph gusts of wind driven by Hurricane Lane shepherded flames towards Lahaina,

Before the 2018 wildfires, Hawaii was more commonly impacted by tsunamis hitting the islands. The worst natural disaster in its history was the tsunami that struck on 1 April 1946. Caused by an 8.4-magnitude earthquake off Alaska, the tsunami killed 165 people, wiping out the Hilo Bay waterfront on the Big Island and prompted the establishment of the Pacific Tsunami Warning Center in the state. More tsunamis followed in November 1952, August 1960 and March 1964.

Now, fires are becoming both more frequent and more extreme. The Hawaii Wildfire Management Organization (HWMO) now estimates that 0.5 per cent (or 20,000 acres) of the state's land mass burns every year, which is at least equal to or greater than the proportion of every other state in the union. The HWMO reports that 98 per cent of those fires are instigated by humans, which compares unfavorably with the US Forest Service's 85 per cent estimate for the nation as a whole.

Contributing to increased fires are the carelessness of man, global warming and the state's growing vulnerability from its abundance of unmanaged dry vegetation providing the ideal fuel. Much is accounted for by invasive species like Guinea grass that are non-native to Hawaii but have colonized areas of former farmland and forest.

The savannas now cover about a million acres across the main Hawaiian Islands, mostly the legacy of land clearing for plantation agriculture and ranching in the late 1800s/early 1900s. The transformation to savanna makes the landscape more sensitive to bad 'fire weather' – hot, dry, windy conditions. It also means Hawaii gets huge buildups of fuels during rainy periods. Agriculture declines also mean less help for firefighters – less maintenance of roads, irrigation and water storage and even fewer people with knowledge of the land. This "benign neglect" has placed too great a burden on emergency responders to tackle the inevitable consequences, emphasizing that prudent investment in "fuel reduction projects, agricultural land use, restoration and reforestation" could do a great deal to avert further tragedy.[2]

Fire is increasingly recognized as an important natural disturbance in the tropics. However, little is known about the evolutionary history of fire in shaping the structure and function of tropical forests, particularly wet forests. In addition, many tropical forests are now heavily impacted by nonnative species which can disrupt ecosystem processes and services, and alter successional trajectories and disturbance regimes.

Nonnative grasses such as guinea grass, (Megathyrsus maximus) also known as green panic grass) is a large perennial bunch grass that is native to Africa and Yemen. It has been introduced in the tropics around the world. Guinea grass grows naturally in open grasslands, usually under or near trees and shrubs and along riverbanks. It can withstand wildfire and drought. The species has broad morphological and agronomic variability, ranging in height from 1.6 to 11.5 ft, 2.0–3.9 in stems. The plant can reproduce without fertilization of the seed, effectively cloning itself through up to 9,000 seeds per plant.

It can be used as a long-term foraging grass if grazed consistently and if fertilized. It is well suited for cut-and-carry, a practice in which grass is harvested and brought to a ruminant animal in an enclosed system. Shade tolerance makes it suited to coexisting with trees in agroforestry. Some varieties have been used successfully for making silage and hay. The leaves contain good levels of protein (6–25% depending on age and nitrogen supply). *Wikipedia*

Nonnative grasses typically degrade remnant native plant communities, and preclude the establishment and restoration of native species assemblages. Most wildfires in Hawaii are ignited by humans. In order to continue to utilize natural resources while simultaneously protecting remnant native species and communities, the invasive grass-wildfire cycle needs to be managed and ultimately eliminated.[3]

It's a typical Los Angeles scene: the Pacific Ocean sparkling under a crystal-clear, bright blue sky, with miles of golden sandy beaches stretching as far as the eye can see. There's also a herd of goats precariously perched on a clifftop, enjoying the multimillion-dollar view. These aren't just any goats, though – they're California's new secret weapon in the fight against wildfires, and they're being put out to graze across the state.

Using goats to clear land is a centuries-old practice in European countries such as Italy, Greece, and Spain. A study into how effective goat grazing in the Mediterranean is in preventing fires found it is probably the most ecologically sound technique for creating discontinuities in fuels, mainly at the shrubby layer, and disrupting fuel ladders. Although the practice hasn't been around for quite so long in California, experiments to enroll the ungulates in fire management have been taking place for more than a decade.

Factors such as hotter, drier conditions due to climate change are key drivers in increasing the risk and severity of the fires. But there are also studies suggesting that land management can play an important role, as the build-up of dead trees and dry shrubs creates dangerous fuel that can lead to big, severe fires. Land managers traditionally relied on herbicide and manual labor to thin out brush and reduce dry fuel, but agencies and city officials are also trying out other, potentially more sustainable and cost-effective methods – such as goats.

Goats are especially useful in places like California and the Mediterranean because of the shrubs – goat's mouths are very well equipped. Unlike other ungulates, goats have narrow, deep mouths which allows them to selectively harvest woody shrubs. They stand on hind legs to graze at an average height of 6.7ft, and have dexterous tongues and lips. They also have the ability to detoxify compounds and so they can eat poisonous plants. When we started researching this, we didn't know where it was going to go. And now there's enough work for people making a living out of it. More city officials and land managers are open to trying goats as a new method of mitigating wildfire risk. Now there's enough work for people making a living out of being a grazer – and cities and counties are willing to pay for it because they know it makes a difference.

Goats have insatiable appetites, and devour weeds, bushes, low hanging leaves, and dry brush – all of which are fuel for fires. California's wildfire preparedness guidelines instruct residents to remove all dead vegetation, and mow grass down to four inches – everything a goat would do naturally, enthusiastically, and without being reminded. Goats also are unperturbed grazing away in triple digit heat (100F and above), and have no problem scaling steep mountainsides which can be difficult to access for laborers.

Goats are natural mountaineers. They can climb up steep hills with no problem, they get all into the nooks and crannies that would normally be very difficult for people, and they eat almost everything.

One of the greatest benefits is reducing the risk and potential workplace injuries in difficult to access areas. Levees are sloped and forested heavily in places and they can put staff at a high risk of injuring themselves even just with a slip or fall.

Goats are also useful when it comes to controlling invasive species, such as non-native black mustard plants. When the seed comes out the other end of the goat, it's nonviable, meaning it doesn't grow again – unlike when other animals digest seeds.[4]

Using goats to clear land has been a centuries-old practice in many parts of the world. It appears to be one of the most ecological methods to control wildfires by disrupting the accumulation of dry vegetation. However, that may not always be the case.

The series of wildfires in August of 2023 in Hawaii predominantly occurred on Maui. Wind driven fires devastated the city of Lahaina and killed more people than any other US wildfire in the past 100 years. In addition to poor land-use decisions, which facilitated the proliferation of combustible invasive species, the effects of feral goat grazing on the landscape played a central role in fueling the blaze. Removing invasives and restoring native plants is crucial to fire suppression efforts. To achieve these goals, Hawaii must better control the feral goat population.

Feral ungulates, especially goats, have played a substantial role in the disappearance of Hawaii's native dry forest ecosystem. First introduced in 1789 as a gift to King Kamehameha I, goats later escaped domestication. Feral goats are notoriously destructive, consuming native plants and stripping away the bark from native trees. The damage goats have done to native species, combined with previous fires and the end of Maui's plantation industry, has left large swaths of land open for the spread of invasive fire-adapted species, creating a cycle of ever-increasing fires and opportunities for invasive species.

Intensive cattle grazing, one fire prevention option, would reduce the quantity of invasive species that serve as fuel for fires. However, this solution would require perpetual management and water allocation and would undermine the global push for reforestation and carbon sequestration. Furthermore, grazing intensive enough to suppress fire would increase the risk of erosion and flooding during winter rains, leave a barren landscape, and fail to support Hawaii's native biota, itself a critical Hawaiian biocultural resource.

Hawaiian dry forest as a biocultural resource is a more sustainable solution. Native Hawaiian dry forests burn less quickly than invasive shrubby grasslands, and plant communities with more canopy layers and deeper root systems prevent erosion and flooding. The ongoing restoration of native vegetation in areas such as the Hawaiian cultural reserve on Kahoʻolawe could not succeed without eradicating goats. Protecting native species from goats will allow them to regenerate, giving them a chance to replace the invasive species that benefit from the goats' presence. To suppress and slow landscape-scale fires, communities should restrict feral goats to areas far from population centers and implement landscape -scale native Hawaiian dry forest restoration.[5]

Lahaina means "merciless sun." That's because even when it rains in Kapalua and Ka'anapali, the sun is probably still shining in Lahaina. Sometime around 1794 King Kamehameha the Great conquered Maui and later named Lahaina the capitol of his kingdom. It remained the capitol of Hawaii until King Kamehameha III moved it to Honolulu in 1840. Lahaina's history is rich with chief's, kings, queens, ship captains and whales. For the better part of the 1800's Lahaina was a whaling port and today it's still famous as a whaling port, mostly for whale watching. During its early whaling days Lahaina was a wild town. When the first missionaries arrived, they were appalled at what they saw and immediately set out converting the heathens to Christendom. Needless to say, the whalers and the missionaries were always at odds with each other. Once the whalers even cannonballed the missionary's homes from their ships. To protect themselves, a fort was built at the Lahaina Harbor.

For most of the late 1800's, until Hawaii became a state in 1959, Lahaina laid dormant. Mostly a company town for the sugar cane plantations during that period. Then in the 1960's when Amfac started developing Ka'anapali as a destination did Lahaina again become alive. Old tin-roof buildings were again converted to shops, restaurants and grog shops, much like the whaling days of old. Many of the kings, queens and missionaries who settled Lahaina are buried in a small cemetery located at the Waiola church on Waine's Street in Lahaina.

Lahaina's famous Banyon tree was planted in 1873 by the sheriff of Maui and is now the largest in the state. As July 2024, the 150-year-old Lahaina banyan tree continues to show signs of recovery, since the August of 2023 Maui fires. Today Lahaina is a bustling seaport. The Lahaina harbor is the center for most ocean activities including whale watching, fishing, snorkeling trips, even the ferry to Lanai. Front street runs about a mile, is loaded with restaurants, souvenir shops, art galleries and t-shirt stores. *A little history about Lahina*

In 2016 Shauna and I took her parents on a cruise around the Hawaiian Islands. Her father, Nate, years ago had damaged his ankles working for a sugar beet factory in Nampa Idaho and I mostly remember his face, voice and hands. He could use a walker some to get around his house, but I mostly remember him sitting or using a battery-operated scooter when out and about.

One of the ports of call on our cruise was Lahaina. The ship tendered us to the Lahaina Harbor near Warf Street and we were enjoying the rich history of the Hawaiian people and its whaling industry when Nate's scooter began to slow down – indicating the battery charge was nearly exhausted. What to do? We were blocks from the tendering boats, finding special transportation for our family that could carry the scooter was in doubt and pushing the scooter with Nate was next to impossible. Fortunately, we found a restaurant that would allow us to charge his scooter battery while we had lunch. We pushed the scooter alongside an opened window, passed the charger cord through and plugged it into a wall socket. We had a very long lunch, the cruise ship was not scheduled to depart until late and all was good.

I first met George Nathen (Nate) Karren in 2004 when his son Tim took him and me to pick cherries at the LDS Stake Farm near Nampa, Idaho. Nate was limping, using a cane and Tim tantalized him to climb a ladder to pick the fruit. To me - Nate wisely declined. Tim seemed to have that "I can do anything spirit of youth" and he worked on Nate to do the same. Over the years Nate learned more and more the effects of limitations in sight, arthritis and mini strokes would have on his body. However, his hearing remained acute and he always seemed to know where he was in a car, whether we did or not.

Over the last fifteen years I have gotten to know Nate mostly from the back seat of a car running with the air conditioner on in the summer and the heater going in the winter. We had wonderful visits waiting in the car while the women folk went into various stores for various reasons. He told me stories about his growing up on a farm/ranch, his adventures in the Korean War, his almost insane courting and eventual capture and marriage to Olivia during a winter blizzard in Idaho Falls, Idaho and about the travels and good times he spent with his family.

I listened while he discussed his family and concerns about things that were or were not happening in his relationship with his family or the relationship's they had between each other. We talked about how there were times in our lives when we were "the heroes in our children's life" and missed opportunities when we could have shared our testimony as to the things that are really important in this life. Also, the frustration when we could see events with warning lights for disaster in our children's lives and our words were not heard or heeded. Listening to the words spoken at Nate's funeral it was obvious he was the rock and patriarch of his family and they were his primary concern.

He often discussed his relationship with his family in his youth and their up and down events that at times led to bitter feelings. I discussed my family memories and how I was fortunate enough to resolve most the growing up bummers I had particularly with my father before his passing. It seemed to me that bad feelings occurred not because our fathers didn't care about our wellbeing but happened during times of stress in our family's that led us to think we were unloved or just another burden for the family to deal with. My discussions with Nate helped me look over my life with dad and see how blessed I really was. *George Nathen Karrin thoughts (2019/07/27)*

I would like to share comments made by Jeffrey R. Holland who has been an intellectual leader, president of a major university, and an Elder and Apostle of his church. I found this discussion about our Father in Heaven and how much he knows and cares about us while spending time on this earth. It was too late to share with Nate but I thought of him when I read it. I pictured what a great experience it was for him when he went through the veil and seeing not only his Father in Heaven but his dad and grandpa through spiritual eyes. When he would see and feel the true character of those men who cared for him and looked after him on this and the other side of the veil: "Among the most important testimonies I could bear is that of God's love for you. I wish to stress at some length that God is good, as any father worthy of the name will always be to his children.

That fact has important implications for our making and keeping covenants. I worry that many sometimes feel too detached from God, seem too convinced that there is too great a distance between Kolob and Kanab. You fear that God in His heaven, with all of His urgent national and international, galactic and intergalactic business, is certain to be occupied with things other than your hopes and happiness. Well, I do not know exactly how He does it but my testimony is that He does know us and does love us and that He hears our personal prayers. My testimony is that nothing in this universe is more important to Him than your hopes and happiness. Nephi wrote, 'The Lord God... doeth not anything save it be for the benefit of the world... He inviteth them all to come unto him and partake of his goodness.' When we pass through the veil, it will be thrilling to learn how God watches over us and cares for us, how He knows our every thought. For now it is enough to know simply that He does it." *Jeffrey R. Holland, April 28, 1994, BYU Women's Conference.* Nate was a special person and we were fortunate to have him be a part of our lives. Let us keep & make our memories of him an ever part of our lives...

Grandpa Nate, some ninety plus years, sat feebly in his wheel chair on the porch in the sun. He didn't move, just sat with his head down staring at his hands. His world had been reduced mostly to his acute mind, hearing, hands and failing sight. When I sat down beside him, he didn't acknowledge my presence and the longer I sat, I wondered if he was all right. Finally, not really wanting to disturb him but wanting to check on him at the same time, I asked him if he was OK.

He raised his head and looked at me and smiled. "Yes, I'm OK. Thank you for asking," he said in a clear strong voice. "I didn't mean to disturb you, Nate, but you were just sitting here staring at your hands and I wanted to make sure you didn't need anything," I explained to him. "Have you ever looked at your hands," he asked. "I mean really looked at your hands?" I slowly opened my hands and stared down at them. I turned them over, palms up and then palms down. No, I guess I had never really looked at my hands as I tried to figure out the point he was making. Nate smiled and related this story:

"Stop and think for a moment about the hands you have, how they have served you well throughout your years. These hands, though wrinkled, shriveled, and weak have been the tools I have used all my life to reach out and grab and embrace life. They put food in my mouth and clothes on my back.

... As a child my mother taught me to fold them in prayer.

... They tied my shoes and pulled on my boots.

... They have been dirty, scraped and raw, swollen and bent.

... Decorated with my wedding band they showed the world that I was married and loved someone special.

... They were uneasy and clumsy when I tried to hold my newborn children.

... They trembled and shook when I buried my parents and my son Tim and danced with my daughter Shauna at her wedding reception.

... They have covered my face, combed my hair, and washed and cleansed the rest of my body.

… They have been sticky and wet, bent and broken, dried and raw.

… And to this day, when not much of anything else of me works real well, these hands still can feed me, let me reach out and touch the ones I love and continue to fold in prayer.

… These hands are the mark of where I've been and the ruggedness of my life.

… Throughout my life I used my right hand to receive the sacrament in remembrance of Jesus Christ's atonement for my sins.

… But even more importantly it will be this right hand that I will reach out to God in hopes that he will help lead me home through the veil to be reunited with my loved ones who have passed before me.

… And that He will point the way with his right hand where I can witness the presence of the resurrected Christ, "Jesus standing on the right hand of God." Acts 7:55-56

I will never look at my hands the same again. Often when my hands are hurt or sore I will think of Nate. *2019-07-18: Grandpa Nate's Hands. Author Unknown and changes made by Walter R. Hoge. In memory of George Nathen (Nate) Karren (09-29-1928 / 07-18-2019)*

And the Lord said: "Nevertheless I am continually with thee: thou hast holden me by my right hand." *Psalm 73:23* Nate was a special person and we were fortunate to have him be a part of our lives. Let us keep & make our memories of him an ever part of our lives…

Thoughts on my Thoughts VI

1   *Why Hawaii's sugar plantations have disappeared, CBS News, 2016/01/08.*

2   *Independent (US edition), Hawaii wildfires: A brief history of natural disasters…, Joe Sommerlad, 2023/08/18.*

3   *Invasive grasses, wildfire, and native forest restoration in Hawaii, University of Hawaii Manoa.*

4   *The goats fighting fires in Los Angeles, BBC, Lucy Sherriff, 09/26/2023.*

5   *The role of feral goats in Maui fires, Science, Daniel Rubinoff and Sam O. Gon III, 09/21/2023.*

CHAPTER 29

STRANDED ASTRONAUTS

Air Force Maj. Nichole Ayers, who completed two years of initial astronaut training in 2024, was the pilot for NASA's SpaceX Crew-10 mission to bring back a pair of NASA astronauts who have been on the International Space Station since June 2024. A SpaceX Falcon 9 rocket propelled the Dragon spacecraft into orbit, March 14, 2025, carrying Ayers, along with Army Col. Anne McClain, who was serving as mission commander. Also on board was Takuya Onishi, an astronaut with the Japan Aerospace Exploration Agency and Russian cosmonaut Kirill Peskov. The spacecraft autonomously docked to the space station March 15, 2025, after approximately 28.5 hours of travel at 17,000 mph in orbit around Earth. The crew undocked and return to Kennedy Space Center in Florida the next day.

Ayers has flown missions around the globe, including more than 200 combat hours during Operation Inherent Resolve over Iraq and Syria and more than 1,400 flight hours in the T-38 Talon and F-22 Raptor. This is her first spaceflight. Previously stationed at Joint Base Elmendorf-Richardson, Alaska, Ayers served as the 3rd Wing, 90th Fighter Squadron assistant director of operations before receiving the call to join NASA four years ago. She said her military training and experiences had shaped her readiness for this next step. "Most of my training has been in the operational realm; learning to make split-second decisions under intense pressure is a skill we learn throughout our time as Air Force pilots. We train for the worst and hope for the best — training to go to the International Space Station is no different. We learn about the space station systems and how to react when something doesn't go as planned. We are well-trained and prepared for any contingency along the way to or from the space station, as well as during our time living there." Ayers said her Air Force experience taught her the importance of teamwork in high-pressure environments, a lesson she believes will be invaluable during her time aboard the space station.

"Taking care of your teammates in adverse or austere environments is something every airman learns throughout their career. My time in the Air Force prepared me well for this mission. Representing the Air Force at NASA is an honor she cherishes deeply." Growing up, Ayers was inspired by the space shuttle program and the idea of becoming an astronaut. "As a child, I always loved flying, space and grew up during the shuttle era. When I learned you could fly the space shuttle, I knew I wanted to be a pilot in the Air Force and pursue my dreams of becoming a NASA astronaut through that path. I absolutely loved every minute of my time at the [U.S.] Air Force Academy and throughout my entire flying career in the T-38A and F-22. Representing those communities and the Air Force as a whole as we embark on our mission to the International Space Station is truly special and one of my greatest honors."

For Ayers, the most meaningful aspect of her career has been the people she's met along the way. She credits the bonds formed during her time in the Air Force with helping her succeed in the toughest moments. "It is the people who matter the most. Take care of your people, and they will take care of the mission. That lesson is no different in space flight. Crew-10 is made up of some of the most intelligent, efficient and caring people I've ever worked with. We make an amazing team because we take care of each other and back each other up on everything, both operationally and personally."

As she embarks on this new chapter, Ayers is focused on the future while honoring the lessons and relationships that have shaped her career. "If you are a good team player and you're willing to work hard, you'll get anywhere you want in this life. Find something you are passionate about, dig in and work hard at it. Take care of others and be a good human along the way, and you'll be unstoppable."[1]

Walter G. Hoge, MD biography recalls WWII: "The day the Japanese attacked Pearl Harbor, 7 December 1941, I heard the news by radio while dissecting a cadaver with some other students in anatomy laboratory. This was on a Sunday morning (in Honolulu), and I could picture such a morning – the sailors a little worn out from the Saturday night festivities and probably only skeleton crews on duty. Anyway, although there have been persistent rumors to the contrary, the Navy apparently was caught by surprise and flat-footed. Practically all of the ships in Pearl Harbor were sunk, along with many, many men drowned, burned or blown up, leaving us without much of a Pacific Fleet and launching us into WWII. Pressure was applied to all medical students to enlist in the Army or Navy. I applied to the Navy, but the examiner thought I was too much underweight. For all I know, this may have been for the best. I joined the Army as Pvt (lowest rank they have) and they took us to camp for a couple of weeks and returned all of us with rank of private first class. Duty consisted of marching around in the park across the street from the school, learning military courtesy, marching commands and procedures, and attending weekly lectures by army personnel. I was discharged from the Army upon graduation from school and was back in about the day after I finished my internship, this time as a first lieutenant (MD received 09/14/1945 – war ended May 1945, Walter R. Hoge was born 02/23/1946). Soon after, I found myself in the USS General Anderson ship, that had been built or converted to carry as many troops as possible, and was completely filled with soldiers. I am not entirely sure now, but it seems that the bunks were stacked about eighteen inches apart and about six deep. If one unthinking started to sit up in bed he would get his forehead bumped. Some of the troops were quartered in the lower compartment of the ship. Gambling and smoking were strictly forbidden because of the possibility of fighting or fire, and there was supposed to be no liquor aboard. I got the duty, at least once, of compartment officer, which meant that I had to stay in the compartment all night to see that the rules were enforced. I tried to do just that, but was careful not to be too obnoxious about it because I was the only officer among one or two hundred potentially unruly troops and someone could have easily stuck a knife in me, a practice that was not unknown. A great many became seasick due to the roll of the ship and they were occupied going to and from the "head." The drains in the urinals became stopped up with cigarette butts and the urine slopped out onto the floor as the ship rolled from side to side. Fortunately, I did not become ill at all, which gave me a certain advantage."

In the 1930s and 1940s, Nazi Germany saw the possibilities of using long-distance rockets as weapons. Late in World War II, London was attacked by 200-mile-range V-2 missiles, which arched 60 miles high over the English Channel at more than 3,500 miles per hour. After World War II, the United States and the Soviet Union created their own missile programs. In a 1950s lecture hall, celebrating the 1945 blasts that ended WWII, held in the Manhattan Project's secret laboratory in the Los Alamos Ranch School in New Mexico, there is posted a quote: "Now I am become Death, the destroyer of worlds." *Hindu scripture the Bhagavad Gita*. "...hasten the day when fear of the atom will begin to disappear...this atomic agency would devise methods whereby this fissionable material would be allocated to serve the peaceful pursuits of mankind...A special purpose would be to provide abundant electrical energy in the power-starved areas of the world." *President Dwight D. Eisenhower, 12/08/1953*

I grew up within 60 miles of the Atomic Energy Commission near Arco Idaho where nuclear reactor power was first used in 1951 to produce electricity and lived in a home where my parents built a fallout shelter. My first awareness and nightmares about nuclear power was as an eight-year-old when I was exposed to several films that explored the themes of atomic bombs and the nuclear age, reflecting anxieties and fears about the potential consequences of nuclear war, including 'The Day the Earth Stood Still' and 'Godzilla'. Godzilla, was dubbed the King of the Monsters. During my pre high school years, I spent a fair amount of time drawing fighter jets and dreaming of flying planes. I would secretly open an old military trunk in our basement and put on my dad's army uniform with captain bars pinned above each shoulder. In high school I worked for a local crop duster, as a flagger, helping him align his plane where the chemicals needed to be sprayed. As part of my pay the pilot, Mr. Galbreth, would give me flying lessons when the environmental conditions made it unsafe to fly close to the ground. He often would nod off during my "lessons." I'll never forget the feeling when I first soloed around the airport and the fear when I was landing the Piper Cub – once was enough for me. During the summer of 1968, entering my below ground graduate school office at Purdue University for the first time, I noticed near the stairway a civil defense looking sign which read: "In case of nuclear attack - 1-Stand clear of all windows; 2-Keep hands free of glasses, bottles and cigarettes etc.; 3-Stand away from bar and tables, orchestra, equipment and furniture; 4-Loosen necktie, unbutton coat and any other restrictive clothing;5-Remove glasses, empty pockets of all sharp objects such as pens, pencil etc.; Immediately upon seeing the brilliant flash of nuclear explosion, bend over and place your head firmly between your legs; 7-Then kiss your ass goodbye."

The open yet restricted rivalry that developed between the US and the Soviet after WWII is known as the Cold War. It was waged on political, economic, and propaganda fronts and had only limited recourse to weapons. The term was first used by the English writer George Orwell in an article published in 1945 to refer to what he predicted would be a nuclear stalemate between "two or three monstrous super-states, each possessed of a weapon by which millions of people can be wiped out in a few seconds." It was first used in the United States by the American financier and presidential adviser Bernard Baruch in a speech at the State House in Columbia, South Carolina, in 1947.

Following the surrender of Nazi Germany in May 1945 near the close of World War II, the uneasy wartime alliance between the United States and Great Britain on the one hand and the Soviet Union on the other began to unravel. By 1948 the Soviets had installed left-wing governments in the countries of eastern Europe that had been liberated by the Red Army. The Americans and the British feared the permanent Soviet domination of eastern Europe and the threat of Soviet-influenced communist parties coming to power in the democracies of western Europe. The Soviets, on the other hand, were determined to maintain control of eastern Europe in order to safeguard against any possible renewed threat from Germany, and they were intent on spreading communism worldwide, largely for ideological reasons. The Cold War had solidified by 1947–48, when U.S. aid provided under the Marshall Plan to western Europe had brought those countries under American influence and the Soviets had installed openly communist regimes in eastern Europe.

The Cold War reached its peak in 1948–53. In this period the Soviets unsuccessfully blockaded the Western-held sectors of West Berlin (1948–49); the United States and its European allies formed the North Atlantic

Treaty Organization (NATO), a unified military command to resist the Soviet presence in Europe (1949); the Soviets exploded their first atomic warhead (1949), thus ending the American monopoly on the atomic bomb; the Chinese communists came to power in mainland China (1949); and the Soviet-supported communist government of North Korea invaded U.S.-supported South Korea in 1950, setting off an indecisive Korean War that lasted until 1953.

From 1953 to 1957 Cold War tensions relaxed somewhat, largely owing to the death of the longtime Soviet dictator Joseph Stalin in 1953; nevertheless, the standoff remained. A unified military organization among the Soviet-bloc countries, the Warsaw Pact, was formed in 1955; and West Germany was admitted into NATO that same year. Another intense stage of the Cold War was in 1958–62. The United States and the Soviet Union began developing intercontinental ballistic missiles, and in 1962 the Soviets began secretly installing missiles in Cuba that could be used to launch nuclear attacks on U.S. cities. This sparked the Cuban missile crisis (1962), a confrontation that brought the two superpowers to the brink of war.

Having promised in May 1960 to defend Cuba with Soviet arms, the Soviet premier Nikita Khrushchev assumed that the United States would take no steps to prevent the installation of Soviet medium- and intermediate-range ballistic missiles in Cuba. Such missiles could hit much of the eastern United States within a few minutes if launched from Cuba. The United States learned in July 1962 that the Soviet Union had begun missile shipments to Cuba. By August 29 new military construction and the presence of Soviet technicians had been reported by U.S. U-2 spy planes flying over the island, and on October 14 the presence of a ballistic missile on a launching site was reported. After carefully considering the alternatives of an immediate U.S. invasion of Cuba (or air strikes of the missile sites), a blockade of the island, or further diplomatic maneuvers, U.S. Pres. John F. Kennedy decided to place a naval "quarantine," or blockade, on Cuba to prevent further Soviet shipments of missiles. Kennedy announced the quarantine on October 22 and warned that U.S. forces would seize "offensive weapons and associated material" that Soviet vessels might attempt to deliver to Cuba. During the following days, Soviet ships bound for Cuba altered course away from the quarantined zone. As the two superpowers hovered close to the brink of nuclear war, messages were exchanged between Kennedy and Khrushchev amidst extreme tension on both sides. On October 28 Khrushchev capitulated, informing Kennedy that work on the missile sites would be halted and that the missiles already in Cuba would be returned to the Soviet Union. In return, Kennedy committed the United States to never invading Cuba. Kennedy also secretly promised to withdraw the nuclear-armed missiles that the United States had stationed in Turkey in previous years. In the following weeks both superpowers began fulfilling their promises, and the crisis was over by late November. Cuba's communist leader, Fidel Castro, was infuriated by the Soviets' retreat in the face of the U.S. ultimatum but was powerless to act.

The Cuban missile crisis showed that neither the United States nor the Soviet Union were ready to use nuclear weapons for fear of the other's retaliation (and thus of mutual atomic annihilation). The two superpowers soon signed the Nuclear Test-Ban Treaty of 1963, which banned aboveground nuclear weapons testing. But the crisis also hardened the Soviets' determination never again to be humiliated by their military inferiority, and they began a buildup of both conventional and strategic forces that the United States was forced to match for the next 25 years.

On Oct. 4, 1957, the Soviets launched the first artificial satellite, Sputnik 1, into space. Four years later on April 12, 1961, Russian Lt. Yuri Gagarin became the first human to orbit Earth in Vostok 1. His flight lasted 108 minutes, and Gagarin reached an altitude of 327 kilometers (about 202 miles). The first U.S. satellite, Explorer 1, went into orbit on Jan. 31, 1958. In 1961, Alan Shepard became the first American to fly into space. On Feb. 20, 1962, John Glenn's historic flight made him the first American to orbit Earth.

"Landing a man on the Moon and returning him safely to Earth within a decade" was a national goal set by President John F. Kennedy in 1961. The Saturn rockets, including the Saturn I, Saturn IB, and the iconic Saturn V, were developed and launched by the United States between 1961 and 1975, with the Saturn V first flight occurring in 1967. "I remember in 1964-65, getting up early in the morning with classmates at the University of Idaho to watch rocket tests for the Saturn rocket. We would place bets as to whether there was going to be a successful blast off or failure."

During the height of the space race in the 1960s, legend has it, NASA scientists realized that pens could not function in space. They needed to figure out another way for the astronauts to write things down. So, they spent years and millions of taxpayer dollars to develop a pen that could put ink to paper without gravity. But their crafty

Soviet counterparts, so the story goes, simply handed their cosmonauts pencils.

This tale with its message of simplicity and thrift - not to mention a failure of common sense in a bureaucracy - floats around the Internet, hopping from in-box to in-box, and even surfaced during a 2002 episode of the West Wing. But, alas, it is just a myth. Originally, NASA astronauts, like the Soviet cosmonauts, used pencils, according to NASA historians. In fact, NASA ordered 34 mechanical pencils from Houston's Tycam Engineering Manufacturing, Inc., in 1965. They paid $4,382.50 or $128.89 per pencil. When these prices became public, there was an outcry and NASA scrambled to find something cheaper for the astronauts to use. Pencils may not have been the best choice anyway. The tips flaked and broke off, drifting in microgravity where they could potentially harm an astronaut or equipment. And pencils are flammable--a quality NASA wanted to avoid in onboard objects after the Apollo 1 fire.

The Fisher Pen Company had already been working on a pressurized pen. That said, it would never have reached the heights it did, in orbit or in popularity, without NASA's testing. The original ballpoints were terrible. They tended to leak, skip, and dry up. To help solve the problem, they had already invented the first universal ink cartridge refill, that worked on a sealed cartridge with pressurized nitrogen at the top pushing a tiny piston against the ink. But the pressure caused the pens to leak. When NASA reached out to them looking for a pen that didn't require gravity, they felt this pressurized ink cartridge could be just the thing – if they could solve the leaks. With NASA's interest spurring them on, the Fisher Pen Company finally succeeded when they added resin to the ink to make it "thixotropic" – almost solid until friction with the ball at the point of the pen liquefied it. They called the result the AG7, for anti-gravity, and sent several to NASA. NASA's Manned Spacecraft Center tested the pens extensively. The space agency found the pens worked in all positions, in extreme heat and cold, and in atmospheres ranging from pure oxygen to vacuum. And they held enough ink to draw a solid line more than three miles long – well beyond NASA's half-kilometer (.3-mile) ink requirement. That testing accelerated the pen's development from a prototype to a proven high-performance product.

The Fisher Space Pen made its television debut in October 1968, as Apollo 7 mission commander Walter Schirra demonstrated weightlessness by blowing on a pen to control its movement as it floated about the capsule. It was one of the first live video transmissions from an American spacecraft. Once it had flown in space, they decided on the name Space Pen. "I thought it was a terrible name," Fisher's son recalled. "I said it's going to sound like a toy. But my father was right, as he often was." The pens are known in part for their reliability, but they also came to symbolize American ingenuity: at a time when NASA was struggling to overcome countless obstacles to put astronauts on the Moon, an inventor and small business owner stepped up and solved the pen problem. The pens have been used on every crewed NASA mission since Apollo 7 – dozens are currently on the International Space Station. NASA originally purchased 400 pens from Fisher at $2.95 apiece (equivalent to $28 each in 2024). The Soviet Union subsequently also purchased the space pen for its Soyuz spaceflights. The Space Pen line now comprises about 80 models and they are especially in-demand among members of the military and law enforcement, as well as outdoor enthusiasts, plane manufacturers, and oil workers, all of whom, like astronauts, appreciate their ability to write in many conditions.

On July 20, 1969, astronaut Neil Armstrong took "one giant leap for mankind" as he stepped onto the Moon. Six Apollo missions were made to explore the Moon between 1969 and 1972. During the 1960s, unmanned spacecraft photographed and probed the Moon before astronauts ever landed. By the early 1970s, orbiting communications and navigation satellites were in everyday use, and the Mariner spacecraft was orbiting and mapping the surface of Mars. By the end of the decade, the Voyager spacecraft had sent back detailed images of Jupiter and Saturn, their rings, and their moons.

Skylab, America's first space station, was a human-spaceflight highlight of the 1970s, as was the Apollo Soyuz Test Project, the world's first internationally crewed (American and Russian) space mission. In the 1980s, satellite communications expanded to carry television programs, and people were able to pick up the satellite signals on their home dish antennas. Satellites discovered an ozone hole over Antarctica, pinpointed forest fires, and gave us photographs of the nuclear power plant disaster at Chernobyl in 1986. Astronomical satellites found new stars and gave us a new view of the center of our galaxy.

In April 1981, the launch of the space shuttle Columbia ushered in a period of reliance on the reusable shuttle for most civilian and military space missions. There were twenty-four successful shuttle launches that fulfilled many scientific and military requirements until Jan. 28,1986, when just 73 seconds after liftoff, the space shuttle Challenger exploded. The crew of seven was killed, including Christa McAuliffe, a teacher from New Hampshire who would have been the first civilian in space. The Space Shuttle was the first reusable spacecraft to carry people into orbit; launch, recover, and repair satellites; conduct cutting-edge research; and help build the International Space Station. On Feb. 1, 2003, the shuttle broke apart while reentering the Earth's atmosphere, killing all seven crew members. The disaster occurred over Texas, and only minutes before it was scheduled to land at the Kennedy Space Center. An investigation determined the catastrophe was caused by a piece of foam ceramic tile insulation that broke off the shuttle's propellant tank and damaged the edge of the shuttle's left wing. It was the second loss of a shuttle in 113 shuttle flights. After each of the disasters, space shuttle flight operations were suspended for more than two years. Discovery was the first of the three active space shuttles to be retired, completing its final mission on March 9, 2011; Endeavour did so on June 1. The final shuttle mission was completed with the landing of Atlantis on July 21, 2011, closing the 30-year space shuttle program.

In the beginning the foam ceramic tiles appeared to be the best answer that materials science could devise for a problem that seemed nearly intractable in 1972. That was when President Richard M. Nixon announced plans to develop a reusable spaceship to replace the throwaway rockets and capsules that first carried humans beyond Earth's atmosphere. In the old days like with Apollo you had a system that would actually melt away and it could only be used once. Now they were trying to do a new system that could be used over and over. Lockheed Missiles and Space Company's Sunnyvale CA Plant won the contract in 1973 (the year I moved to CA) with a lightweight silica formulation that could be thought as rigidized fiberglass - pure silica fiberglass. I took care of a client's pet at Camden Pet Hospital, that worked at Lockheed. I was overwhelmed by the details she tried to explain of the complicated procedures of attaching around 23,000-30,000 heat-resistant tiles that were used as part of the Thermal Protection System (TPS), to withstand the extreme temperatures of re-entry. I asked my client if she could get me just a little itsy, bitsy piece of one of those tiles – she told me that we shouldn't even be talking about it! The tiles, invented in the 1960s, would need to withstand the extreme vibration of liftoff and acceleration to 17000 miles per hour. In space temperatures could drop to 240 degrees below zero Fahrenheit. During reentry the heat could build to 3000 degrees. It couldn't have extreme thermal expansion like a metal; it couldn't go from an amorphous silica to a crystalline form and it had to survive the temperature change without cracking. It had to be lightweight, inhibit thermal radiation, made mostly of air and a smooth solid coating so water couldn't penetrate, and you wouldn't have frictional heating. If you were to pick up a tile it would feel like you were holding a piece of Styrofoam and in terms of how well it insulates it was excellent. Stanford University calculated that the tiles contributed 10 percent of the risk of accident on any given shuttle flight. To improve the odds NASA implemented a series of recommendations. It boosted installers' pay to attract better workers, reduced pressure on them to work too fast and made the foam insulation on the external tank less likely to break away. It took forever to glue on the thermal tiles that shielded the space shuttle from the scorching heat of reentry - nearly two man-years of work for every flight - and the glue dried so fast that technicians had to mix a new batch after every couple of tiles. But they came up with a solution, spit in the glue so it took longer to harden. The trouble was that spit weakened the adhesive bond between the tiles and the shuttle's aluminum shell making the tiles more likely to fall off during the stresses of space flight. When NASA officials found out about this home remedy they put an end to it.

The Gulf War proved the value of satellites in modern conflicts. During this war, allied forces were able to use their control of the "high ground" of space to achieve a decisive advantage. Satellites were used to provide information on enemy troop formations and movements, early warning of enemy missile attacks, and precise navigation in the featureless desert terrain. The advantages of satellites allowed the coalition forces to quickly bring the war to a conclusion, saving many lives. Space systems continue to become more and more integral to homeland defense, weather surveillance, communication, navigation, imaging, and remote sensing for chemicals, fires, and other disasters.

The International Space Station is a research laboratory in low Earth orbit. With many different partners contributing to its design and construction, this high-flying laboratory has become a symbol of cooperation in space exploration, with former competitors now working together. The station has been continuously occupied since the arrival of Expedition 1 in November of 2000. The station is serviced by a variety of visiting spacecraft: the Russian Soyuz and

Progress; the American Dragon and Cygnus; the Japanese H-II Transfer Vehicle; and formerly the Space Shuttle and the European Automated Transfer Vehicle. It has been visited by astronauts, cosmonauts, and space tourists from 17 different nations.

Space launch systems have been designed to reduce costs and improve dependability, safety, and reliability. Most U.S. military and scientific satellites are launched into orbit by a family of expendable launch vehicles designed for a variety of missions. Other nations have their own launch systems, and there is strong competition in the commercial launch market to develop the next generation of launch systems.

Modern space exploration is reaching areas once only dreamed about. Mars is focal point of modern space exploration, and manned Mars exploration is a long-term goal of the United States. NASA is on a journey to Mars, with a goal of sending humans to the Red Planet in the 2030s. NASA and its partners have sent orbiters, landers, and rovers, increasing our knowledge about the planet. The Curiosity Rover has gathered radiation data to protect astronauts, and the MARS 2020 Rover will study the availability of oxygen and other Martian resources. *Aerospace, AI + others*

NASA astronaut Sunita Williams was stuck at the International Space Station (ISS) for over 9 months. A short space mission which was initially planned for just 8 days turned into 286 days of wait to be rescued after the spacecraft carrying them faced technical glitches - making their return unsafe. However, on 03/31/2025, the astronaut along with Barry 'Butch' Wilmore returned to Earth aboard SpaceX's capsule. Although their safe return brought smiles to the faces of fans and family members, experts warn that the real challenge for the astronauts is just beginning. The astronauts' bodies struggled to readjust to gravity, facing significant challenges in adapting to the forces. When the human body is exposed to microgravity for a prolonged period of time it can suffer from severe muscle loss and bone mass reduction. Basically, without the need for gravity-dependent movement, muscles weaken over time and there is increased bone mass reduction resulting in increasing the risk of fractures. The heart, accustomed to functioning in a weightless environment, has to adapt to pumping blood against gravity again, and the astronauts suffer from fluid re-distribution - all the body fluid shifts to the lower body, leading to dizziness and swelling.

1– Sunita Williams holds the record for the longest spacewalk by a woman, spending a total of 50 hours and 40 minutes outside the International Space Station (ISS).

2– In 2007, Sunita Williams became the first person to run a marathon in space. She participated in the Boston Marathon while orbiting the Earth, running the 26.2 miles on a treadmill aboard the ISS.

3– Before joining NASA, Sunita Williams served as a helicopter pilot in the U.S. Navy. She flew helicopters during the Gulf War and later served as an instructor at the Naval Test Pilot School.

4– Sunita has a total of seven spacewalks, setting a world record for the most spacewalks by a female astronaut.

5– In addition to her marathon, Sunita Williams also completed a triathlon in space. She swam in a rigged contraption, biked on a stationary bike, and ran on a tread mill, all while orbiting the Earth, helping her stay fit, even in zero gravity.

6– Sunita was a part of the first crew rotation mission aboard the Russian Soyuz spacecraft after NASA's Space Shuttle program ended. This mission was crucial in continuing human presence aboard the ISS.

7– During one of her spacewalks, Williams lost a camera that floated away into space. It was a poignant reminder of how even the smallest errors in space can lead to significant losses.

8– She has adopted numerous dogs and often speaks about her love for animals, making her relatable to animal enthusiasts around the world. She appeared on Dog Whisperer – Season 7, Episode 6 Astronaut Dogs & Mongo program.

9– She is a role model for women and girls around the world, especially in India and the United States. Her achievements have inspired countless women to pursue careers in STEM (Science, Technology, Engineering, and Mathematics) fields.

Air Force Maj. Nichole Ayers who completed two years of initial astronaut training in 2024, and was the pilot for NASA's SpaceX Crew-10 mission to bring back a pair of NASA astronauts who had been on the International Space Station since June 2024, said: "If you are a good team player and you're willing to work hard, you'll get anywhere you want in this life. Find something you are passionate about, dig in and work hard at it. Take care of others and be a good human along the way, and you'll be unstoppable."

Determined, tireless, patient, purposeful and unstoppable, Sunita Williams has shown those characteristics even as a young girl. During an interview when she was 52-years-old she stated: "Everywhere I go I always have a pair of running shoes with me. That's just part of the standard package." Her parents encouraged her to lead an active lifestyle while she grew up in Needham, Massachusetts, a suburb of Boston. She was a long-distance swimmer who "grew up doing the 5 a.m. swimming thing." It wasn't until her senior year of high school that she started running track in the spring—and even then, it was more to prepare for college at the Naval Academy, which required cadets to run. As a 17-year-old, Williams ran the 1983 Boston Marathon as a bandit. She didn't have a pair of running shoes, so she wore basketball sneakers. "I shortly figured out that wasn't a good idea," said Williams. Towards the end of the race the shoes literally disintegrated and fell from her feet. Unstoppable, she finished the race bare footed. She has run Boston five times, including once orbiting the earth – 2007. [1]

1   *Military Pilot's First Spaceflight is Mission to Rescue Astronauts, Maria Galvez, 03/17/2025, AI + others.*

CHAPTER 30

NEIL EVAN'S STORY FROM 60TH CLASS REUNION BLACKFOOT

All conscience acts set in motion changes in a person's life. Some create life changes that will affect every day of one's life. Others might nag you from time to time, make you feel some guilt, wish that you had never made such a decision and wish you could turn back the clock. On June 27th 2019 I wrote this letter concerning a thought I requested be presented to my 55th year High School Class Reunion. I was my senior class vice president in high school. Our president Jerry Smith died the year before, I had a stroke on April 23, 2019 and felt it wise not to travel to Blackfoot Idaho.

Dear Tom Richardson,

There is only one thought you might share with our class that has bothered me every time we prepare for a class reunion. When I ran for senior class vice president I did it because I felt I could do a better job than the other candidate, Jim Smith. This was not a particularly bright move on my part since I'm not good speaking in front of an audience or of a political nature. This decision might have been influenced from my attending the American Legions Gem Boy's State in Boise (think I have the name correct). Here we learned about running for political office and contributing to our community. Not long after graduation we lost Jim in Vietnam. My parents were good friends with Jim's and it seemed like every time I was home with my parents during social events the Smiths were there. Jim's mom would always say to me, "Rich, would you turn around for me? I would like to imagine what Jim would have looked like if he were here." This request would tear my heart out. And every thought of a reunion brings me back to thoughts of Jim. Why did I run against him, he couldn't have made a worse VP than me, he would more than likely have lived near Blackfoot where he could help our class more, and it would have been nice for his parents to have added Vice President of the Blackfoot High School Senior Class to their memories of Jim.

I hope there is a good turn out this year. We were fortunate to have grown up in an isolated and protected area and the teachers helped us be able to take on the world no matter where we landed. Please plan another class reunion. I noticed this year's event has a wheel chair ramp – that boosts my confidence that I will make the next one. If you get the opportunity, give a toast to Jim Smith for me. *Thoughts on my Thoughts… Book I, Walter R. Hoge, Pg's 205-212.*

Who is likely to be happier and healthier at 90? A woman who moves across the country to live with her daughter and sees a grandchild every month, but rarely interacts with friends—or a woman who socializes with friends all the time, and sees family members mainly on holidays? With any two real people, the answer depends on all kinds of factors. But most people assume that strong family ties are a bigger influence on well-being in old age than friendship. If you don't have much family, you might worry that you're likely to end up old and sick and alone. That assumption is wrong, according to an April, 2017 study sponsored by the National Institute on Aging. Actually, as you age, friendship is thicker than water.

Over the years, much research shows, your friends influence your happiness and habits—whether you'll smoke or drink, work out, stay thin or become obese. The new research found that the importance of friendship increases with age. This works both ways—quarrels with friends, it suggests, are tied to chronic health problems. The key is to keep friendships in good order. You may need to repair, or replace, friendships as you age.

The study, designed by Michigan State University psychology professor William J. Chopik, looked at two sets of data—one drawn from people around the world at different ages, and another from older Americans. The first data set came from more than 270,000 volunteers ages 15 to 99, from nearly a hundred countries. The volunteers answered questions about how highly they valued different kinds of relationships and how happy they were. Instead of tracking the same people over time, it tracked "representative" groups of different ages at intervals over the years.

The result: from about age 65 on, valuing friendship highly turned out to make a bigger difference than it did when you were younger. Strong family ties were linked to happiness, but their importance stayed about the same over the life span.

In a separate analysis, researchers examined data from close to 7,500 American volunteers in their sixties and seventies. This time, the data followed the same people over time. Getting support—be it from spouses, children and friends—predicted greater well-being over an eight-year period, although more extended family didn't seem to make much difference.

These questionnaires asked about "strain" within relationships, among other questions. It turned out that people who experienced strain within friendships were more likely to suffer from chronic illnesses like diabetes, heart disease, and psychiatric problems. This was true even if they also had support from immediate family. Strain with family, surprisingly, wasn't tied to more illness.

To add this all up, valuing your immediate family is good for your health and happiness at any age. But the older you become, the more important it is to have strong friendships. You're happier and healthier when they're happy--and you're more likely to be sick when you don't value friendship or your friendships are in trouble.

Other research has found what might seem to be a contradictory observation—we tend to socialize with fewer people as we age. But, as Chopik points out, we also invest more in a choice few. Those choice few help to keep us healthier, not just happier. "Friendship quality," he writes, "often predicts health more so than the quality of other relationships."

Some of us take friendship for granted—friends are supposed to be "easy," while we work at family relations. But over the years, friendships run into trouble as well. You can decide to work through those trouble spots—ideally, getting closer—and move away from friendships that drag down your health. Don't meet the old drinking buddies at the bar if you overdrink; see your girlfriend who eats a box of cookies at midnight for a morning walk instead.

As you get older, people move away, divorce and die. You no longer may see work buddies if you retire. You may find yourself needing to make new friends. Community organizations, religious groups and volunteer work may make all the difference.[1]

A literature review reported in the Journal of Gerontology concerning encounters with friends and daily experiences summarized:

- Pleasantness: As hypothesized, older adults reported greater pleasantness during their encounters with friends than during encounters with other types of social partners. Socioemotional selectivity theory predicts that close social partners (e.g., family members, friends) among older adults generate more positive emotional experiences than do acquaintances. Our current study parallels with these studies and finds that encounters with friends are the most pleasant, even beyond the encounters with romantic partners or family members. This is possible because older adults spend more time with their romantic partners or family members; they may habituate to encounters with these people. An encounter with a friend, on the other hand, may represent a positive change in daily activities.

– Stressful experiences: Our findings also revealed that older adults were less likely to discuss stressful experiences in their encounters with friends than in their encounters with romantic partners or family members. These findings are consistent with the relational ambivalence literature, which suggests older adults are less likely to have negative exchanges with friends than with family members. However, it is worth noting that discussing stressful experiences does not necessarily indicate the encounter per se was stressful. Individuals may discuss stressful issues with friends as a way to garner support. Nevertheless, we were also surprised to find that encounters with other social partners (who were not family or friends) were even less likely to discuss stressful experiences than encounters with friends, romantic partners, or family members. This lower rate of discussing stressful experiences may reflect a lack of investment and commitment in these distal social partners, such that older adults do not bother to raise annoying issues or generate conflicts with these distal social partners.

– Mood: Consistent with prior retrospective studies, we found that encounters with friends and family members were associated with increased positive mood throughout the day. Encounters with friends were more strongly associated with positive mood than encounters with other social partners, but did not differ significantly from romantic partners or family members. It appears to be the case that both encounters with friends and family members play an equally important role in enhancing positive mood among older adults. However, we did not observe a reduction in negative mood when older adults encountered friends. This might due to a lack of variability in negative mood among older adults.

– Closeness of Friendships and Daily Experiences: Socioemotional selectivity theory suggests older adults tend to retain their closest social partners and engage more often with these partners. Likewise, older adults are expected to engage more often with close friends than less close friends. Surprisingly, our findings revealed the opposite. Our finding provides evidence that older adults maintain some "dormant" friends who are viewed as important but are not frequently encountered.

The social convoy literature documents the influential role of social convoy partners (someone to relax with) on one's well-being. Yet, our findings revealed no association between closeness of friendships and momentary ratings of pleasantness or discussions of stressful experiences in their encounters with friends. However, interestingly, although encounters with non-convoy friends were associated with increased positive mood and reduced negative mood, we found that encounters with convoy friends were not. Our findings added support to the literature on the importance of peripheral ties, which suggests less close ties are beneficial in terms of social integration, diverse activities, and novelty. Further, relational regulation theory posits that global perceptions of support are not based on the actual instances of support, but on other pleasant exchanges in the relationship. In this case, although less close friends are unlikely sources of support, encounters with these friends are associated with better mood because these encounters may entail fun and companionship. Indeed, encounters with non-convoy friends may involve novel experiences compared to more routine activities with closer friends and family. Several studies have documented that novelty is associated with happiness. Our findings parallel those findings by revealing that contact with less close friends (who may be sources of novelty or encourage novel behaviors) was associated with better mood in older populations.[2]

During my comments to our 60th high school reunion on 11/10/2024 I mentioned my frequent breakfast visits for over five years with our classmate, Milton Belnap, who was suffering from cancer. What touched me was the attempts he had made to keep accurate classmate records and his insistence that I continue this effort after his death. He passed in 2013 leaving me with thoughts about my own mortality and an ongoing guilt that I was not making the effort he wished me to do.

I also mentioned during our 50th reunion rekindling a friendship with a friend I had known before our teens and lasted through several of our college years at the University of Idaho. He went off to fly helicopters in Vietnam, supplying oil platforms in the Gulf of Mexico and medical patient transfers.

We had such a good time that before the night was over, he and his wife arranged to join us on our upcoming annual anniversary cruise. During the cruise, they renewed their marriage vows on our wedding date (Sept 3rd) and most years we have taken a cruise together. Unknown to us, we even had a heart monitor placed under the skin on the same day.

Two days following our high school class reunion (08/12/2024) a classmate, Neil Evans, posted these comments on our class email. They expressed thoughts I would like to share: "Diane and I just got home from the 1964 Blackfoot High School Reunion. I had never been to a class reunion before. I have been in contact with only a couple of you over the years. Thus, the majority of my high school classmates I have not seen for sixty years. I was surprised that some people remembered me.

As a young man I was a combination of shyness and blind selfishness that didn't really take life very seriously. Of course, I enjoyed things but without much genuine care about what was presently or eternally good for myself or others. Thankfully, over the past sixty years I have changed, or more accurately God has changed me.

I had only a few close friends while in High School, and I, like many others moved away from my hometown, so it is understandable that I would neither miss or be missed, especially after sixty disappearing years.

So, why did I choose to go to this reunion after so long? I thought, even talked, about going to a reunion throughout the years. I always had what I considered good reasons not to go back to a past which I assumed, had little influence on me, or on which I had such little influence. But as I have matured, or as God has graciously taught me, I realize that these thoughts and feelings are not unusual. Thankfully most people grow out of the blind arrogance of youth. I believe that none of us deserve the credit for any good changes in our lives. I was curious about how God has changed the people I knew in my youth.

It is not surprising that beyond, and much more significant than, gray hair and "wrinkles," amid the variety of vocations and accomplishments I witnessed sincere interest in and appreciation of each other. One man, (Rich) summarizing our time together, mentioned that our shared youth had more influence on who we have become than we tend to realize. I agree and admit that I have been slow to learn how God uses every circumstance and every person in our lives.

Thank you, Lou for sharing your music and giving us your CD! Thank you Richard and Sharon for the fun song! Thank you, Janet and all the others who worked at planning and leading this fun time!

Thank you, Blackfoot High School class of 1964 for the reminder that God can grow and change us, when we let Him." Neil and Diane Evans *havelife.us* or *truesaint.us*

A group of retired friends for years have met together on Mondays to just visit and discuss events that are affecting their lives. The name of the group is ROMEOs (Retired Old Men Eating Out). Being a veterinarian, most clients presenting their companion animals for care were females. When their spouse was retiring, I would often ask them how they felt about their prince charming being at his castle 24/7. One wife made the comment: "It's my castle and I don't want him home for lunch!"

My visits to ROMEOs have become more frequent over the last ten years. We have met at Costco until Covid, at various homes of the group and in a senior care facility lunch room. I was the youngest at first, am currently middle aged and we have fond memories of the five members that have passed since I joined the group.

"Oil and perfume make the heart glad, and the sweetness of a friend comes from his earnest counsel *Proverbs 27:9.* Behold, how good and pleasant it is when brothers dwell in unity *Psalms 133:1.* A friend loves at all times, and a brother is born for adversity." *Proverbs 17:17*

---

1 *To Age Well, You Need Friends – Your health depends on stable friendships, Psychology Today, Temma Ehrenfeld, 06/19/2017.*

2 *Encounters With Friends and Daily Experiences, J Gerontol B Psychol Sci Soc Sci. 2021 Mar; 76(3): 551–562.*

CHAPTER 31

WHO IS RIGHT

I was once asked to visit the home of an inactive member of my church using the principle of ministering. It is a concept that encompasses a wide range of activities, from preaching and teaching to acts of charity and hospitality, all aimed at glorifying God and edifying the body of Christ. In the biblical context, ministering is deeply rooted in the teachings of both the Old and New Testament. The Old Testament lays the groundwork for understanding ministering as service, often describing the service of priests and Levites in the tabernacle and temple. The New Testament extends the meaning of ministering to all believers, with Jesus Christ exemplifying the ultimate model of service.

I was in my late 20's, just graduated from college, and very busy trying to learn my duties as a veterinarian, husband and father. I knocked on the door of a young inactive member breaking the cardinal rule of always protecting oneself by visiting with at least one other member of the church. Advice given in the New Testament: Jesus sent his disciples out two by two, emphasizing mutual support and accountability in their mission (Mark6:7). A principle I also learned at work – a door cracked open or a technician present was always a good idea.

She appeared to be about my age, very pleasant and responded to small talk. I then mentioned to her that I had been asked by the bishop of my ward (the presiding High Priest, that oversees the spiritual and social needs of the members) to see if there was anything, spiritual or temporally, that we could do to help her? Her response raised up the hair on the back of my neck, I had a cold dark feeling and wanted only to flee her home. The feeling reminded me of young Joseph Smith's description of darkness that occurred soon after Joseph determined that he would pray to God for guidance and knelt in a small grove of trees he'd been clearing in the days previous, where he knew he'd be left alone. There, praying aloud for the first time seeking truth and asking for guidance. Almost as soon as he began his pleadings, a thick darkness gathered around him, and he found it difficult to speak. The sunlight disappeared, and as the darkness, pain, and threat of destruction pressed down on him, he begged God for deliverance.

The woman told me that she had never seen God, but she had seen Lucifer. He had been in her bedroom several times and presented her a written document, saying - "If you will sign this, everything will be well with you." I felt much like Joseph fleeing Potiphar's wife when she attempted to seduce him!

The universal salvation or reconciliation principle posits that all souls will ultimately be saved and reconciled to God. This doctrine has been a subject of debate within Christian theologians with various interpretations and implications for salvation and judgment. Proponents often cite biblical passages, such as 1 Timothy 2:4 and 2 Peter 3:9, to support their view, suggesting that God's ultimate will is for all humanity to be saved. Critics argue that this doctrine undermines the seriousness of sin and the necessity of faith, pointing to passages like Matthew 25:46, which speaks of eternal punishment. The concept has historical roots in early Christian thought, with Origen being one of the first to propose it. Origen was an early Christian scholar and theologian who was born and spent the first half of his career in Alexandria. He was a prolific writer who wrote roughly 2,000 treatises in multiple branches of theology. He was one of the most influential and controversial figures in early Christian theology, apologetics, and asceticism (severe self-discipline and avoidance of all forms of indulgence, typically for religious reasons). He has been described as "the greatest genius the early church ever produced", but has been largely rejected by mainstream Christian denominations.

Lucifer's plan, often associated with his rebellion against God, involved an alternative proposal to save all of humanity while seeking glory for himself, contrasting with God's plan of agency and redemption through Jesus Christ. Lucifer, originally a high-ranking angel, proposed an alternative plan during the pre-mortal existence, which is often referred to in theological discussions. His plan aimed to ensure that all of God's children would be saved, but it came with the condition that he would receive the glory for this salvation. This proposal was made during a grand council in heaven, where God presented His plan for humanity's progression and salvation through agency and the Atonement of Jesus Christ.

Lucifer's universal salvation principle claimed he could save all souls, which undermined the principle of agency that God intended for His children. He sought to eliminate the possibility of failure or sin, which would ultimately strip individuals of their free will.

Because our Heavenly Father chose Jesus Christ to be our Savior, Satan became angry and rebelled. There was war in heaven. Satan and his followers fought against Jesus Christ and His followers. The Savior's followers "overcame [Satan] by the blood of the Lamb, and by the word of their testimony."

In this great rebellion, Satan and all the spirits who followed him were sent away from the presence of God and cast down from heaven. A third part of the hosts of heaven were punished for following Satan. They were denied the right to receive mortal bodies.

Because we are here on earth and have mortal bodies, we know that we chose to follow Jesus Christ and our Heavenly Father. Satan and his followers are also on the earth, but as spirits. They have not forgotten who we are, and they are around us daily, tempting us and enticing us to do things that are not pleasing to our Heavenly Father. In our premortal life, we chose to follow Jesus Christ and accept God's plan. We must continue to follow Jesus Christ here on earth. Only by following Him can we return to our heavenly home. *AI + others*

Years ago, my company used the services of an accountant that in his words, actions, and behavior was willing to express his ideas and beliefs concerning his faith. Retiring in his 60's (as most accountants do) he announced that he and his wife were leaving their home and family, serving as lay mission leaders for The Church of Jesus Christ of Latter-day Saints (LDS), and serving in a foreign country for three years. A lay minister in the LDS church refers to a member of the Church who serves in a leadership or service capacity without being a paid, professional clergy member. This means that all leadership positions within the Church, from local ward (congregation) leaders to those who oversee larger geographical areas, are filled by volunteer members. These members are called to their positions, and they dedicate their time and talents to serving their congregations and communities. My accountant has a firm testimony, belief in the Gospel of Jesus Christ, served as a missionary in his early 20's and also served in other lay callings throughout his life.

He has a brother has no strong feelings about his LDS faith and hasn't felt a "Burning in the bosom," a phrase often used by LDS to describe a feeling of spiritual confirmation or revelation, and often associated with the Holy Spirit. It's described as a warm, comforting, and peaceful sensation that confirms the truthfulness of a particular idea, belief, or principle. This feeling is considered a personal witness of the Holy Ghost, guiding individuals towards what is right. My accountant's brother is considered to be a "good person," cares for and loves his family, goes through the motions of attending church, follows the doctrine, and waits for a confirmation.

For more than 50 years, death was a poignant part of Stephen Hawking's remarkable life. The physicist, who died at age 76, wasn't expected to see his 25th birthday, after being diagnosed with the incurable neurodegenerative condition ALS at age 21. Though Hawking beat the odds for more than five decades, death was never far from his mind. Once he said: "I have lived with the prospect of an early death for the last 49 years. I'm not afraid of death, but I'm in no hurry to die. I have so much I want to do first."

The scientist took a pragmatic view of what happens to the brain and body after death. "I regard the brain as a computer which will stop working when its components fail. There is no heaven or afterlife for broken down computers; that is a fairy story for people afraid of the dark."

He believed in an 'impersonal God,' but not a creator. Hawking invoked the name of God in his seminal book A Brief History of Time, writing that if physicists could find a "theory of everything" — that is, a cohesive explanation for how the universe works — they would glimpse "the mind of God."

But in later interviews and writings, such as 2010's The Grand Design, which he co-wrote with Leonard Mlodinow, Hawking clarified that he wasn't referring to a creator in the traditional sense. "Spontaneous creation is the reason there is something rather than nothing, why the universe exists, why we exist. It is not necessary to invoke God to light the blue touch paper and set the universe going. God is the name people give to the reason we are here. But I think that reason is the laws of physics rather than someone with whom one can have a personal relationship. An impersonal God."

Hawking considered himself an atheist. "Before we understand science, it is natural to believe that God created the universe. But now science offers a more convincing explanation. What I meant by 'we would know the mind of God' is, we would know everything that God would know, if there were a God, which there isn't. I'm an atheist."

Though Hawking rejected the conventional notion of God or a creator, he fundamentally believed that the universe and life have meaning. "Remember to look up at the stars and not down at your feet. Try to make sense of what you see and wonder about what makes the universe exist. Be curious. And however difficult life may seem, there is always something you can do and succeed at."

One of the main debates in the philosophy of religion is between theists, who believe that God exists, and atheists, who believe there is no God. However, not everyone interested in God's existence is a theist or an atheist. The term "agnosticism", coined by Thomas Henry Huxley in the 1860s, describes the view of some of the people who do not fit into these two camps.

One is agnostic about something when one suspends judgment on it, i.e., is neutral or undecided about the issue in question after considering it. For example, most people, when they begin wondering whether the number of leaves on a nearby tree is odd or even, become agnostic on the matter. Within the contemporary philosophy of religion, the word "agnosticism" usually refers to the position of those who suspend judgment on the existence of God. Agnosticism is not necessarily incompatible with religious faith. According to some, agnostics can have non-doxastic faith. This is faith without theistic belief, with some other positive attitude (e.g., hope) at its core. Another positive option for an agnostic is to embrace fictionalism and treat religion like a fictional narrative that guides one's actions. However, agnosticism does not entail any specific positive or negative attitude towards religion; agnostics may or may not actively seek or hope to acquire evidence about the existence of God. Agnosticism entails neither being a 'seeker' nor spiritual indifference.

Agnosticism is not the same thing as apophaticism, which states that God is essentially unknowable: on most accounts, apophaticists are a subgroup of theists; agnosticism is not the same thing as religious non-cognitivism – the position that the question of whether God exists (like all statements which involve the term "God" or other religious terms) does not make sense (because it does not refer to anything empirically observable) and thus cannot have a meaningful answer. Both agnostics and non-cognitivists are neither theists nor atheists, but agnostics believe that the question of whether God exists does have an answer, even though they suspend judgment on what it is.

The main argument for agnosticism can be described as the evidential argument. One of its premises is the view (called evidentialism) that one should believe something if evidence supports it, disbelieve it if evidence supports its negation, and suspend judgment on the matter if evidence is neutral. The other premise states that evidence about whether God exists is neutral between theism and atheism, prompting the agnostic conclusion.

Why consider the evidence about God's existence to be neutral? Some argue that there is an equal amount of evidence for theism and atheism (which includes the view that there is no evidence for any of the two). Others prefer to say that the evidence is ambiguous: it is not clear how much evidence there is on each side or how to measure it. For example, it is hard to say how the existence of evil, which supports atheism, measures against the ontological arguments for God's existence.

Every argument for theism or atheism, considered in itself, is also an argument against agnosticism, but there have also been attempts to directly challenge the evidential argument. One answer to the evidential argument for agnosticism is that suspending judgment on the existence of God is psychologically or practically impossible (or identical to atheism in psychological or practical terms). The reason for this would be that whether we are theists or not determines our actions and attitudes (e.g. our expectations about the afterlife) in such a way that one cannot have neutral position on God's existence – just like one cannot be neutral about performing an action: one can only perform it or not perform it.

Another common answer to the evidential argument is noting that the evidence for a lot of things is ambiguous, but it is generally considered unreasonable to suspend judgment on all of them. Especially in areas such as ethics or politics, where a lot is at stake, we routinely have strong beliefs even though evidence allows for different readings, and it seems counterintuitive to say that these beliefs are not rationally justified. If we are justified in having such beliefs despite neutral or ambiguous evidence, the burden of explaining why this is not the case with theistic or atheistic belief is on the agnostic.

Two types of agnosticism, strong and weak, have been distinguished. The views on the nature of the difference between them vary. One proposed criterion of the distinction is whether agnosticism is considered to be universally rationally required: weak agnostics believe that, for some people at some times (which includes themselves at the current moment), rationality allows suspending judgment on God's existence; strong agnostics state that everyone is always obliged to do that if they are to remain rational. On this account, weak agnosticism is preferable if some people at sometimes may have neutral or ambiguous evidence, and strong agnosticism is the right option if evidence available always and to everyone is neutral or ambiguous. As a consequence, weak agnostics believe it is possible to have evidentially justified theistic or atheistic belief, while strong agnostics take it to be an impossibility.

Agnosticism has often been perceived as an "empty" position – nothing more than an inability or unwillingness to take a stance. In spite of that, philosophers are increasingly interested in its positive aspect: the possibility and nature of perspectives resulting from suspending judgment on God's existence.

While some philosophers explore the consequences of combining permanent agnosticism with some form of religious commitment or its absence, others analyze the nature of agnosticism as a stage on the way to a more robust (theistic or atheistic) position. In any case, agnosticism seems to be the key to the epistemic and spiritual borderland which extends between theistic and atheistic realms. *Agnosticism about God's Existence, 1000-Word Philosophy, Sylwia Wilczewska, 01/05/2022*

I wonder if theistic, atheistic and agnostic debates haven't been going on time immemorial, referring to a point of time in the past that was so long ago that people have no knowledge or memory of it. Maybe these debates began during the pre-existence when we were spirits living with God and Lucifer debating who would become our savior (Lucifer or Christ). Consider these thoughts:

- In a mother's womb were two babies. One asked the other: "Do you believe in life after delivery?" The other replied, "Why, of course. There has to be something after delivery. Maybe we are here to prepare ourselves for what we will be later." "Nonsense" said the first. "There is no life after delivery. What kind of life would that be?"

The second said, "I don't know, but there will be lighter than here. Maybe we will walk with our legs and eat from our mouths. Maybe we will have other senses that we can't understand now." The first replied, "That is absurd. Walking is impossible. And eating with our mouths? Ridiculous! The umbilical cord supplies nutrition and everything we need. But the umbilical cord is so short. Life after delivery is to be logically excluded."

The second insisted, "Well I think there is something and maybe it's different than it is here. Maybe we won't need this physical cord anymore." The first replied, "Nonsense. And moreover, if there is life, then why has no one has ever come back from there? Delivery is the end of life, and in the after-delivery there is nothing but darkness and silence and oblivion. It takes us nowhere."

"Well, I don't know," said the second, "but certainly we will meet Mother and she will take care of us."

The first replied "Mother? You actually believe in Mother? That's laughable. If Mother exists then where is She now?" The second said, "She is all around us. We are surrounded by her. We are of Her. It is in Her that we live. Without Her this world would not and could not exist."

Said the first: "Well I don't see Her, so it is only logical that She doesn't exist." To which the second replied, "Sometimes, when you're in silence and you focus and you really listen, you can perceive Her presence, and you can hear Her loving voice, calling down from above." *A parable from Your Sacred Self by Dr. Wayne Dyer.*

My day-old child lay in my arms.
With my lips against his ear
I whispered strongly, "How I wish?
I wish that you could hear."

"I've a hundred wonderful things to say
(a tiny cough and a nod)
"Hurry, hurry, hurry and grow
So I can tell you about God."

My day-old baby's mouth was still
And my words only tickled his ear.
But a kind of a light passed through his eyes
And I saw this thought appear:

"How I wish I had a voice and words;
I've a hundred things to say.
Before I forget I'd tell you of God?
I left Him just yesterday." *Carol Lynn Pearson, 10/10/2009*

CHAPTER 32

WHO WAS THAT MAN

My brother-in-law, Dr. Michael (Mike) Retford, is a veterinarian who during veterinary school stayed at my home, in San Jose CA, during a summer internship. During that time, I spent the weeks working and he observed while his creative mind displayed his ability to mimic animal and human sounds, used clipped fur from an angora rabbit as facial hair and pulled rubber gloves over his head to create weird facial designs. Many years later he was a guest at a radio station where the announcer would take callers that would ask Mike to impersonate the sounds of famous people, cartoon characters and animals. During his internship, he also spent his time creating activities to keep us away from church on the weekends. One of these was a trip to the California gold fields where my son, Chris, found a small nugget of gold near the bank of a creek and we visited Moaning Caverns.

Moaning Caverns got its name from the distinctive moaning sound that emanated from the cave entrance. This sound, caused by dripping water echoing within the cavern, was loud enough to be heard on the surface. Early miners and explorers were drawn to the cave by this peculiar sound, which also led to the MiWok Indians creating a legend about a stone giant named Yayalli residing within. Thousands of years ago, the first inhabitants of North America were just making their way into the continent. A common belief is that they came over the "land bridge" from what is now Russia to Alaska and migrated south. In their travels, some of them passed by the entrance to the cavern and may have even lived nearby. A chert outcrop lies near Moaning Cavern (when heated, chert hardens to a material that can be chipped into sharp-edged flakes for excellent arrowheads and other points for tools). It appears to have been quarried many years ago for its hard rock. Near the outcrop, fired bits of chert and partial points have been found. The large size of the quarry may mean the first humans to live around the cavern arrived thousands of years ago. Other evidence of early human residence is skeletal remains. Some of the human bones found in the cavern have been estimated to be at least 12,000 years old, based on the thickness of the calcite layers found on the bones and the results of carbon and uranium-thorium dating techniques. Anthropologists dug a trench in an area of the main room in 1952 and removed a number of fragmented human bones from an area of mud that had been covered by layers of dripstone. Many of these bones had layered films of calcite covering them. Calcite layering builds in thin layers, similar to the growth rings of trees. The extensive amount of time it takes for the deposits to build up gives evidence as to the age of the bones. There is no evidence these early residents explored the cave voluntarily. No remnants of pine or reed torches or ladders of any kind have been found in or near the cavern. The more likely explanation for the presence of the bones in the cavern is that they resulted from accidents. The entrance may have been hidden by plants and the shape of the cavern would make it easy to slip into and impossible to get out of without ropes or ladders. Some of the artifacts that were found among the bones also help with dating, as well as give us some insight into these ancient people. The age of the bracelet displayed at the visitor center has been dated within the past 500 years. It is made of sea-snail shells and suggests regular trading with other people over a wide region. The mother-of-pearl necklace was found in the clay layer and estimated to be over 8,000 years of age.

Before our oldest child reached the age of ten, during vacation trips, Mike had introduced my and his two oldest boys to the stories and interesting areas of Arizona's history. Included was a boat trip where we put in at the Saguaro Lake boat ramp and camped overnight at the base of the dam. We placed our belongings in a tent above the water line and slept in the boat. Mike relates this story: "It was at Saguaro Lake which is formed by a dam on the Salt River. The lake dropped overnight due to irrigation and household water demands, as I understand it. It rises and falls in response to the downstream demands. I doubt if any of the boys were over 10. I believe the dam is still the same. We put in at the Saguaro Lake boat ramp. I remember the feeling of terror as the water level fell early in the morning and the boat started to tip. I was asleep and for some reason, in that moment I thought that a tidal wave was washing us away. I remember pushing the boat down the bank to the new lower water level. Lots of grunting. I may have caused some of the first tears in my inguinal ring which later herniated."

Mike also introduced us to the Superstition Mountains, the Lost Dutchman's Mine legend and took us to various old mine sights and mining towns. He has a way of telling stories that make fables, legends and proverbs reality:

Fables are short, fictional stories often featuring animals or inanimate objects with human-like qualities, typically used to teach moral lessons. Aesop's Fables contain many moral fables and "The Crow and the Pitcher" is one of the most cited. The fable is about a thirsty crow that finds a pitcher with water at the bottom. Unable to reach the water, the crow devises a clever plan: it drops in pebbles, one by one, until the water rises to the top of the pitcher, allowing the crow to drink. The fable illustrates the importance of using one's wits in tough situations and the value of intelligence and adaptability.

Legends, on the other hand, are traditional stories believed to be rooted in history, though they may involve fantastical elements and have been passed down through generations. An example of a legend is the story of Dr. Michael Retford's encounter with a large footprint in the snow where he lived in Island Park, Idaho. In book III of my *"Thoughts on Thoughts"* series of books, chapter 10 - Yeti Myths Legends, Mike is quoted: "We sent the pictures of the 'giant footprints' (we found in the snow) to Dr Jeff Meldrum at Idaho State University. He is without a doubt one of the world's leading crypto zoologists and a well-respected scientist and professor. He said he had no doubts as to their authenticity and agreed with my conclusions." The legend of the "Wandering Jew" is one of the most enduring legends and enigmatic myths in Western culture. Rooted in medieval Christian folklore, the tale recounts the story of a man cursed to wander the earth until the Second Coming of Christ. In Matthew 16:28, Jesus promises that some of those present would not experience death before witnessing the "Son of Man coming in his kingdom." This is generally understood to refer to either the Transfiguration or the establishment of the Church and the outpouring of the Holy Spirit at Pentecost, rather than the final, eschatological coming of Christ. The phrase "coming in his kingdom" can also be interpreted as a reference to the ongoing reign of Christ through his Church. The events in Matthew 17:1-13 describe the Transfiguration, where Jesus, Peter, James, and John witnessed a glimpse of his glorified glory. This is a common interpretation of the "Son of Man coming in his kingdom". The establishment of the Church and the outpouring of the Holy Spirit at Pentecost (Acts 2) are seen as the fulfillment of Jesus' promise that he would be with his followers until the end of the age. Some interpret "coming in his kingdom" as referring to the ongoing reign of Christ through his Church, where he is present with his followers and they witness the power of his kingdom. Most theologians agree that this promise is not referring to the Second Coming, where Jesus will return at the end of time, but rather to a manifestation of his glory and power within the lifetime of some of his apostles. Over the centuries, this myth has evolved, absorbing diverse cultural narratives and sparking debates about its religious, moral, and social implications. The earliest recorded references to the Wandering Jew appear in 13th-century Christian texts. The story likely emerged from biblical interpretations and apocryphal tales surrounding the Passion of Christ. One of the most common versions centers on a Jerusalem shoemaker or doorkeeper named Cartaphilus, who mocked Jesus on his way to crucifixion. In response, Christ cursed him to "tarry until I return." As the myth spread across Europe, the identity of the Wandering Jew varied. Some versions referred to him as Ahasuerus, while others linked him to figures like Malchus, the servant of the high priest Caiaphas. Each iteration reinforced the idea of perpetual wandering as divine punishment, a narrative that resonated deeply with medieval Christian audiences. The Wandering Jew came to symbolize the consequences of faithlessness, pride, and cruelty. His ceaseless journey became a cautionary tale, warning against moral transgression and the denial of divine truth. Additionally, the legend echoed broader Christian themes of repentance and redemption, as the Wanderer's suffering served as a penance for his actions. In some interpretations, the Wandering Jew represented the Jewish people as a whole, reflecting the medieval Christian belief in Jewish displacement as divine retribution. This association fueled antisemitic narratives that persisted through the centuries, casting a long shadow over the myth's cultural legacy. The Wandering Jew's story permeated literature, art, and folklore throughout Europe. In 17th-century Germany, chapbooks circulated widely, depicting his encounters with historical events and figures. Romantic writers like Goethe and Shelley explored the theme of eternal wandering, weaving it into broader existential inquiries. In visual art, the Wanderer's image evolved to reflect contemporary anxieties and curiosities. Artists portrayed him as a solitary, weathered figure, eyes heavy with the weight of centuries. His image often embodied the archetype of the eternal outsider, a symbol of both alienation and resilience. In modern contexts, the Wandering Jew continues to inspire reinterpretations. Contemporary writers and filmmakers have recast him as a tragic hero, grappling with immortality and the burden of memory. The myth's adaptability speaks to its profound resonance, as each era finds new meanings in his unending journey. Critics and scholars also examine the legend through the lens of cultural critique. The antisemitic undertones of earlier versions have prompted reexaminations, challenging audiences to confront the prejudices woven into the fabric of the tale. The myth of the Wandering Jew endures as a poignant narrative of eternal restlessness and moral reckoning. From its medieval origins to its modern reinventions, the tale offers a mirror through which societies reflect on faith, punishment, and the human condition. As long as stories are told, the Wanderer will continue his journey, a timeless symbol of the search for redemption and belonging. The Wandering Jew plant, also known as Tradescantia zebrina, offers both practical and aesthetic benefits. It's an easy-care houseplant that can help purify indoor air by filtering out toxins. Additionally, it's known for its vibrant, trailing foliage, adding visual appeal to homes. Some traditional uses, though not scientifically proven, suggest it may have medicinal properties like helping with gastrointestinal issues and fighting bacterial infections.

A parable is a short fictitious story that illustrates a moral attitude or a religious principle. It is a simple narrative that sketches a setting, describes an action, and shows the results. Parables are often used to teach or explain ideas, especially moral or religious ones. The parable presents different ways people react to the Gospel message (the parable of the Sower is among the most cited and shared biblical parables. It can be found in Matthew 13:3-23, Mark 4:1-20, and Luke 8:4-15. The parable presents different ways people react to the Gospel message. Contained in the Book of Mormon - the three Nephites is a "type of parable" that illustrates a religious principle about translated beings. Few, in the church, have not heard about these translated beings. Like the apostle John, these three disciples of Christ chose to "live to behold all the doings of the Father unto the children of men" (3 Nephi 28:7), meaning they are translated beings who will live on the earth until the Second Coming. However, beyond 3 Nephi 28, there is not much else written in the scriptures about these three, translated disciples. In fact, the prophet Mormon was even forbidden from writing their names. But there are a few fascinating things we know about these disciples and their purposes on this earth. The Book of Mormon contains the names of the 12 disciples—including the three Nephites. Assuming their names have not changed or were not altered by Mormon, we do have the names of the 12 disciples chosen by Christ in the Book of Mormon—including the three Nephites. In 3 Nephi 19:4, we learn the names of the 12 disciples Christ chose among the people after appearing to the Nephites and Lamanites in the Americas. Of those 12, we know three chose to be translated and become what we refer to as the three Nephites. In fact, we know from 3 Nephi 28:25 that Mormon was about to write the names of the three Nephites but "the Lord forbade; therefore I write them not, for they are hid from the world." While we do not know the names of the three Nephites specifically, it is possible that their names could have been among those of the apostles called by Christ. While we know there were at least three translated Nephites, there is evidence in the scriptures and from commentary from Church leaders to suggest that there could be more. When Alma the younger departed out of Zarahemla into the land of Mulek, there isn't much to suggest that he was seen again, at least not as a non-translated being. From Alma 45, we know he was "never heard of more" and "his death or burial we know not of" (Alma 45:18). And in Alma 45:19 we learn "the saying went abroad in the church that he was taken up by the Spirit, or buried by the hand of the Lord, even as Moses." The last part about being "taken up by the Spirit" or "buried by the hand of the Lord" sound contradictory when paired with Duet. 34:5-7, which states that Moses was buried in a "valley in the land of Moab" (v. 6) and that he was "one hundred and twenty years old when he died" (v. 7). However, according to Bruce R. McConkie: "Moses, Elijah, and Alma the younger, were translated. The Old Testament account that Moses died and was buried by the hand of the Lord in an unknown grave is an error. (Deut. 34:5–7.) It is true that he may have been 'buried by the hand of the Lord,' if that expression is a figure of speech which means that he was translated. But the Book of Mormon account, in recording that Alma 'was taken up by the Spirit,' says, 'the scriptures saith the Lord took Moses unto himself; and we suppose that he has also received Alma in the spirit, unto himself.' (Alma 45:18–19.) It should be remembered that the Nephites had the Brass Plates, and that they were the 'scriptures' which gave the account of Moses being taken by way of translation. As to Elijah, the account of his being taken in 'a chariot of fire ... by a whirlwind into heaven,' is majestically set out in the Old Testament" (2 Kings 2.) (Mormon Doctrine, 2nd ed. [1966], 805). Similarly, Nephi, son of Helaman, also disappeared while traveling out of the land of Zarahemla. Though there is less evidence here that he was translated, it appears he was not planning to return, having given "charge unto his son Nephi, who was his eldest son, concerning the plates of brass, and all the records which had been kept, and all those things which had been kept sacred from the departure of Lehi out of Jerusalem" (3 Nephi 1:2). Similarly to Alma the younger, no one knew where Nephi went, and no one knew anything about his death or his burial save it "could nowhere be found in all the land" (3 Nephi 2:19). From 3 Nephi we learn that the three Nephites can choose to be seen or not be seen by whomever they desire. This isn't because of anything they do on their own volition; they must ask for it in prayer and the power to do this comes from Heavenly Father. "And they are as the angels of God, and if they shall pray unto the Father in the name of Jesus they can show themselves unto whatsoever man it seemeth them good" (Nephi 28:30). Furthermore, Satan and evil men and women have no power over translated beings, including the three Nephites. In fact, when the three Nephites were in mortal peril at the hands of those who wished them harm, they escaped each time unscathed. Their ministry is ultimately determined by Heavenly Father. As the iniquity grew among the Nephites and the Lamanites after Christ's appearance in the Americas, the three Nephites were eventually taken out of the land to an unknown location. But wickedness did prevail upon the face of the whole land, insomuch that the Lord did take away his beloved disciples, and the work of miracles and of healing did cease because of the iniquity of the people (Mormon

1: 13). And I did endeavor to preach unto this people, but my mouth was shut, and I was forbidden that I should preach unto them; for behold they had wilfully rebelled against their God; and the beloved disciples were taken away out of the land, because of their iniquity (Mormon 1: 16). Though the three Nephites were taken out of the land of Zarahemla at about 326 AD, we know that they could, in fact, appear to those they wished because they ministered to Mormon and Moroni. But behold, I have seen them, and they have ministered unto me (3 Nephi 28:26). But behold, my father and I have seen them, and they have ministered unto us (Mormon 8:11). When describing the state of the three Nephites, Mormon uses the word "transfiguration," but in 3 Nephi 28:17, he seems unclear about whether or not the three Nephites were mortal or immortal after they were "caught up into heaven" (v. 13). However, Mormon later writes that he inquired of the Lord to know what state the three Nephites were in and learned "that there must needs be a change wrought upon their bodies, or else it needs be that they must taste of death;" (v. 37) and that this change "was not equal to that which shall take place at the last day;" (v. 39). Mormon also writes that "in this state they were to remain until the judgment day of Christ; and at that day they were to receive a greater change, and to be received into the kingdom of the Father to go no more out, but to dwell with God eternally in the heavens" (v. 40). *5 Things You Probably Didn't Know About the Three Nephites, LDS Living, Katie Lambert, 01/12/2018.*

In 2020 D. L. Ashliman wrote about encounters with the three Nephites: "According to the Book of Mormon (3 Nephi:28), a book given scriptural status by the Church of Jesus Christ of Latter-Day Saints, Jesus Christ appeared to the inhabitants of the western hemisphere immediately following his death and resurrection in Palestine and promised three of his New World believers that they would never taste of death. The following unedited stories are typical of the numerous accounts recorded by faithful Mormons of appearances by one or more of these three deathless saints, known as 'The Three Nephites'."

In the month of November 1867, my parents, William H. and Mary Laidlaw Seegmiller, were married in Salt Lake City. My father and mother were among a number of L.D.S. people who received calls to colonize the southeastern part of Nevada. The group settled on what was known as the Muddy River, in a place called St. Joseph, in the Moapa Valley, Nevada. Late one afternoon while my father was just outside their tent home chopping wood, he was approached by a rather distinguished-looking person of Jewish type, having a large Roman nose, who accosted father in the German language, father's parents being German, that language, as well as English, was familiar to him. The visitor asked for something to eat to take along in his bag that he carried across his shoulder, and also for some patches of cloth with which to mend his clothes. Father told the man they had not yet eaten their evening meal and for him to come in the tent and rest and mother would prepare supper and they would all eat together. To this the man replied he did not have to stop and would prefer to have some food just to take along with him. Father asked him where he was going. He pointed to the southwest. Father then warned him not to go in that direction as it was barren desert and no water within sixty miles. To this the man replied, "I have traveled in the north, south, east and west, in heat and in cold, and I have no fear of suffering from thirst." Father then asked him his name, to which he replied, "They call me the Wandering Jew." The stranger was given the things he asked for and father stepped into the tent. Mother said, "Don't let that man start over the desert this late in the day." So, father hurried out to call him back to spend the night with them. The road stretched out for miles without obstruction, but the man could not be seen. A neighbor, Brother Fairbanks, had also seen the man as he approached my parents' tent, but had no conversation with him.

Father and mother always thought their visitor was John the Beloved, or one of the three Nephites, who had been promised by the Savior to tarry upon the earth until He returns again. -William A. Seegmiller. Published in Heart Throbs of the West, vol. 3 (1947), pp. 351-52.

An Experience of Mrs. Alyda Abbott Squires: It was on a hot summer day in the year 1874 at WaWa Springs in the state of Utah. The springs being an oasis in the desert and nothing only sage and bunches of grass and hot sand it was here in a little lumber shack on their homestead Mr. and Mrs. Edwin Squires lived with their 3 small daighters. They owned horses and cattle and Mr. Squires had 2 or 3 men hired to help take care of these. And it was on this day in 1874 they had gon on around up leaving Mrs. Squires and the children a alone and they were miles from any one else and her husband had told her he would be back at a sertain time and to have dinner ready for them. And from the house they could see for miles in any direction. And it being about time for them to come she went to the spring for water and look in ever derection to see if they were comming but there was nothing in sight and she took the water in and set it down and turned around and there to her amazement was a man standing in the door and he ask her if she would kindly give him a bit to eat and altho she was frightened she set the table it was humble but good meal. I remember there was cheese bread butter cold milk and an apple pie and she told him to eat he was welcome and he did eat as though he was hungry. And while eating he conversed with her and said Sister you are not well and she said No I have had apain in under my shoulder. Which bothered me a great deal and he said that is your liver but you wont be bothered any more with that. Then he got up and started off and thanked her for her kindness and fine meal and said Got bless you sister You will never want for any thing you will always be blessed with plenty and he left. As soon as she thought he had had time to turn the corner of the house she went out to see in what direction he had gon and there was no sighn of him any where. This worried her more than ever. She went back in the house and to her suprize the table was just as she had set it And she had seen him eat and drink the milk. But it was there and she then thought how he looked and he was dressed so neet and his eyes were so bright and just twinkled when he talked and he had long white beard his hair was gray. She was still worring when her husband and the men came and she ask them if they had seen him but they hadent. She told them the story but she couldent get it off her mind and it went on for about 3 moths and her Mother Mrs. Abigal Abbott came to make her a visit and she told her the story and she smiled and said Why Lyda hove you forgote your Patriochal Blessing. You was promised that one of the Three Nephits would dine at your table thats who it was. Well, she never had any more trouble with her liver lived a good old age and always had plenty and her husband died first and when she died she left a good start to her children and we have right here in our town a family of grand-children there mother being a daughter. And dieng before her mother her children got her share and it set them all up in business. When she died she was 89 years old

This story was told to me by my mother it was her fathers sister and she heard her tell it and also Mr Bowman he is the father of the family here in our town a son in law of Mrs Squires. A he also tell the same story. This story was written in 1943 by Mrs. Elsina Robison, Bunkerville, Nevada. (Her age was about fifty.) It is reproduced here exactly as the informant wrote it.

My grandmother, Mary Biddlecome, was a famous midwife with an art of healing that amounted almost to a gift. Before she came to Ferron and Castle Dale, she lived in Nevada and was taking care of a woman whose breasts had caked. The woman was in great pain and nothing Grandmother did seemed to give her any relief. Grandmother was standing at the stove heating some water for hot packs when there came a knock at the door and an old man entered. He asked for something to eat and as he sat eating the lunch she set out for him, he asked what the trouble was in that house. Grandma told him and he said to take a piece of tobacco the size of his thumb and he measured off an exact amount and boil it in lard and rub that on the woman's breast. Grandma hurried to do it and didn't pay much attention to the old man. The woman was so immediately relieved that Grandma went to call her thank you to the old man and he had disappeared completely. The house sat out on a plain and she should have been able to see him. This is told as a Nephite story. Oral version written from notes. Green River, Utah, March 29, 1946.

This story was told to Mrs. Eggett by Mr. Larsen who was a former bishop in Bountiful. The story was about two girls who were down in Southern Utah near Richfield. They were walking down a mountain where there was slate. It was late and had been raining so that the slate was slippery. It was dark and they had lost the trail and didn't know how they were going to get off the slate. A man appeared to them and said, "Follow me." He got them down the trail and when he was quite a ways ahead of them, he switched around the corner of the mountain. The girls went around the corner of the mountain to thank him but he was nowhere to be found.

Bishop Morgan was telling about a Greek family that weren't converts of the Church but were sure that they had met one of the Three Nephites.... They were riding from Price to Salt Lake around conference time and met an old man on the road around Soldier Summit. They offered him a ride. He got in and they pushed the catch on the door down because they were used to having children in the car. They got on the way and were talking among themselves and turned around and looked but they couldn't see him. He had said just before that he was going to the gathering of the Saints. They turned around and went all the way back to Soldier Summit but they couldn't find him. Oral version from shorthand notes. Price, Utah, July 24, 1946.

The "Lost Dutchman's Gold Mine" is a legendary, unproven rich gold mine said to be hidden in the Superstition Mountains of Arizona, a story fueled in the 1800s by the claims of German immigrant Jacob Waltz who supposedly discovered it before dying without revealing its exact location. Waltz was nicknamed "the Dutchman" because he was German (Deutsch), and his gold discovery led to the legend of the Lost Dutchman's Mine. Waltz allegedly died in 1891 without fully revealing the mine's location, leading to decades of treasure hunts and speculation. The mine is said to be located somewhere within the Superstition Mountains, a rugged and remote area east of Phoenix, Arizona. Despite numerous expeditions and theories, the Lost Dutchman's Mine has never been found, fueling the legend and its enduring fascination. Lost Dutchman State Park, located at the base of the Superstition Mountains, is named after the legend and offers hiking, camping, and other outdoor activities. The Lost Dutchman's Mine has been featured in various forms of media, including books, movies, and video games. Over the years, various theories and clues have emerged about the mine's location, but none have been definitively proven. The story of the Lost Dutchman's Mine continues to draw people to the Superstition Mountains, seeking the legendary treasure. The Lost Dutchman State Park is located at the base of the Superstition Mountains, 40 miles east of Phoenix. The Superstition Mountains in Arizona have been the site of numerous mines, most notably known for the legendary Lost Dutchman's Gold Mine. While the location of this mythical gold mine remains unknown, many other mines have been documented in the area. In more than a century of searching, none have found the fabled mine - though more than 30 people have died exploring the 160,000-acre Superstition Wilderness Area in hopes of making it rich.

Even today, the search continues. Notable Mines in the Goldfield Mining District are: The Mammoth Mine; near it the Black Queen Mine; the Bulldog Mine, where some believe this mine was the source of the ore in the Lost Dutchman story; the Silver King Mine, which is also known for its silver production; and The Vulture Mine, was once the most productive gold mine in Arizona. Other mines in the area also boasts a number of other gold, lead, and zinc mines, as well as prospects for mercury, silver, and magnetite. The Superstition Mountains are composed of various rock types, including welded tuff, breccia, granite, and basalt, some of which contain gold deposits. By the 1860's large discoveries of gold were occurring in the Bradshaw Mountains, especially along the Hassayampa River. The early prospectors and fledgling mining companies added pressure to the movement to make Arizona a territory which happened in 1863. The Bradshaw Mountains and Superstition Mountains are not located near each other. The Bradshaw Mountains are located in central Arizona, southwest of Prescott, while the Superstition Mountains are in eastern Phoenix, in the Superstition Wilderness Area.

During Easter break when our four oldest boys were still under 10 years of age, Mike and I decided to camp in the Superstition Mountain Park Area. The day before Easter we filled our back packs and, as I recall, used empty liter soda bottles for canteens. As we were walking up the trail, we passed people huddled under trees that didn't provide much shade. Mike recalls using his impersonation skills: "On the superstition hike, I remember getting to a spot slightly above the trail to watch the sunset. While we sat there perched in silence, the other hikers who we had passed earlier came passing by under our "perch" and I made the mountain lion sound. I remember one of them dropped to the ground as his knees buckled and the other looked up at us and cursed." At camp Mike and I discussed concerns about not having a map of the area, knowing which trail to take the next morning, where we were to find safe water to drink and the stupidity of bringing our young children on a potentially disastrous expedition. We didn't want to become one of the Superstition Wilderness Area's statistics listed as "rescues or deaths."

As the Easter morning's light began to fill the dry cool mountain canyon, we found a small dirty lake with stagnant water. First elated finding that there was water, our excitement soon became gloom when we realized that we had not packed a water filter. Our choices were to filter the water through our clothing and take the chance of drinking dangerous flora or fauna, or start down an unknown trail without water that could lead to disaster? As we were contemplating our situation, we began discussing with our boys how the third day after Christ was crucified, He was resurrected as all man will be after tasting death. Then, just as the sun started to break over an out cropping of rock over the lake, we saw a man perched there with his legs crossed, eyes closed, facing the rising sun with his hands clasped together in prayer. When finished, he came down from the out cropping of rock and approached us. He had long hair, beard and was not dressed as a hiker. I don't remember our conversion with him – however, I do remember him filtering the lake water and filling all our water bottles and I felt a comfortable inner peace about taking the chosen path we decided to follow down the mountain. It eventually led us safely to our car.

Was he the "Wondering Jew" that biblical interpretations and apocryphal tales occurred from the Passion of Christ? A Jerusalem shoemaker or doorkeeper named Cartaphilus, who mocked Jesus on his way to crucifixion? That in response, Christ cursed him to "tarry until I return." Had he become penitent, humbled and was trying to help others in any way he could until the resurrected Savior comes again? Or was he one of the "Three Nephites" that when Jesus Christ appeared to the inhabitants of the western hemisphere, immediately following his death and resurrection in Palestine, had promised the three of his New World believers that they would never taste of death? Or was it just a "stroke of luck?" Whatever it was, I felt a warmth deep inside that I have felt from time to time during special experiences in my life. When I asked Mike about that experience, he wrote: "Good times to be sure! Cherished memories…"